CW01465196

Barry Hines

MANCHESTER
1824

Manchester University Press

Barry Hines
Kes, *Threads* and beyond

David Forrest and Sue Vice

Manchester University Press

Published by Manchester University Press
Altrincham Street, Manchester M1 7JA

www.manchesteruniversitypress.co.uk

British Library Cataloguing-in-Publication Data
A catalogue record for this book is available from the British Library

ISBN   978 1 7849 9262 0   hardback

First published 2018

Typeset in 10/12 Sabon by
Servis Filmsetting Ltd, Stockport, Cheshire

Contents

Figures

Foreword

Tony Garnett

This book is the first academic account of Barry Hines's work. It will surprise those who know him as the writer of the novel *A Kestrel for a Knave* and the BBC drama *Threads*. They captured the imaginations of millions and are now permanent fixtures in the national memory. But Barry was productive over many decades, and his work extended from short stories, to novels, to cinema and to television. Varied as they were, three elements drew them together into a coherent body of work.

First was Hoyland Common, the small semi-rural community near Barnsley in South Yorkshire. Here almost every man walked through beautiful countryside as he made his way to the darkness and danger of the local coal-mine. Barry's father and grandfather were coal-miners. Indeed Barry himself started work down a pit, until he was abruptly told by a miner to get out and do something with his life.

His writing never leaves Hoyland Common. It is either set there, or he uses the sensibility and values he found there wherever it is set: a deep respect for and identification with the miners, and, by extension, all working people. He nourished an unromantic, but poetic, appreciation and understanding of the lives and sensibilities of the people there. This sense of where he comes from and where he belongs gave him a firm identity.

I first met Barry in the mid-1960s. Alfred Bradley, a radio producer in Leeds, had tipped me off about this likely lad. From the first moment I could see a man I could deal with. His bright blue eyes shone out at me like headlamps: I knew I was under scrutiny too. He turned me down. He knew who he was and he knew what he wanted to do. Go to Hoyland Common even now, observe and talk to the people there and you begin to understand the source and the strength of Barry's writing. The more particular and concrete the focus, the greater the general truth: the wisdom in that paradox is borne out in Barry's work.

Second, Barry was a socialist writer. Not a reformist, not a soft liberal, not a Stalinist hack. He was from the working class, identified with it and fought the class war. He never wavered or trimmed. His political convictions were in his bones. They were his lodestar and they succoured everything he wrote, even pieces that seemed to have no political theme.

Barry's life coincided with the collapse of coal production, a painful adjustment leading to a cruel defeat, to bitterness and depression. Living communities were destroyed. Over the years we talked extensively of the symbolic and practical significance of the miner in the labour movement: the National Union of Mineworkers, organised around groups of pits, was the most disciplined, most solid and formidable group of workers in Britain; what they produced was essential to powering the economy from the start of the Industrial Revolution right up to the middle of the twentieth century; the daily dangers they faced and their courage made them formidable. Whenever Capital needed a decisive victory over the organised working class, it knew that it had to beat the miners into submission: the rest would meekly follow.

His two linked films, *The Price of Coal*, showed both Barry's affection for the miner and his cold anger that it should still be a hazardous and life-threatening occupation. His response to the Thatcher confrontation in 1984–85 was bitter. He was particularly exercised by the events at Orgreave and their consequences. He mourned the wanton destruction of close communities, as he marked the solidarity in the face of a cruel state apparatus. His writing about it was not produced. One grieves that it will never be produced.

The third element surprises those who know of him only as a writer in the tradition of provincial realism. They clearly have not read him attentively. Barry was a poet. He was not 'poetic'. He would never use a poetic image, however beautiful, if it did not feel necessary. In that sense he wasn't a 'writer', revelling in his command of words. His words are used sparingly. Each one has to earn its keep. They were tools of his trade, to be used precisely. Their job was to create a believable world. In giving his readers necessary information he also fed their imaginations, usually with the use of arresting similes, a product of his detailed observation, particularly of the flora and fauna of the Yorkshire countryside. One should place him firmly in the English pastoral tradition.

Barry went to work each morning, faced a blank sheet of paper and almost literally mined words, rejected some, then rearranged them, like most other professional writers. But Barry saw himself as a man literally hacking them out, mining black gold. It was a romanticising conceit, if you will, but it tells one much about where his sensibilities lay. He was a worker at the service of other workers.

He was always humble in his home environment. He never liked being away from Hoyland Common. He was the laureate of his own people and praise from a miner, brief and rarely spoken, would fill him with pride. He will be read in a hundred years' time by his own Yorkshire people. Reputations come and go, but one suspects that Barry's evocations of a lost world will always find a reader from the wider world.

Acknowledgements

The authors would like to thank the following, who have contributed to and supported this project in a variety of ways: Amanda Bernstein, Val Harding, Jacky Hodgson, Chris Loftus, Jane Mason and Mary Sackett in Special Collections, University of Sheffield Library; our students James Ashby, Lucy Barnes, Chloe Bolton, Ryan Bramley, Jed Dixon, Emily Flint, Katie Goody, Jessica Hammonds, Louise Hooper, Iona Johnson, Linnea Pettersson, Jemma Roffey and Dominic Sims; Emily Parsons at the Willy Russell Archive; Kathleen Dickson and Steve Tollervey at the BFI; Jonny Davies at the BFI Reuben Library; Nick Bentley, Julia Dobson, Hugh Escott, David Etherington, Kate Flannery, Tony Garnett, Mark Hanna, Margaret Hines, Richard Hines, Sally Hines, Tom Hines, Jane Hodson, Rachel Hughes, Ian Nannestad, Beth Johnson, Pete Lyons, Seàn McCorry, Robert McKay, Michael Mangan, Scott Marshall, John Miller, Eleanor Mulvey, Jean Penchion, Charlie Pritchard-Brennan, Jonathan Rayner, Willy Russell, Dave Silver, Andrew Smith, Gemma Thorpe; Paul Clarke, Matthew Frost and everyone at Manchester University Press; and all our family members and friends.

Note on referencing: throughout, 'BHP' (Barry Hines Papers) precedes all references in endnotes to archival material, followed by details of box and folder.

Introduction

Kes, *Threads* and beyond

While this book is by no means a biography, the importance of environment in Barry Hines's writing means that insight into his background and the journey to his writing career introduces us to the recurrent preoccupations of his work. The son and grandson of a miner, Hines grew up in Hoyland Common, a pit village between Rotherham and Barnsley in the heart of South Yorkshire's Dearne Valley. Hines passed the 11-plus examination and attended Ecclesfield Grammar School, on the outskirts of Sheffield, from 1950 to 1957. This experience shaped Hines's long-standing and vociferous criticism of the grammar school system: 'Just because I sat down one morning when I was 10 years old and got a few more sums right than my mates seemed no reason for trying to make me into a snob', he observed in 1975.[1] Notwithstanding a brief stint as a mining surveyor, Hines did, however, stay on at school to study for O-levels and A-levels and subsequently took up a place at Loughborough College of Education, graduating in 1963 with a Certificate in Physical Education.

Hines was a talented footballer and athlete. He had been offered trials for Manchester United, played in the reserves at Barnsley, and represented the English FA's School Week XI (effectively a national Grammar School Boys team) in a 3–0 loss to Scotland, an experience which enabled him to see 'the class system close up', and 'to place football into some kind of social perspective'.[2] Having previously suggested that he was not 'an academic boy', and that 'football and running were the only things I was any good at', Hines's response to the match was an early sign of the subtle notion of sport as a site of intellectual reflection and practice that would inform much of his writing.[3]

Undoubtedly, this appreciation was cultivated throughout Hines's time at Loughborough, where in the football team he played along-side Bob Wilson, who would go on to represent Scotland and to play for Arsenal. He also played alongside Dario Gradi, one of the longest-serving managers of all time and the architect of the cel-ebrated Crewe Alexandra academy, and Ted Powell, who as a youth coach with England developed future stars such as Paul Scholes, Gary Neville, Robbie Fowler and Sol Campbell. The point here is not to indulge in trivia about Hines's social network of footballing personalities, but to point out that at Loughborough he was sur-rounded by others who were also thinking conceptually about the game, none more so than his coach, Allen Wade, who went on to publish the definitive coaching manual, *The F.A. Guide to Training and Coaching*.[4] Wade's approach was notable for its integration of a theoretical dimension into the practice of football, and it was clear that Loughborough was for Hines a similar crucible of the intellec-tual and the physical. Indeed, Hines's undergraduate dissertation, a piece of creative writing entitled 'Flight of the Hawk', explored and sought to bridge the tensions between legitimised academic pursuits and the apparently more down-to-earth pleasures and struggles of football. Following the gender division that frequently appears in Hines's writing, according to which mothers prioritise academic skills, fathers sporting ones, in 'Flight of the Hawk' it is the protago-nist Jack's mother who considers that her aspiring footballer son 'was wasting his time and should be studying instead of watching 22 men running round after a bag of wind'.[5]

The spark for Hines's literary career began when his room-mate at Loughborough, Dave Crane, lent him a copy of George Orwell's *Animal Farm*, 'the first novel I'd read in my own time, and of my own volition … I was 21', as he noted later.[6] The experience unlocked Hines's passion for reading and writing, which led to his submitting short stories to the college magazine and finding 'some-thing special' in the 'simple style' of Ernest Hemingway.[7] Hines, in short, became a writer. In all of his work after this point, Hines dis-carded the Modernist style of free indirect discourse that had char-acterised 'Flight of the Hawk' and his early stories. Instead, he can be seen to follow Hemingway's 'principle of the iceberg', by means of which a surface clarity and simplicity of expression conveys a deeper significance without expounding it.[8] Hines valued the fiction of such British writers as Stan Barstow, who acted as the younger writer's mentor in getting his work published, and Alan Sillitoe. In

Hines's BBC Play for Today *Speech Day* (John Goldschmidt, 1973), Sillitoe's short story collection *The Loneliness of the Long Distance Runner* (1959) is handed out at an English class, yet tantalisingly taken away again after an interruption before it can be read, dramatising the author's disappointment at schooling priorities. Ian Haywood detects another influence, in likening Billy's mother in *A Kestrel for a Knave* (1968) to the character of Helen, the neglectful mother to the protagonist Jo, in Shelagh Delaney's 1958 play *A Taste of Honey*.[9]

By reason of these influences and his own practice, much of the literary reception of Hines's work places him within a canon of working-class writing.[10] However, more nuance has recently been given to such an apparently straightforward categorisation. Dave Russell argues that *A Kestrel for a Knave*, in its focus on a 'dysfunctional' family in place of a more 'clichéd' or romanticised version, is a precursor to what he calls the 'underclass' writing of the 1980s, by such writers as Alan Bleasdale and Andrea Dunbar.[11] This suggests that, ironically, a novel taken to be an archetypal representation of a young boy's working-class life, his experiences at an uninspiring local school to be followed by a future down the pit, is not fully contained by such a definition.[12] In turn, Hines has influenced succeeding generations of writers in terms of his style and concerns, including David Peace, the author of such novels as *Red Riding* (1999–2002), about corruption and murder in Yorkshire, and *GB84* (2004), centring on the miners' strike. Versions of the kestrel imagery itself, as a 'living talisman' of a different kind of life,[13] have appeared in a wide variety of texts ranging from Stephen Kelman's 2011 novel *Pigeon English*, shortlisted for the Booker Prize of that year, to the BBC television drama *Nature Boy*, scripted by Bryan Elsley (Joe Wright, 2000).

Hines spent the period from 1960 to 1962 working at a school in London's Paddington, and, after graduating from Loughborough, returned to Hoyland Common to continue teaching physical education, a role in which he remained until 1972. Soon enough he set about writing his first work, *Billy's Last Stand*, a radio play about a coal-shoveller whose life is interrupted by an outsider with commercial interests, which was broadcast on the BBC's 'Third Programme' in 1965. In the words of John Hall, who interviewed the author for a *Guardian* profile in 1970, Hines approached the play 'with no medium in mind, and at epic length'.[14] Although traces of the

Beckettian tenor of *Billy's Last Stand* are evident in some of Hines's later works, including his screenplays for the television film *Two Men from Derby* (1976) – which he claimed to be the favourite of all his works – and the unproduced *Fun City* of the mid-1980s, Hines developed what would become his trademark style of poetic realism in *The Blinder*. This first novel, about the teenage footballing prodigy Lennie Hawk, was published in 1966, fittingly also the year of England's World Cup win, and is structured according to the familiar narrative of conflict between intellectual and sporting life which underlay Hines's own biography.

On the strength of this novel, the television and film producer Tony Garnett invited Hines to write a Wednesday Play for the BBC, but the author turned this offer down in order to complete a different project: his novel *A Kestrel for a Knave* of 1968. This novel, which was filmed as *Kes* by Ken Loach the following year, is not only Hines's best-known work, but, with its plot about a misunderstood 15-year-old schoolboy who gains solace from training a kestrel, has taken up a permanent place in British cultural history. Ian McMillan's description of the novel's protagonist Billy Casper as 'a South Yorkshire Icarus', who attempts to rise above his unfulfilling environment, reveals that the story's power lies in its being at once identifiably local yet also universal.[15] McMillan's invocation of Icarus is apt, given the significance from Hines's earliest writing onwards of the metaphor of attempted flight. The imagery of birds is used to show the effect of jazz on its audience in 'I Went to a Concert', a short story Hines published while a student. It is also used to convey prowess at 'the beautiful game', as we see in the hawk imagery that furnishes the title for Hines's football-focused dissertation and the protagonist's surname in *The Blinder*.[16] Birds equally embody a wish for transcendence and escape more broadly, as is evident in *A Kestrel for a Knave* itself, in the surname of the schoolteacher Tom Kite in the unproduced film script of that name, and in *The Gamekeeper*, where the protagonist George Purse, the gamekeeper of the title, watches with secret envy when a young pheasant flies away, out of reach of the Guns on a shoot. The aviary tended by Jimmy, the boyfriend of the central character Ruth, in *Threads* (Mick Jackson, 1984) conveys the idea of lost values of nurture when his *Handbook of Foreign Birds* is discarded by his daughter Jane a generation into post-apocalyptic life on Earth; while the pet budgerigar owned by Karen and her mother in *Looks and Smiles* (Ken Loach, 1981) acts as an emblem of their own experience of constriction, living as they do in a high-rise flat without the chance to keep such birds as pigeons or chickens.[17] In Hines's customary method, allegorical and realist codes are inextricable in these instances.

After *A Kestrel for a Knave*, Hines published *First Signs* (1972), another novel about education in a South Yorkshire setting, followed, in what became an exceptionally productive decade, by a series of film and television screenplays. The Play for Today *Speech Day* of 1973 continued Hines's exploration of education's role in perpetuating class inequality. This was followed by *The Gamekeeper* in 1975, Hines's novel about class in relation to private landownership, and the Loach-directed film version was released in 1980. The contradictions of the gamekeeper's life, as a liminal figure living between the two 'estates' of ducal woods and council housing, makes this individual, and the narrative as a whole, especially enigmatic. Garnett commissioned Hines's next project by inviting him to write about what was 'on his mind': the answer was 'mining'.[18] This resulted in the screenplay for a pair of Plays for Today, *The Price of Coal*, broadcast in 1977, the year of the Queen's Silver Jubilee, about the implications for a mining community of a royal visit followed by a fatal pit accident. In a change from what had been his usual practice, Hines wrote the screenplay before the novel, and repeated this pattern with *Looks and Smiles* (Ken Loach, 1981), about the early days of Thatcher-era unemployment in Sheffield. The aesthetic priority of the screenplay in each case shows that Hines had uncovered a talent for drama, based on his feeling for dialogue and setting as well as filmic technique, and he frequently included directions for camera movements in his scripts. As well as this, in all four of his collaborations with Loach, Hines was involved in casting decisions alongside the director, attended the process of location filming, and even took part in that of cutting and editing, making his role in these works transcend that simply of writer.

In 1983, Hines published *Unfinished Business*, a novel that is unusual in his body of work in placing centre-stage the experiences of a working-class woman whose life is fundamentally altered by going to university as a mature student. By this time, Tony Garnett had left Britain for a decade-long sojourn in the USA, one of the reasons, alongside its apparent resemblance to the film version of Willy Russell's *Educating Rita*, also released in 1983, why the novel was never adapted for the screen. The Northern city-setting of *Unfinished Business* goes unnamed. However, Hines had been a Yorkshire Arts Fellow in Creative Writing at the University of Sheffield from 1972 to 1974, and its distinctive buildings, including the Brutalist high-rise Arts Tower, are clearly depicted. Hines describes his office on the ninth floor of the Arts Tower, and the view of the nearby steelworks and council estates it afforded and which 'inspired' his writing, in the title essay to the anthology *This Artistic Life*.[19] Hines was an Arts Council Fellow at Sheffield City Polytechnic, now Sheffield Hallam University, from 1982 to 1984, meaning that the city was the consistent backdrop to the composition of *Unfinished Business*.

Hines's largely convincing effort to respond to the era's gender politics in *Unfinished Business* emphasises how important the retention of an up-to-date symbiosis of real-world events and writing was for him. In his works of the 1990s, including *Shooting Stars* (Chris Bernard, 1990) and *Born Kicking* (Mandie Fletcher, 1992), some elements of a nascent engagement with other aspects of contemporary Britain, including its multicultural nature, appear. However, the plot of *Shooting Stars* is a preliminary and sometimes uncomfortable examination of a concern with the elements of intersectional identity-formations, including that of ethnicity, which Hines's writing life did not continue long enough to address fully. Hines's responsiveness to political contexts meant that he had brought great commitment to writing the screenplay for the 1984 nuclear-attack drama *Threads*, for which his script provides the extreme generic and narrative disruption of a nuclear bomb falling on Sheffield and destroying the known western world. *Threads* was a shocking cautionary tale which prompted widespread political debate on its television broadcast in both the UK and USA. The miners' strike of 1984–85 followed this, and affected Hines's writing in a traumatic and contradictory manner. Although he drafted no less than three plays on the topic, the difficulty Hines experienced in attempting to represent these exceptionally divisive events meant that none of the plays was ever produced or filmed. His next published work was *The Heart of It* (1994), an elegiac look back at the strike a decade on in the form of a novel.

The era of deindustrialisation which followed the miners' strike during the Thatcher years meant that Hines had to branch out from what had been his usual explorations of Northern working-class communities, and bring his concern with inequality and injustice instead to the effects of redundancy and unemployment. This was not always such a sure task, as is evident in the television film *Shooting Stars* and Hines's final novel, *Elvis Over England* (1998), where his customary themes are refracted, respectively, through narratives about youth crime and middle-aged regret. Hines's screenplay for the 1993 film *Born Kicking* marked a return to a football narrative, but this time it is a London-set one in which the protagonist who is torn between academic and sporting success is a woman. Despite its realist look, Garnett describes the film as a 'fantasy', so distant was its premise of a woman playing for the England team.[20] Even relatively late in his writing career, Hines's focus remained with representing such flights of political and aesthetic fancy.

Writing in the *Observer* in 2005, Richard Benson records asking Hines about the apparent paradox in his work, that it regrets alike the terrible hardship, and equally terrible absence, of hard manual labour. As Benson puts it, '*Looks and Smiles* seemed to evoke nostalgia for old industrial communities even as *The Price of Coal* clearly rues the associated hardships'.[21] Benson evokes here what could be described as the central structural principle of Hines's work: that of ambivalence. Both manual work, most paradigmatically mining, and school education, are represented in Hines's writing in terms of a 'polarisation of feelings, thoughts, actions' that are 'interpreted as in principle irresolvable', as Kurt Lüscher defines ambivalence.[22] Rather than revealing to young people new capacities in themselves and others, education is instead shown, in Foucauldian fashion, to be inextricable from, and meant to accustom young people to, the actuality of work and inequality. In many of Hines's works we witness the 'disappointments' suffered by those who should be experiencing 'the wonderful life force of teenage optimism'.[23] In his last works, Hines's representation of former miners and steelworkers faced with 'modern, call-centre-world anomie' is perhaps even bleaker than his revelation of that manual work's dangers and hardships, as his response to Benson reveals.[24]

After a diagnosis of dementia in 2008, Hines moved from Sheffield back to his native Hoyland. While the headline '*Kes* Comes Home'[25] with which the local newspaper greeted him conveys a self-consciously hyperbolic conflation of author, bird and book on the part of journalists, it also acknowledges the lifelong significance for

Hines of a specific location. His commitment to South Yorkshire's representation stayed with him even when he was living away, and this invariably took a personal and a political form. The county appears both on its own geographical and historical account, yet also as a synecdoche for, or even, in Mikhail Bakhtin's term, a chronotopic realisation of, class relations under capitalism.[26] When Hines died in 2016, many obituaries returned to the cultural importance of *A Kestrel for a Knave* and its continuing significance for contemporary readers. Our aim in the present volume is to endorse such a claim, while arguing for the equal value of Hines's other works.

Hines's archive, the Barry Hines Papers, on which we have drawn throughout this study, reveals that no less than ten projects from the extent of his writing life remained in draft or unproduced form. Among these are his three miners' strike plays, as well as *Slate*, a play about a Welsh mining village into which he transposed elements from the miners' strike, and *Private Fears*, a film script about the nuclear power industry. As was the case for *Slate*, in *Springwood Stars* (2000), another of Hines's unproduced plays, the writer adopted a historical perspective which would never be realised in his broadcast or published work. The account in *Springwood Stars* of a young working-class footballer who escapes the depression-hit North through his footballing talents, playing for Herbert Chapman's Arsenal side in the 1920s, witnessed Hines returning to familiar thematic terrain, albeit set in the pre-war past. In this sense, it is possible to see variations on his preoccupations as well as preliminary sketches for later ideas in the archival material. For instance, Hines's unproduced play 'The Last Shift' of the mid-1970s is a realist parable ostensibly about the impending retirement of a pit pony, in which the parallel injustice meted out to animals and to manual labourers, which appears in fully realised form in *The Gamekeeper*, is a matter overtly debated by the characters. Other works contained in Hines's archive did appear in the public realm, yet have slipped out of cultural memory. These include the 1967 radio play *Continental Size Six*, a precursor to *Two Men from Derby* in its centring on a blackly comic portrait of football fanaticism, the title referring to the fan's expensive football boots; while neither *Speech Day* nor *Two Men from Derby* is currently available to view, despite their both having been commissioned for the BBC Play for Today television strand. Even more of a definitive loss of this kind has been undergone by the television version of *Billy's Last Stand*, also a Play for Today (1971), and which no longer exists at all. Our sense of its appearance relies entirely on cast lists and contemporary press reviews.

The very fame of *A Kestrel for a Knave* – Hines was always insistent that the novel be referred to by its original title – has meant that much of his other writing has been overlooked. Even *Threads*, for which the director Mick Jackson asked Hines to write the screenplay in order to ground the atomic-disaster drama in a socially realist setting, is not always associated with the author.[27] Our aim in the present book has thus been twofold: to bring to wider attention all the rest of Hines's work, and to argue that his writerly contribution to films such as *Kes* and *Threads*, as well as to his other collaborations with Garnett, Loach and such directors as Chris Bernard and Mandie Fletcher, should be given its full due.

Notes

1 Barry Hines, *This Artistic Life*. Hebden Bridge: Pomona 2009, p. 86.
2 Ibid., p. 90.
3 Ibid., p. 85.
4 Allen Wade, *The F.A. Guide to Training and Coaching*. S.l.: Trafalgar Square Publishing 1967.
5 Barry Hines, 'Flight of the Hawk', unpublished dissertation, Loughborough College 1964, BHP BLX/1.
6 Anonymous, 'Loughborough Team Photo'; John Hall, 'Barry Hines 1970 Interview – from the Archive', the *Guardian* 21 March 2016.
7 Hall, 'Barry Hines 1970 Interview'.
8 George Plimpton, 'An Interview with Ernest Hemingway: The Art of Fiction', *Paris Review* 18 1958, pp. 60–89: 74.
9 Ian Haywood, *Working-Class Fiction: From Chartism to Trainspotting*, London: Northcote House 1997, p. 106. Hines later described his regret at not having paid more sympathetic attention to the circumstances of either Mrs Casper or Jud, both of whom appear through Billy's disenchanted viewpoint: see Nigel Armitage, 'Interview with Barry Hines', *Yorkshire Magazine* 13 November 2011.
10 See for instance Simone Turnbull, 'The Portrayal of the Working class and Working-class Culture in Barry Hines's Novels', unpublished PhD thesis, Sheffield Hallam University 2014.
11 Dave Russell, *Looking North: Northern England and the National Imagination*, Manchester: Manchester University Press 2004, p. 91.
12 See also Roberto del Valle Alcalá's argument in the terms offered by

Gilles Deleuze and Félix Guattari that Billy's bodily and intellectual being exceeds a working-class identity, in his 'Class, Embodiment and Becoming in British Working-Class Fiction: Re-reading Barry Hines and Ron Berry with Deleuze and Guattari', *College Literature* 43 (2) 2016, pp. 375–96.

13 Dominic Head, *The Cambridge Introduction to Modern British Fiction, 1950–2000*, Cambridge: Cambridge University Press 2002, p. 57.
14 Hall, 'Barry Hines 1970 Interview'.
15 Ian McMillan, 'Yorkshire found its voice in *Kes*', the *Guardian* 21 March 2016.
16 Mr B. Hines, 'I Went to a Concert', *Thesaurus: A Magazine of Creative Writing by Loughborough Students*, May 1963, pp. 8–10.
17 See Hines, *This Artistic Life*, p. 2.
18 Tony Garnett, interview with the authors, 19 October 2015.
19 Hines, *This Artistic Life*, pp. 1–4.
20 Garnett, interview with the authors.
21 Richard Benson, 'When we were heroes', the *Observer* 4 December 2005, reprinted in Hines, *This Artistic Life*, pp. 159–69: 168.
22 Kurt Lüscher, quoted in Dagmar Lorenz-Meyer, 'The Politics of Ambivalence: Towards a Conceptualisation of Structural Ambivalence in Intergenerational Relations', *Gender Institute New Working Papers*, 2, February 2001, pp. 1–23: 3.
23 Garnett, interview with the authors.
24 Benson, 'When we were heroes', p. 166.
25 This *Barnsley Chronicle* headline is reproduced in Hines, *This Artistic Life*, p. 175.
26 See Mikhail Bakhtin, 'Forms of Time and Chronotope in the Novel', *The Dialogic Imagination: Four Essays*, ed. Michael Holquist. Austin: University of Texas Press 1981.
27 Some of the fullest analyses of Hines's work take place at a remove, and without much mention of the writer himself, in those studies of Ken Loach in which their four collaborative film projects are discussed. These include not only Jacob Leigh (2002) and John Hill (2011) but also French critical studies of the director, which focus on the cinema releases and thus omit *The Price of Coal*; see for instance Francis Rousselet, *Ken Loach: un rebelle* (Paris: Le Cerf 2002), and Erika Thomas, *Le cinéma de Ken Loach* (Paris: Harmattan 2005).

Poetry with purpose and the journey to *Kes*

Billy's Last Stand, The Blinder, A Kestrel for a Knave and *Kes*

In this chapter, we trace the roots of Barry Hines's literary mode of poetic realism in those works of the 1960s that preceded *A Kestrel for a Knave* (1968). These include the 1965 play *Billy's Last Stand*, which gives an absurdist form to its social-realist content, and Hines's first novel *The Blinder* (1966), its title invoking the concept of a sporting move characterised by its excellence – ironically so, given the introduction this novel offers to Hines's consistent theme of the stand-off between sporting and intellectual pursuits in an individual's life story. The literary promise Hines showed in *The Blinder* led to the filming of his novel *A Kestrel for a Knave* as *Kes* (Ken Loach, 1969). We argue that the roots of this novel's cinematic realisation are already apparent in Hines's prose, meaning that the film, so significant in British cultural history, is more of a writerly and collaborative venture than has yet been acknowledged.

Billy's Last Stand (1965, 1970, 1971)

Billy's Last Stand was first broadcast as a radio play on the BBC's 'Third Programme' in 1965. The play is a sparse duologue in which a coal-shoveller, Billy (Arthur Lowe), has his simple but impoverished life interrupted by a manipulative outsider, Darkly (Ronald Baddiley). Darkly becomes Billy's business partner, forcing him to adopt increasingly laborious and almost literally 'back-breaking' working practices; Billy then persuades Darkly to join him in violently assaulting and leaving for dead Starky, a competing worker who threatens their trade. At the play's end Billy himself murders Darkly, in a desperate attempt to return to the simplicity of his past. The play thus presents an allegorical critique of enterprise and consumer culture, a familiar concern of course to working-class writers of the period, yet, as we will see, its minimalism distances it from the social realism of Hines's contemporaries. To approach *Billy's Last Stand* as a 'lost play' – on the basis that no recording of the TV play exists – therefore is to begin to develop a fuller and multi-dimensional understanding of both Hines's complex creative agency and the traditions of post-war working-class writing in which his work is included.

The play was written while Barry Hines was a PE teacher at the St Helen's Secondary Modern School in the Athersley area of Barnsley, South Yorkshire, where he worked between 1963 and 1968. It was Hines's first broadcast work and was developed along-side his debut novel *The Blinder* in his spare time. Like almost all of his plays, films and novels, it was inspired by his class background and the community in which he lived and worked, as Hines put it in an interview to support the broadcast: 'There is a man in this village who gets in coal for a few shillings. I just happened to think of him when I started writing … Billy has a coal shifting business and this other man tries to get into the business and eventually takes it over. The man represents society and Billy, the outsider.'[1] Even in the infancy of his writing career, we can begin to identify in Hines's own interpretation of his work the development of central themes and emphases that would underpin his later, more widely known novels and screenplays, namely the relationship between marginalised individuals and the social and economic forces beyond their control. It is therefore significant that, following the broadcast, the play's producer, Alfred Bradley, persuaded the BBC's Northern Region to award the then 25-year-old Hines a bursary to develop his writing, giving him the time and space to write *A Kestrel for a Knave*.

While learning more about the context of *Billy's Last Stand* and its origins helps us to gain a greater sense of Hines's development as a young writer, a consideration of the play's diverse modality offers a way to understand the author's ambiguous status within discourses about working-class and regional post-war writing. After its beginning as a radio play, Hines adapted *Billy's Last Stand* as a theatre production, first for regional theatre in Bolton, and then 'upstairs' at the Royal Court, directed by Michael Wearing in 1970, where Darkly was played by Ian McKellen. The play was received extremely well by critics, so that Hines was praised for his 'considerable literary touch'[2] by Milton Shulman; his mastery of the 'small, closely observed subject'[3] by Pearson Phillips; and for producing 'a story told with the intensity and detail of D.H. Lawrence at his best'[4] by Rosemary Say. The near-universal acclaim for the play is telling: this was to be Hines's only theatrical production, although *Kes/Kestrel for a Knave* has repeatedly been adapted for the stage, as have *The Price of Coal* and *Two Men from Derby*, but with a range of different writers and never with Hines taking the lead. Knowledge of Hines's brief but successful career as a playwright – the play was also performed in Germany and reproduced for publication in the United States – further reveals the complex and multi-layered nature of his authorship. In chronological terms, Hines was first a radio writer, then a novelist, before adapting *Kes* as a screenplay, and then working on *Billy's Last Stand* for the theatre, and finally for his first television play in 1971. While Hines shifted between mediums during this frenetic early period of writing, *Billy's Last Stand* also shows a new willingness to experiment with genre. Indeed, the BBC Play for Today production, directed by John Glenister, who would collaborate again with Hines five years later on *Two Men from Derby*, differs very little from the radio play and theatre versions, although, predictably, the violence appears to have been toned down. Thus the play maintains the earlier version's stark aesthetic and formal structure, its minimal use of location and its symbolic rather than multi-dimensional or realist characterisation.

In *Billy's Last Stand*, Hines can be seen to work outside the generic tropes that would characterise his work with Loach. For example, Darkly and Billy are avowedly unrepresentative figures: Billy is a self-confessed 'rag man'[5] who lives in a shed, and Darkly, we are told, used to 'get bad heads and have dos … a kind of mental strain' (32). Both men are thus at the very margins of society and while familiar thematic interests of Hines's characterise the narrative, including the emphasis on coal and a wider meditation on labour, and the effects of the market on the dignity of individuals and communities, there can be little doubt that *Billy's Last Stand*'s allegorical nature and stark focus on just two characters constitute an experimental dimension within Hines's oeuvre.

The play's moral, and by extension socioeconomic, themes are communicated through Billy's worsening physical condition and increasingly uncertain mental state as his relationship with Darkly develops. He begins the play happy with the simplicity and freedom of his working pattern, but Darkly tells him 'it's getting harder working on and off like tha does, things are changing' (11). Billy, despite his suspicions of Darkly's intentions, seems grudgingly to accept his new acquaintance's view of the world: 'Ar, things are closing in as tha says, tha closing in on me' (11). Billy's personal sense of wellbeing is thus inextricably linked to the socioeconomic determinism represented by Darkly. As the second act begins, three months have passed and we are told that:

> *BILLY IS SHOVELLING COAL AS AT THE BEGINNING OF ACT I, ONLY THIS TIME SLOWLY, MAKING HARD WORK OF IT. HE TAKES FREQUENT RESTS, STRAIGHTENENING UP AND RUBBING THE SMALL OF HIS BACK.* (29)

Billy's body thus itself becomes a symbol of his exploitation and subordination to the demands of the market: the more he works, the more money he makes, and the more his body (and soul) decays:

> DARKLY: Thi money's building thi security for thi.
> BILLY: An' it's building my worries an' all.
> DARKLY: Tha talks t'opposite way round to everybody else.
> BILLY: But I act same. I never used to, but I do now.
> DARKLY: Nowt wrong wi' that, is there?
> BILLY: There is! There is! It means that I'm not t'same bloke anymore. I'm nowt but a bloody fool now. What do I do first time I get a bit o'money in my pocket? I rush out an' buy myself a few extras. Luxuries they call 'em, but before I know where I am they've become necessities an' I'm on t'scrounge for summat else.
> DARKLY: It's all part of modern living, Billy lad.
> BILLY: What, being in a turmoil all along? Worrying about growing old, about saving, thi mind sharpened to a razor's edge through constant contact wi' cash, cash! Cash! *(Bangs his fist into his own palm three times).* (23–4)

Billy's anger is not just because of his self-recognition as a capitalist subject but it also enables Hines to explore, in a broader sense, the very nature of labour. Billy, we learn, used to be a miner (a byword for masculine virtue in many narratives of working-class lives, but for Hines something altogether more ambivalent), and this memory of collective working life enables Billy to philosophise on the distinction between fulfilling, autonomous labour and employment as exploitation:

> BILLY: I can't remember my back ever being as bad as this in all my years on this job.
> DARKLY: That'll be some, won't it? When did tha start?

BILLY: I don't know, but I can remember sweatin' cobs ont' face one day, and thinking, if King don't work why should I?

DARKLY: You daft bugger.

BILLY: What's daft about that?

DARKLY: We' what's getting coals in if it's not working?

BILLY: Ar, but I wa' employed before. And there's a big difference in work and being employed ... I enjoyed getting coals in, whereas before I wa' employed an' that's different, it's just different.

DARKLY: I don't know what tha on about.

BILLY: I can't explain it right, it's just t'way I feel. (*Pause*) Looking back I've had some good times getting coals in. (33)

This reminiscence of simpler times, itself contributing to the play's elegiac tone, leads Billy to describe his treasured collection of coals: 'Everyone o' them lumps brings back a memory. I spend hours looking o'er remembering' (34); in contrast, Darkly is incapable of understanding the symbolic, affective meaning of Billy's emotional investment in coal: 'I've never heard owt as bloody ridiculous in my life' (34), as he puts it. After the murder of Starky, Billy is provoked to kill Darkly by the latter's threat to destroy the coals and by extension Billy's attachment to memory and place. As the row escalates, another moment of self-recognition and clarity hits Billy: 'Inside me, it's all gone. There's nowt left but a shattered crumbling shell, I'm no good to man nor beast now' (46).

Billy's 'last stand' (to kill Darkly) is a destructive act which confirms his acceptance of, and his adherence to, an inevitable and ruthless capitalist reality. To reorder Hines's statement, Billy has now come to represent 'society' and he is no longer the 'outsider'. The play's allegorical tone, undoubtedly increased by its original conception as a radio play, invites further such readings of the representative rather than multi-dimensional facets of the characters. Thus, we might see Darkly as a reflection of Billy's own divided self, as a wholly symbolic entity representing his anxiety about the changing world. It is also possible to see Starky as a doubled version of Darkly (the linguistic similarity is clearly intentional) or indeed as the inverse of Billy, as Darkly describes him: 'He belongs to that breed o' men outside o' things. (*Pause*) Summat like thee, only nasty wi' it' (42).

The television broadcast of *Billy's Last Stand* was met with acclaim equal to that which had greeted Hines's stage version. Nancy Banks-Smith identified its allegorical tenor and symbolic patterns, deploying similar devices in her own review: 'An agent, our Darkly, a manager, a time-and-motion man, a would-be boss in an embryo. Having nearly broken Billy's back, cracked his integrity and essentially killed him, Darkly is himself killed by Billy. As if the tree falling crushed the insect.'[6] Virginia Ironside was also attentive to the play's political scope and singled out Hines for specific praise: 'The play was a cry on behalf of humanity against materialistic progress and was splendidly written by Barry Hines',[7] and an anonymous review in the *Sunday Times* suggested that *Billy's Last Stand* 'recalls Beckett's commentaries on human existence'.[8] While the popular press responded positively to Hines's first work since *Kestrel for A Knave*, Raymond Williams saw in *Billy's Last Stand* the work of a highly effective political dramatist, who was able to make tangible and human the dynamics of capital and labour in a way which was both dramatically convincing and ideologically coherent, as he argues:

> The lively and convincing common talk was not a theatrical cover, but the slow creation of a world of work and precarious survival. And the stranger came, not from an undefined area of threat, but from a real social condition. ... What Darkly was taking away was the freedom and self-respect of that kind of work, and he was doing it in the name of the modern idols: increased productivity and a rising standard of living.
> [...]
> There was at once immediacy and resonance: the facts of labour and of human identity, the destructive intrusion of a familiar alienation.[9]

Williams's reading of *Billy's Last Stand* illuminates significant aspects of Hines's thematic agenda as evident in all his work, including a highly politicised focus on class aided by a broader exploration of everyday life. Alongside the critical enthusiasm for the play in its various forms, it is clear that in 1971, at the age of just 32, Hines was building a reputation as a writer of some standing, one not solely based on his connection to *Kes*, or drawn from reductive conceptions of realism and 'working-class' writing. Indeed, as we argued at the outset, the anti-realist nature of *Billy's Last Stand* underlines Hines's willingness to challenge the traditional associations of working-class writing and the accompanying discursive formation of his art. Yet, the recordings of the TV play are not in existence, the play script is long out of print, and the radio play is available only at the whim of schedulers. Thus the 'lost' status of the text and its subsequent absence from Hines's available oeuvre fragments our wider understanding of his work. It is important to recall that the radio version of *Billy's Last Stand* was Hines's first work as a professional writer, completed just four years after he first began reading novels, let alone writing them. That a work of such originality and formal experimentalism emerged at such an early stage in his career was a significant creative achievement.

The Blinder (1966)

Following the broadcast of *Billy's Last Stand*, Alfred Bradley and Stan Barstow, the author of *A Kind of Loving* (1960) and by this point Hines's mentor, worked to gain a publisher for Hines's first novel *The Blinder*, and in June 1965 Hines was offered a contract by Michael Joseph. Hines acquired an agent in the same month, Sheila Lemon, who was again one of Alfred Bradley's contacts. It is important to note, however, that despite the apparent professionalisation of Hines's writing career, he was still at this point a full-time teacher, and remained so until 1972.

The Blinder was published in 1966, a fitting year for the release of a football novel, although the protagonist Lennie Hawk is by no means an exemplar for the national game and its successes. The teenage Hawk is on the one hand a gifted young player, and on the other a highly capable, albeit unenthusiastic, scholar – in both pursuits he is an outspoken maverick, increasingly aware of his class status. In the novel, Lennie wrestles with the dilemma of whether to go to university or to pursue a professional football career. In the process, and seemingly as a means of reinforcing in narrative terms his split interests, Lennie has an affair with the wife of his oppressive teacher, and embarks on a sexual relationship with the daughter of the corrupt chairman of the football club, Jane, who ends up pregnant with his child. The love triangle between an articulate, upwardly mobile young man, a sexually inexperienced younger woman of higher social standing, and a repressed older woman, recalls the regressive sexual politics of *Saturday Night and Sunday Morning* and *Room at the Top*.[10] Here, the chairman's proprietorial view of his daughter's relationship is strongly reminiscent of the transactional pragmatism of the factory owner, Mr Brown, in the novel and film of *Room at the Top*. *The Blinder*'s derivative nature and surface appearance as a by now tired Angry Young Man/New Wave narrative thus marks out *The Blinder* from the political allegory of *Billy's Last Stand* and the institutional critique and poetic realism of *A Kestrel for a Knave*, as Luke Spencer argues: '*The Blinder* contains some characteristic Hines ingredients – insubordinate working class male versus the system; the unsatisfactoriness of male-female relations; the arrogance of power – but they are not organised into a coherent ideological structure.'[11] However, while the novel's closeness to the earlier cycle of British working-class fiction makes it one of Hines's least distinctive works, it offers much in relation to one of his most significant recurring themes: that of sport, specifically football.

As we will show throughout this book, Hines's appreciation and knowledge of football is central to a number of his works, and was shaped by a multi-layered view of the game. Hines saw football in three distinct dimensions: as a mass leisure pursuit and central tenet of working-class life; as a site of working-class expression and performance; and as a way of understanding and organising social, political and economic relations. Football, for Hines, is never merely a fictional device; it is a subject worthy of exploration and representation in its own right.

Hines played the game to a high level throughout his youth, representing England at schools level and Barnsley F.C.'s A team, before studying PE at Loughborough College of Education, where he played for the college first team alongside others such as Bob Wilson, who would go on to have a long career for Arsenal and Scotland. It was at Loughborough that Hines began reading novels and taking an interest in literary fiction, and, rather than displacing his enthusiasm for the game, his emerging tastes added an intellectual dimension to it. This was made explicit in Hines's dissertation 'Flight of the Hawk', undertaken, rather boldly, as a piece of creative writing, as he puts it:

> My thesis was a novel. I don't know how I got away with it … It was all about aesthetics and sport being an art. Then I started my first novel (at school) which was a second draft of my thesis … He was a boy like I was, from a mining background, he played in the second division. It was the conflict between going to college or university or becoming a professional footballer … The thesis was a dry run for *The Blinder*: instead of having him a decent player, I'll have him absolutely brilliant, good enough to play for Manchester United.[12]

Hines's dissertation was therefore an embryonic version of *The Blinder*, underplaying the dramatic tension in favour of a more cerebral exploration of football as an aesthetic practice, and using the protagonist's dilemma as a way of putting forward an interface between apparently discrete and disparate physical and intellectual practices. As the preface states:

> The growth of aesthetic appreciation to me is vitally important and I feel that if Physical Education can awaken the appreciation of the arts, then it has performed a task which is of equal importance, if not greater, than many of its more boosted by-products.[13]

This contention is developed through the thirst of Jack, the protagonist of 'Flight of the Hawk', for a more expressive and less formulaic academic culture and, in turn, a yearning for an appreciation of football that goes beyond the adversarial and physical, and which instead privileges the aesthetic and emotional dimensions of the game. These points coalesce most effectively when Jack learns about the Ancient Greeks at school:

> I can just see me now playing football, stripped to t'waist in sun, big game; I'll bet they'd have been fair footballers them Greeks. I can tell by looking at 'em, good movers, they look like ball artists to me quick and agile. I'll bet they'd have had judges and awarded prizes for ball control and t'way you moved with it and I'll lay 6 to 4 that when a player got t'ball crowd wouldn't have yelled Get rid of it, get rid, they'd have wanted more than crunchers in their games, they'd have expected t'same kind of response as they felt in't theatre and from poetry and music, and it takes more than crunchers to give you that, it takes artists. That is if they'd have played at football.
>
> Then a good long bath. Talking with people and going to listen to a philosopher, chirping up and arguing [sic] if I'd owt worth saying. All this talk, seemed to me about everything music, drama, wrestling, philosophy, athletics, maths; that's what I like about it, a real mixture, not cutting one thing off from another, everything to do with people seemed to be important not just one side of him as seem t'case wi' a lot of people today.[14]

Jack's academic engagement here enables a deeper appreciation of football, which in turn sparks off an imaginative meditation on ancient history. Here Hines, albeit idealistically, initiates the philosophy of sport and art that underpins Lennie's idiosyncratic but full appreciation of the game as high culture in *The Blinder*, and, more broadly, 'Flight of the Hawk' offers a starting point in setting out Hines's deeply-held views on education and class: Jack, like many of his young protagonists, develops an enthusiasm for learning when he is given the freedom to do so independently in a non-institutional and anti-elitist fashion.

The Blinder's attempt at a nuanced examination of class and sport has naturally drawn comparisons with David Storey's 1960 novel *This Sporting Life*. Storey, like Hines, was well positioned to find the poetry in sport: he was a professional rugby league player and an art student, which Ian Haywood sees as generating 'inner tensions and conflicts' which 'could be seen as aesthetically productive as they informed much of his later fiction'.[15] As Peter Stead puts it, *The Blinder* was 'football's response' to Storey's novel, and there can be no doubt that elements of *This Sporting Life* bear comparison with the football text, and more broadly with Hines's use of and interest in sport. As Jeffrey Hill argues, *This Sporting Life* shows that the 'commercial relationships that governed the sport reproduced those present in work. As Storey shows, employers buy labour power through wages. The rugby players are commodities who symbolize the power of their employers.'[16] Indeed, just as Arthur's (Frank in the film) love for sport is polluted by his recognition that he is himself a commodity, Lennie's attempt to defy the board of his team, specifically the chairman and father of his lover, Mr Leary, shows a similar awareness of sport's potential as an allegorical mechanism to explore capitalist exploitation, a theme picked up in a number of Hines's later football narratives. Moreover, the tensions between an affluent sporting life and a hard (and economically deprived) working one also appear in *The Blinder*. While in *This Sporting Life*, this conflict is brought out through contrasts between Arthur's fortunes and those of his landlady, Mrs Hammond, Hines has Lennie's meteoric rise occur alongside his father's redundancy in *The Blinder*:[17]

> As she walked into the kitchen Mr Hawk passed the front window like someone crossing the screen.
> 'There's my dad here.'
> 'Where?' She came to look as though he was pointing to a photograph in the paper. 'Are you sure? He's only just gone.'
> 'Course I'm not. I've never seen him before.'
> Mr Hawk hung his jacket under his cape behind the kitchen door, and turned the lapel back to his snap from the inside pocket. He

walked into the living-room and placed the greaseproof packet on the corner of the table.

'What's a matter, Arthur?'

'We're on strike. What's up wi thee?'

'I've sprained my ankle.'

'What doing?'

'I went over in t'corridor.'

'Are they after more money again?'

'Is it bad?'

'Doctor says I've to have a month off.'

'Doctor says you've to have nothing of the kind. Who's to blame this time?'

'There's trouble over a new contract, and there's talk of 'em laying some men off.'

'What about you?' (47–8)

Hines deliberately makes no distinction between Lennie's injury and his father's, and making the provenance of the dialogue ambiguous in this way draws out the tragic juxtaposition between the structural inequality and precarious working conditions of Lennie's community and the individuating nature of his talent. In this sense, the novel succeeds in becoming what Lee McGowan terms 'a forceful and searing commentary on British working-class culture and its attachment to and the inflated value it places on football'.[18] However, *The Blinder* does more than merely critique the politics and economics of sport.

Although 'Flight of the Hawk' shows a fuller examination of Hines's aim to aestheticise sporting practice than the published novel, *The Blinder* contains a number of central scenes in which Hines attempts to invite an appreciation of football as a creative and, indeed, beautiful pursuit. It is important to reiterate, however, that this aim was avowedly political and can be connected, as implied at the outset, to Hines's wider project of imagining the possibilities and acknowledging the latent potential of working-class lives and cultures, as he reflected: 'You never hear anyone denigrating ballet dancers. It's ok if you've got no O levels, and you're a ballet dancer, but if you're a footballer and you've got no O Levels, you're thick.' This sentiment finds articulation in *The Blinder*, particularly in passages where Lennie is playing football:

> The ball had beaten the full back for him. All he had to do was dribble it down the line and centre. The forwards moved up in anticipation.

The centre half ran across to tackle. The centre was low and hard, travelling at knee height parallel to the ground. Lennie pivoted on his left leg and swung his right, pointing his foot like a ballet dancer. The ball would have gone a long way if the net hadn't stopped it. (12)

Hines's description of Lennie's goal moves beyond narrative reportage and is almost self-consciously poetic in its lingering attention to detail. In comparing his movement to that of a dancer, Hines seeks to elevate Lennie's craft to an art and transform the process of football into a performance. Yet this poetic transformation is not reserved solely for Lennie. While the narrative focus is very firmly on his football career, by means of the tensions in his school life, and in his duplicitous sex life, Hines also shows a separate, distinctively lyrical appreciation of the spaces and places that Lennie occupies. At the end of an early match, the 'crowd poured out of the gates like water from a sluice gate' (19), and, later when a conflicted Lennie walks alone, he observes cars passing 'in a glaring rush, slicing the night with their lights' (19) and a town that from above 'glittered in the valley like a shower of fallen stars' (154). Crucially, Hines also imbues the football ground itself with poetic significance as a theatre of communal participation, rather than just a backdrop for Lennie's performance on the pitch, as the stage for the expression of Lennie's individual talent:

The sun was dropping dead behind the kop and the big blue sky was already pink round the edges. A sharp wind cut across the pitch into the empty terrace, shaking and breaking the drops of melted frost hanging under the cross-bars of the crush barriers. The pitch was still greasy in the sun, but in the shadow, the frost was already sprinkling and sparkling the grass. Under the turf the earth was gripped tight by cold. (147)

This meticulously heightened rendering of a distinctive feature of working-class iconography (and topography) connects *The Blinder* to Hines's later works by showing a willingness to invite poetic interpretations of everyday spaces, places and practices. Thus, while *The Blinder* can be seen as derivative of earlier working-class fiction, it does signpost some of the most distinctive features of Hines's style and the thematic interests that would go on to find more successful execution in his next novel.

A Kestrel for a Knave (1968) and *Kes* (1969)

In the months following the publication of *The Blinder*, Hines began work on his second novel, *A Kestrel for a Knave*. The first draft was written while Hines was still teaching full-time and he was able to complete the second draft during a writing retreat on the Isle of Elba. The sabbatical was funded by a BBC Northern Region bursary and had been requested by Alfred Bradley. Bradley had given Hines his first break with *Billy's Last Stand*, as well as acting as a *de facto* agent along with Stan Barstow in successfully handling *The Blinder* manuscript, and again supported his young protégé, enabling him to take a term off school and complete what would be his most famous and widely revered novel.

A Kestrel for a Knave has been published across the world, in China, Japan, Russia as well as European territories; it has been adapted for the stage; performed as a musical; broadcast as two radio plays; and, most recently, it has been interpreted as a ballet, to great critical acclaim. Since the 1970s it has featured regularly on school curricula in the United Kingdom and continues to be taught to 12–16 year-olds: the novel can comfortably lay claim to being one of the most widely read pieces of post-war English literature. In 1999 it was republished as a Penguin Modern Classic, cementing its status within the national imaginary – indeed, it is significant that this mark of recognition has not been afforded to the work of any of Hines's more critically lauded contemporaries, such as Alan Sillitoe or David Storey. Yet there can be no question that for many, the novel is a mere companion to *Kes*, a film which is a symbol of British cinema – both a founding instance of British social realism and, more broadly, of post-war British film culture. Undoubtedly the visual text, *Kes*, has overwhelmed the literary text *A Kestrel for a Knave* in the popular imagination. It is significant that the Penguin edition carries as its cover the iconic film still of a pensive David Bradley, as Billy Casper, with his kestrel in the foreground – the novel thus appears as a book of the film, rather than as the book that inspired the film. While we will go on to discuss the film, and the significant role that Hines played in its creation, it is essential to begin with the literary text. *A Kestrel for a Knave* is a powerful, complex and lyrical exploration of class, landscape and education and its textual qualities should be acknowledged on their own merits before being integrated within a cross-medium reading of *Kes*.

On the surface, the novel is relatively simple, taking place over one day in the life of its central character, Billy Casper (albeit with significant flashback sections), a schoolboy who keeps and trains a kestrel. The reader is quickly made aware of Billy's routine and soon gains an insight into his familial and social isolation – he is a misfit at school and the stark circumstances of his difficult home life are made worse by his uncaring mother and bullying half-brother, Jud, who eventually kills Billy's beloved hawk after the latter spends Jud's money instead of placing it on what would have been a lucrative winning bet.

While *The Blinder* draws on Hines's experience of teaching and football, *A Kestrel for a Knave* retains the focus on education while relying on Hines's childhood experience of Hoyland Common, the semi-rural village between Barnsley and Rotherham where he grew up. More specifically, Hines's younger brother, Richard (to whom the novel is dedicated), trained hawks as a teenager and would go on to act as technical advisor on *Kes* – the pair read T.H. White's *The Goshawk* (1951), and the novel clearly draws on technical details of falconry gleaned from the book while showing a persistent attentiveness to the spatial characteristics of the South Yorkshire landscape.[19]

Unlike *The Blinder*, however, *A Kestrel for a Knave* breaks significantly from the traditions of working-class writing of the period. Billy is not a brash, conventionally articulate, misogynistic and sexually active protagonist, and the novel is concerned explicitly with environmental and institutional inequalities. While Billy is by no means a representative figure, his coming-of-age arc presents fundamental questions about the economy, and the relationship between labour and the education system.

For Ian Haywood, the familial and social cultures of novels such as *Saturday Night and Sunday Morning* are absent from Hines's bleaker, more precarious and fragmented vision of working-class life:

> Billy has no Aunt Ada to turn to; there is no trace of the nostalgic, older working-class community in the novel. It is as if a Hegelian break in history has taken place, leaving Billy stranded on the bleak fringes of affluence. Though Jud is a miner, the culture of traditional labour and class solidarity is absent from the story.[20]

While *The Blinder*, despite Lennie's father's redundancy, posits a cohesive and partially optimistic view of community aligned with its protagonist's spectacular talent, *A Kestrel for a Knave*, with its 'proletarian dawn opening',[21] strikes an immediately bleaker tone and marks a break with previous, more confident examples of working-class writing. Similarly, Dave Russell, in his analysis of Northern working-class fiction of the period, summarises a range of characteristics that Hines's novel undoubtedly breaks away from:

> They were certainly little concerned with much of the daily texture of northern life and did not engage at any significant level with regionally distinctive topography, labour relationships, workplace practices or any of the other standard concerns of earlier northern fiction. Similarly dialect was generally abandoned in favour of a looser regional demotic. [22]

In contrast, *A Kestrel for a Knave* is notable for its exploration of a regionally specific socioeconomic context; its use of local dialect is conspicuous throughout; and, perhaps most strikingly, the novel draws much of its aesthetic distinctiveness from its sustained engagement with the landscape its characters inhabit.

For Ian McMillan, himself a popular Barnsley writer, what 'the book has, in abundance is poetry'. For McMillan, 'the descriptions of the Lawrentian countryside around the place referred to as the city in the book are strikingly lyrical for a writer known for his straightforward take on socialist realism', and, as McMillan suggests, one of the novel's achievements is to give 'ordinary people … a kind of operatic grace by having their lives elevated to the status of art'.[23] What McMillan describes here might be identified as Hines's approach to 'poetic realism' in the novel, that is, his application of a delicate, lingering treatment of the details of the landscape as Billy experiences it, so that everyday, recognisable spaces are transformed into imaginative, multi-purpose symbols. For example, in the early part of the novel, as Billy goes about his duties as a paper-boy, the narrator breaks away from the functional processes of Billy's day to reflect on the sense of life in the landscape he encounters:

> A thrush ran out from under a rhododendron shrub and started to tug a worm from the soil between the loose asphalt chips. It stood over the worm and tugged vertically, exposing its speckled throat and pointing its beak to the sky. The worm stretched, but held. The thrush lowered its head and backed off, pulling at a more acute angle. The worm still held, so the thrush stepped in and jerked at the slack.

The worm ripped out of the ground and the thrush ran away with it, back under the shrubs.[24]

In one sense, Hines foregrounds the significance of the natural environment and its non-human inhabitants to the novel (we have yet to meet Kes), and in the process the animal world is identified as holding practical, narrative value and simultaneous symbolic potential, since the interplay between the thrush and the worm seems to point towards the spatial dynamics of Billy's and Kes's pleasures and struggles. More broadly, however, the frequency and sustained nature of Hines's 'nature writing' has the effect of centralising the working-class landscape as worthy of poetic interest.

For Ian Haywood, *A Kestrel for a Knave* 'draws on the pastoral tradition by structurally opposing urban corruption and alienation to a redemptive nature,'[25] and there is no doubt that the aforementioned lingering treatments of natural spaces operate as a relief from the hardship of Billy's encounters with the individuals and institutions that seek to contain and oppress him, as the scene below suggests:

> 'Just you wait lad! Just you wait 'til tonight!'
>   She went back in and banged the door. Billy turned away and looked down the garden, over the fence into the fields. A skylark flew up, trilling as it climbed. Higher and higher, until it was just a song in the sky. (25)

This passage, as Billy runs away from his mother, is indicative of the way nature is used as site of partial escape, yet the landscape is never idealised as offering idyllic sanctuary – it is always an in-between space, balancing the rural with the mechanical and the industrial, and thus the distinction that Haywood describes is more nuanced than it might at first appear. In an afterword to the Penguin Modern Classics edition, Hines writes: 'In the village where I lived, the miners walked to work across meadows, with sky larks singing overhead, before crowding into the cage at the pit top and plunging into the darkness' (200). In this sense, the landscape does not function to convey what Raymond Williams terms the 'rural innocence of the pastoral',[26] which denies the turbulent histories and live, socioeconomic dynamics of space. Instead it is positioned as an entity which is not fixed either temporally or pictorially, but constantly in motion through labour (or, indeed, its conspicuous absence). As Williams also observes in *The Country and the City*: 'A working country is hardly ever a landscape. The very idea of a landscape implies separation and observation,'[27] and, despite *A Kestrel for a Knave*'s positioning of the landscape as a site of reflection and poetic contemplation, it is always a 'working landscape',[28] as is the case in all almost all of Hines's works. To return to the earlier passage, the very physical mobility of the animal and plant imagery evokes a sense of the poetic topography as dynamic and evolving, a feature made tangible earlier in the same section:

> The sky was a grey wash; pale grey over the fields behind the estate, but darkening overhead, to charcoal away over the City. The street lamps were still on and a few lighted windows glowed the colours of their curtains. Billy passed two miners returning silently from the night shift. A man in overalls cycled by, treading the pedals slowly. The four of them converged, and parted, pursuing their various destinations at various speeds.
>   Billy reached the recreation ground. The gate was locked, so he stepped back and sprang on to the interlaced wire fence, scaled it and placed one foot on top ready for the descent. He rode it, with one hand and one foot on top, the other arm fighting for balance; but the more he fought, the more it shook, until finally it shook him off, over the other side into the long grass. He stood up. His pumps and jeans were saturated, and there was dog shit on his hand. He wiped it in the grass, smelled his fingers, then ran across the football pitch. (13)

The initial image succinctly combines a sense of the spectacle of the landscape with the impending reality of the 'darkening' presence of the pit. Billy's encounter with the miners is significant not only in the way we described previously – as industrial workers are shown to be inhabiting and operating within the pastoral landscape – but because he is also at work: he is on his paper round, and Hines connects Billy to those with whom he shares the landscape. The second paragraph takes on a more physical, and quite literally earthy, treatment of the space, yet the description is still both lingering and precise, just as it is when capturing the apparent beauty of the worm and the thrush a few pages later. There is here no artificial distinction drawn between reflective poetic imagery and the hardship of everyday labour.

The use of this 'poetic realism' is significant for Hines because of the way he avoids first person narration, free indirect discourse and other subjective literary devices. In an interview with Alfred

Hickling, Hines talked about how, during the writing of *The Blinder*, he drew unlikely inspiration from Evelyn Waugh:

> I saw him being interviewed on television. He was playing the absent-minded eccentric with the ear trumpet and so on, but what he said was that he only revealed who his characters were, where they were, and what they said. Their thoughts were left entirely in the mind of the reader. I thought: 'That's it!' I'd had problems with thoughts and internalised dialogue defeats me completely. I went straight home, scrapped the novel, and started again.[29]

Such an approach therefore places a much greater emphasis on place and space as signifiers of poetic meaning and emotional affect. What results in Hines's writing is a form of image-led narration, as he told Clare Jenkins:

> I can't write thoughts. Nobody thinks anything in my books. It's all at the surface. I think that's why I can write scripts. It's what people say and what they do and where they are, nothing happens inside them … I found that I couldn't do thoughts very well, I'm much better at the external.[30]

While we will go on to suggest that this style plays a central role in giving his screenplays, not least *Kes* itself, a distinctive aesthetic, it is useful to reflect here on Hines's own identification of the filmic nature of his literary style. In a contemporary review of *A Kestrel for a Knave*, Penelope Maslin noted Hines's 'extraordinary visual sense which makes his writing a series of word-pictures, derived not from purplish description but clarity of detail'.[31] Maslin points to qualities that we have already identified: that is, the way in which Hines transforms everyday spaces into sites of poetic value. Yet this image-led approach is not one-dimensional, and it is important – particularly given the aforementioned dominance of the film of *Kes* over the literary text – to note the more unconventional aspects of Hines's prose style.

For example, Hines's repeated use of short sentences, repetitions, and staccato punctuation effects in *A Kestrel for a Knave* is more evocative of contemporary postmodern working-class writers such as David Peace than of the literary tradition from which Hines emerges:

> Enter Mr Farthing, running. The boys mooching around the fringes of the fight, like supporters locked out of a football ground, spread

the word. The word spread amongst the back ranks of the crowd, and the knot slackened as boys hurried away before Mr Farthing could reach them. (95)

To return to Maslin, the passage also carries the quality of a stage direction – a description of an image rather than a literary evocation of it. This coldly static approach to location accelerates towards the end of the novel, as Hines seeks to convey the boy's immediate trauma over the discovery of Kes's death, as a grief-stricken Billy runs through the landscape described so richly at the outset:

> A shadow rippling across a drawn curtain. A light going on. A light going off. A laugh. A shout. A name. A television on too loud, throwing the dialogue out into the garden. A record, a radio playing; occasional sounds on quiet streets. (191–2)

The fragmentation here is in marked contrast to the descriptive detail found elsewhere in the novel and reflects with tragic efficiency Billy's heartbreak and alienation. It is notable that this scene precedes the fantasy sequence found at the novel's conclusion but deemed 'unfilmable' in *Kes*, where the same disjointed but ominously rhythmic style is deployed:

> The Pictures. Warm. Full. Smoky. Big Picture. Billy as hero. Billy on the screen. Big Billy. Kes on his arm. Big Kes. Close up. Technicolor. Looking round, looking down on them all, fierce eyed. (196)

At this stage of the novel, Hines's 'word pictures' are deployed without embellishment, with the sense of a series of still images, and the 'scene's' filmic quality is given added resonance by its placement within a cinema.

When combined with *A Kestrel for a Knave*'s lack of chapters (a feature of all Hines's works), and its flashback structure, the novel carries with it a conspicuous formal sparseness, albeit one which has been obscured through the novel's marginalization by the more narrationally conventional film version. Despite this, the political quality of *A Kestrel for a Knave* is never obscured, with its poetic qualities augmenting its fundamental concerns rather than detracting from them. As Hines himself commented: 'That's what *Kes* is about really – about the fact that Billy Casper's not supposed to be clever, he's not done well at school, but when he gets involved in something, then you get a sense of what his potential could be.'[32] Thus, the lyrical foregrounding of Billy's imagination and emergent literacy by means of falconry, and his subsequent heartbreak, is crucial to the novel's political project. As Luke Spencer puts it: 'Hines shows the boy's struggle to know and to control a small fragment of his world. It is a largely inarticulate process, but it can generate more conventional forms of learning, like the voracious reading of falconry books.'[33] The impossibility of this process is seen in the classroom scene where Hines has Billy teaching the class and the benevolent Mr Farthing about falconry (80), before a creative writing exercise shows us the extent of Billy's tragic home circumstances and the practical shortcomings of his education:

> Once day I wolke up and my muther said to me heer Billy theres your brecfast in bed for you there was backen and egg and bred and butter and a big pot of tea when I had my brecfast the sun was shining out side and I got drest and whent down stairs we lived in a big hous up moor edge and we add carpits on the stairs and in the all and sentrall eeting. (89)

Here, two literacies are presented: one self-taught, dynamic and empowering, the other heavily institutionalized and imposed, what John Kirk terms, 'the life deadening institution of the school'.[34] For Erica Hateley, this aspect of the narrative points to 'the difference between writing and being written',[35] and this is *A Kestrel for a Knave*'s central concern: that the beauty of the imagination and the pleasures of coming-of-age, are, for Billy and others like him, subordinated to the tragedy of environmental determinism.

By the time *A Kestrel for a Knave* was published in 1968, *Kes* was already in development. In July 1967, Barry Hines had signed over the film rights of his as yet unpublished novel to Tony Garnett and Ken Loach's newly formed production company, Kestrel Films. Garnett had met Hines on the recommendation of Alfred Bradley, and, having read *The Blinder*, a book he admired for its 'simplicity' and 'directness',[36] Garnett invited Hines down to London to discuss the possibility of writing a Wednesday Play. Hines was positive about Garnett's offer, but told him 'I've got this book going round in my head, and I've got to write it'.[37] The book, of course, was *A Kestrel for a Knave*, and Garnett asked Hines to send it to him when it was completed. Hines's agent, Sheila Lemon, posted Garnett the manuscript on its completion and the producer's response was emphatic: 'we've got to do this for the cinema.' Garnett's collaborator, Ken Loach, read the unpublished novel, and was equally enthusiastic, whereupon Hines, Garnett and Loach began the process of bringing the novel to the screen. The production was put into doubt when the original backer, National General Corporation, pulled out at an advanced stage leaving Loach and Garnett £165,000 short. Despite much scepticism from Wardour Street executives, who as Garnett says, felt they had 'done the North',[38] Tony Richardson, still holding much sway with American studios following the success of *Tom Jones* (1963), was able to secure funding from United Artists (who had previously rejected Garnett) and filming began in Barnsley in the summer of 1968.

The film faced an even harsher post-production life, and relied on a long campaign from Garnett and Kestrel's Clive Goodwin to secure a general release in the UK. This was helped by friendly quarters in the left-leaning press, most aptly summarised by Penelope Mortimer in the *Observer*, whose headline read: 'BANISHED TO YORKSHIRE ... the picture they won't let London look at.'[39]

These contextual questions of production and distribution are fundamental to a consideration of Hines's work, because in order to understand his contribution to *Kes* it is necessary to take into account the collaborative nature of film production, particularly when critical and commercial discourse invariably constructs the director as the sole author of a text. As Stephen Lacey argues in his study of Tony Garnett's career: '*Kes* (1969) is arguably the most achieved result of Garnett's long-term collaboration with Ken Loach.'[40] There is no doubt that much of the credit for bringing *Kes* to the screen and ensuring an audience for the film should lie with Garnett, and his role in the collaboration is rightly acknowledged by many critics and scholars. This also serves to underline the extent to which Hines's contributions to the film have not been thoroughly considered or discussed.

This critical imbalance is, of course, common in studies and broader understandings of British cinema, and reflects what Andrew Spicer has called 'the major problem that British screenwriters have often faced', which 'is precisely their exclusion from the production process'.[41] As we will show throughout this study, this was rarely, if ever, the case with Hines and was certainly not apparent in the dynamic collaborative context of his relationship with Loach and Garnett on *Kes*, yet, as Spicer goes on: 'the influence of auteurism, which became fashionable in the 1960s, elevated the director often at the expense of the screenwriter.'[42] In the case of Ken Loach, this is particularly acute, given the director's long career and prominence. Andy Willis's thoughtful study of Loach's relationship with another of his long-term collaborators, Jim Allen, illuminates a number of points which are also relevant to our understanding of Hines:

> Undoubtedly, one of the main reasons for Jim Allen's critical neglect is his close collaboration and association with director Ken Loach. Indeed, in much of the writing on British television drama that does touch upon Allen's work, he is most often lumped together with director Loach and producer Tony Garnett, creating a Loach/Garnett/Allen triumvirate. However, ultimately in the case of Allen, this is also somewhat limiting.
>
> [...]
>
> In short, Loach's increased profile as *the* auteur of the Left has had the effect of diminishing that of one of his most important collaborators, Allen.[43]

Willis's reference to television drama is again useful in relation to Hines because, while TV has tended towards a valorization of the writer (and it is important to consider that the majority of Hines's collaborations with Loach were made for the small screen), Hines, like Allen, is indelibly associated with Loach as a critically established cinematic auteur, who, regardless of the medium in which he works, possesses an authorial presence, albeit one that is externally constructed, which overwhelms those of his collaborators.

While it is by no means our purpose to argue that Hines should be regarded as the sole 'auteur' of *Kes*, it is important to make the case for a more nuanced understanding of the collaborations and creative processes that resulted in the film. For example, much of our discussion of Hines's novel focused on the image-led, poetic character of the prose, and it is significant that Garnett seems also to identify the novel's filmic quality when recalling the development of the screenplay: '... the three of us put a screenplay together – not that difficult because Barry Hines had written it so visually, and it was more or less a cut-and-paste job.'[44] Loach echoes Garnett's feeling of the novel's easy cinematic export: 'the script was a collaboration, but I don't want to make anything of that. The film is so close to the book anyway,'[45] and, more recently Garnett has suggested that 'Ken and I should not have had the credit'[46] for the screenplay. These reflections convey a sense of a collaboration which was symbiotic, but respectful of the individual contributions of its constituent members. Jacob Leigh's monograph on Loach, however, strikes a different note:

> The novel's themes, dialogue and structure resemble those in the film, yet this does not necessarily imply that Hines took the majority of creative decisions in adapting the book. Loach attributes his photographic style to Menges, but he chose to work with Menges; similarly, although the subject of *Kes* comes from Hines' imagination and experience, he (and Garnett) chose to film Hines' novel. The 'tight rein' that the director keeps on the structure of *Kes* only partly grows out of the novel's structure; the film benefits from a responsive handling of elements other than the script, particularly … in the casting and directing of actors.[47]

Leigh's interest here is in making the justifiable case for Loach's centrality within the film's organising system, and while he also rightly argues for the importance of Chris Menges and the crucial contributions of the largely untrained cast, his argument for Loach's authorship has the effect of marginalising Hines's contribution to the film. Again, it is important to state that in seeking to account for Hines's contribution we are not replacing one problematic, individuating reading strategy with another, but instead seeking to argue for the writer's place within a broader understanding of the film's collaborative creation. As artists committed to socialist values, Garnett's, Loach's and Hines's attitude to production reflected their politics, as Garnett states in relation to *Kes*: 'all films are social activities, we dissolve ourselves into the social project … a film is a collective work.'[48] These sentiments suggest the need to acknowledge the multi-layered nature of the film's authorship with renewed focus, and to review central moments with Hines's writing at the forefront of our critical perspective.

In an early, deeply arresting scene in the film, Billy reads *The Dandy* after completing his paper round. (See Figure 1.) He sits on a hill absorbed in his comic and oblivious to the significance of the pit that looms ominously beneath him. In his study of Loach, John Hill describes how the scene is illustrative of the way the worlds of nature and industry exist in close proximity, playing a 'role in undercutting the "romantic" strain in the film's treatment of the countryside and in reminding viewers of the industrial realities that continue to impose upon the characters' lives (even on those occasions when they might appear to have "escaped" them)'.[49] Leigh

1 Billy reading *The Dandy* in *Kes*

offers a similar reading: 'The countryside bordering Barnsley is present throughout the film, often in the background of shots; but this is no idealised rural landscape; it is a part of South Yorkshire dotted with collieries and pit villages … it is the first occasion on which *Kes* shows us the place to which Billy swears he will not go.'[50] Both Leigh and Hill identify the pointed, poetic imagery as evidence of Loach's authorship, and earlier Leigh talks of how 'Menges and Loach carefully photograph the landscape' to draw attention to its symbolic quality. Yet the poetic landscape is as much literary as it is cinematic, as much Hines's as it is Loach's and Menges's. We have already discussed the ways in which Hines in the novel emphasises the working nature of the landscape, rather than fetishising and unambiguously beautifying the space, and the same atmosphere is present in the shot. At this point, it is useful to recall the concurrent moment in *A Kestrel for a Knave*:

> A lane cut across the top of Firs Hill, forming a T junction, Billy turned left along it. There was no pavement, and whenever a car approached he either crossed the lane or stepped into the long grass at the side and waited for it to pass. Fields, and a few hedgerow trees sloped down into the valley. Toy traffic travelled along City Road, and across the road, in the valley bottom, was the sprawl of the estate. Towards the city, a pit chimney and the pit-head winding gear

showed above the rooftops, and the back of the estate was a patch-
work of fields, black, and grey, and pale winter green; giving way to
a wood, which stood out on the far slope as clear as an ink blot. (18)

This is typical of Hines's writing and his observation of the contradictions of his local landscape: the poetic evocation of an in-between
space – at once romantic, imaginative, rural, and industrial, layered
with social, political and economic narratives. This is Hines's South
Yorkshire and, as we will see, his novels frequently deploy similarly
long, descriptive and figurative treatments of the regional topography. This approach to writing space is akin to the cinematic representation of location as identified by Leigh and Hill – these passages
are the equivalent of Hines's long takes, his landscape shots. The
poetic imagery we see in the film *Kes* is first felt and imagined in the
novel, *A Kestrel for a Knave*.

Thus the representation of external space is one means of locat-
ing Hines's authorial hand within the cinematic text. Another is
the representation of the domestic realm, that which functions as
the institutional reality against which Billy's (temporary) external
freedom is juxtaposed. Jacob Leigh offers a close reading of a particularly significant encounter between Billy, Jud and their mother,
just before the latter pair embark on their separate nights out. He
describes the 'remarkable … dialogue', as the family argue; he
speaks of how Loach presents their exchanges 'with shot/reverse-
shot patterns', before praising the actors for their use of 'Barnsley
accents'[51] and Loach for the authenticity of his casting. Again,
therefore, Hines's creative contribution is implicitly discounted in
this auteurist analysis of the film, but once more a focus on the
same sequence in the novel reveals significantly similar narrative
and thematic effects to those attributed to Loach. Leigh is interested
in the way the film shows how Billy's private, burgeoning world jars
with his brother's and mother's eagerness for a night out and the
subsequent emotional neglect of the protagonist, yet these qualities
are equally evident in the prose:

> Jud watched him through the mirror, chin up, throat taut as he
> knotted his tie.
>   'I'm hopin' I'll be laid watchin' a bird tonight. But she'll not have
> feathers on; not all over anyway.'
>   He grinned at himself and folded his collar down, covering the back
> of the tie.

'Tha ought to have seen 'em though, Jud.'
'A few pints first.'
'An' that ought to have seen of them dive down.'
'Then straight across to t'Lyceum.'
'It dived straight down behind this wall. Whoosh!'
Billy clawed his fingers, and dived straight down on to the settee. Mrs
Casper came in from the hall, looking down at herself and smoothing
wrinkles out of her sweater. (45–6)

The quick, percussive exchange, punctuated by moments of third
person narration which orient the characters within the space,
carries a similar function to the editing and framing that Leigh
attributes to Loach. Similarly the representation of local dialect can
be seen in line with the casting (and resultant performances) in the
film: as a further marker of authenticity and connection to a place-
specific narrative.

Addressing archival material in relation to the film's production
and conception also offers a means of anatomising the creative
interplay between writer, director and producer. Significantly, the
earliest versions of the screenplay differ markedly from both the
novel and the final film. This confirms an important point: that
the process of adapting the novel was not merely a tightening of
significant elements but, in the first instance at least, constituted a
creative process that triggered an expansion and significant development of *A Kestrel for a Knave*'s key themes and plot lines. For
example, one draft begins with an extended sequence involving
Billy and his classmates, such as MacDowall and Tibbut, engaging
in a 'prank' phone call which involves them ringing the father of
a fellow pupil and pretending to be the head teacher, Gryce. Later,
the boys break into the school and play-act a lesson. In other addi-
tions, there appears to have been a far more developed exploration of the dynamic between the schoolteachers, with an extended
scene in the staffroom (a concept to which Hines returns four
years later in *Speech Day*). It is clear that these added scenes would
have contributed greater complexity to the characterisation of the
ensemble but that such changes might have resulted in diminishing the strong central focus on Billy and Kes, and their sense of
isolation (both positive and negative) from other characters in the
film.

While the final film is ultimately without additional scenes of this
nature, and cuts from rather than adds to the narrative detail of the

novel, both Hines and Loach have since identified the aspects of the adaptation that, in hindsight, they would have changed. According to Loach:

> Something that we didn't get quite right in the film is that Jud, Billy's brother, is provoked to kill the bird because Billy's failure to place Jud's bet meant that Jud lost the equivalent of a week's wages. He could have had a week off work. A week in the sun and the open air, not underground with the coal dust in his lungs. It was important that Jud didn't come off as just a villain, because he's entitled to be angry, but, as I say, we didn't quite pull that off. [52]

Hines adds:

> Looking back on it, I think I was a bit unfair to Jud [...]. In the book all the sympathy is on Billy – when he says 'I could have had a week off work with that', that's one of the crucial lines in the book; he could have done something creative. [53]

Hines implies that in the novel Jud's justified feeling of injustice is more conspicuously foregrounded than it is in the film, and both Loach and Hines express regret at Jud's characterisation as an ambiguous villain rather than as, ultimately, a victim of the wider system of education and labour that so oppresses Billy. This is significant because archival materials reveal that Hines, Loach and Garnett explored ways of humanising and politicising Jud. For example, while in the film we see Jud arriving for work, his dialogue with colleagues is inaudible. Yet in early versions of the screenplay, Jud is given a platform at the pit to express his anger and frustration with his place in the world, in a manner not unlike that of more traditional post-war realist protagonists such as Arthur Seaton and Arthur/Frank Machin. He eloquently and powerfully voices his frustrations during a scene entitled 'JUD AT THE COAL-FACE. JUD AT SNAP TIME':

> 1ST MINER: Never mind, Jud, soon be t'holiday.
> JUD: Ar, they'll soon be over an'all; two weeks at home, a week at Blackpool, then back here for another twelve months. ... And then they talk about an increase in leisure. I'll tell you summat. If some o'them bloody politicians and professors and whatnots had to work down here for a couple of weeks, tha'd see an increase in leisure then. T'bill'd go through Parliament that bloody fast, the bugger'd be red hot. [54]

This foregrounding of the toil of Jud's working life makes explicit an aspect of the novel and film which is otherwise implicit: the hardship felt by miners and, more broadly, Hines's conviction of the need for creativity and productive leisure activities in working-class life. While these early screenplays evidence the degree of experimentation that was involved in bringing the novel to the screen, they also provide further evidence of the extent to which Hines's literary treatment of the landscape informed the cinematic treatment of the narrative. For example, as Billy goes nesting in the film script, subtly adapted extracts from Hines's novel accompany the dialogue: 'A cushion of mist lies over the fields. Dew drenches the grass and the occasional sparkling of individual drops makes Billy glance down as he passes.'[55] The passage extends across a number of pages in the novel and the sections of descriptive prose are equally lengthy in their repositioning as preliminary stage directions in the draft screenplay, thus anchoring the proposed film treatment to both the narrative content and the poetic atmosphere of the original novel.

These elements contribute to the presence of *A Kestrel for a Knave* within *Kes*, a feeling that the novel's poetic sensibility – its sense of place, its rhythms and its implicit but unambiguous politics – is carried forth within the film. Indeed, for Tony Garnett, *Kes*'s enduring legacy and impact can be traced back to a line from the novel, taken up in the film, as Billy describes Kes: 'Is it tame? Is it heck tame, it's trained that's all. It's fierce, and it's wild, an' it's not bothered about anybody, not even about me, right. And that's why it's great' (146). Garnett reflects: 'It was enough to make us want to make the film, that line … He was talking about his own class: a statement of fact about the kestrel, but a statement of hope about working people.'[56]

Notes

1 Anonymous, 'The reward for a teacher's homework', date unknown, BHP/BLS 5.
2 Milton Shulman, 'A parable of take-overs', *Evening Standard*, date unknown, BHP/BLS 5.
3 Pearson Phillips, 'A superb Yorkshire pudding', *Daily Mail*, date unknown, BHP/BLS 5.
4 Rosemary Say, 'Billy's Last Stand', *Financial Times* 1 July 1970, BHP/BLS 5.

5 Barry Hines, *Billy's Last Stand*, radio typescript, BHP/BLS 4, p. 16. All further page references in the text.

6 Nancy Banks-Smith, 'Billy's Last Stand', the *Guardian*, date unknown, BHP/BLS 5.

7 Virginia Ironside, 'Billy's business venture takes all the joy out of coal shifting', publication and date unknown, BHP/BLS 5.

8 Anonymous, untitled, *Sunday Times*, date unknown, BHP/BLS 5.

9 Raymond Williams, 'Billy and Darkly', the *Listener*, date unknown, BHP/BLS 5.

10 Alan Sillitoe, *Saturday Night and Sunday Morning* (1958), *Saturday Night and Sunday Morning* (dir. Karel Reisz, 1960); John Braine, *Room at the Top* (1957), *Room at the Top* (dir. Jack Clayton, 1959).

11 Luke Spencer, 'British Working-Class Fiction: The Sense of Loss and the Potential for Transformation', *Socialist Register* 24 1988, pp. 366–86: 377.

12 Interviewer unknown, 'Interview with Barry Hines', date unknown, BHP/Audio Recordings 14.

13 Barry Hines, 'Flight of the Hawk', date unknown, pages unnumbered, BHP/BLX 1.

14 Barry Hines, 'Flight of the Hawk', pages unnumbered.

15 Ian Haywood, *Working-Class Fiction: From Chartism to Trainspotting*, London: Routledge 1996, p. 111.

16 Jeffrey Hill, *Sport and the Literary Imagination: Essays in History Literature and Sport*, Oxford: Peter Lang 2006, p. 58.

17 Barry Hines, *The Blinder*, London: Michael Joseph 1996. All page references in the text.

18 Lee McGowan, 'Marking out the Pitch: A Historiography and Taxonomy of Football Fiction', *Soccer and Society* 16:1 2015, pp. 76–97: 87.

19 In 2016, Hines's brother published his own memoir, *No Way But Gentlenesse*, which takes as its starting point Richard's training of hawks as a child.

20 Haywood, *Working-Class Fiction*, pp. 132–3.

21 Ibid., p. 132.

22 Dave Russell, *Looking North: Northern England and the National Imagination*, Manchester: Manchester University Press, p. 93.

23 Ian McMillan, 'Introduction' in Barry Hines *A Kestrel for a Knave*, London: Penguin 2010 [1968], p. xi

24 Barry Hines, *A Kestrel for a Knave*, London: Penguin 1968/2000, pp. 16–17. All further page references in the text.

25 Haywood, *Working-Class Fiction*, p. 133.

26 Raymond Williams, *The Country and the City*, Oxford: Oxford University Press 1975, p. 46.

27 Ibid., p. 120.
28 Ibid., p. 56.
29 Alfred Hickling, 'Tales dug deep from the heart', *The Yorkshire Post* 7 May 1994, BHP/HEA 21.
30 Clare Jenkins, 'Interviews for the Millennium Memory Bank', date unknown, BHP/Audio Recordings 13.
31 Penelope Maslin, 'Exception', publication and date unknown, BHP/ KES 2.
32 Mo Bhula, Interview with Barry Hines and Natasha Betteridge, 'Kes: Programme', Spring 1999, BHP/KES 7.
33 Spencer, 'British Working-Class Fiction', p. 378.
34 John Kirk, p. 91.
35 Erica Hateley, '"In the Hands of the Receivers"': The Politics of Literacy in The Savage by David Almond and Dave McKean', *Children's Literature in Education* 43 2012, pp. 170–80: 176.
36 Tony Garnett, interview with the authors, 9 October 2015.
37 Tony Garnett, 'Working in the Field', in Sheila Rowbotham and Huw Beynon (eds), *Looking at Class: Film, Television and the Working Class*, London: Rivers Oram Press, pp. 70–82: 75.
38 Garnett, interview with the authors.
39 Penelope Mortimer quoted in William Stephenson, 'Kes and the Press', *Cinema Journal* 12: 2 1973, pp. 48–55: 51.
40 Stephen Lacey, *Tony Garnett*, Manchester: Manchester University Press 2007, p. 83.
41 Andrew Spicer, 'Restoring the Screenwriter to British Film History', in James Chapman, Marc Glancy and Sue Harper (eds), *The New Film History: Approaches, Methods and Sources*, Basingstoke: Palgrave Macmillan 2007, p. 90.
42 Spicer, 'Restoring the Screenwriter', p. 91.
43 Andy Willis, 'Jim Allen: Radical Drama Beyond *Days of Hope*', *Journal of British Cinema and Television* 12:2 2008, pp. 300–17: 303.
44 Garnett, 'Working in the Field', p. 75.
45 Ken Loach quoted in Graham Fuller, *Loach on Loach*, London: Faber and Faber 1998, p. 42.
46 Garnett, interview with the authors.
47 Jacob Leigh, *The Cinema of Ken Loach: Art in the Service of the People*, London: Wallflower 2002, p. 62.
48 Garnett, interview with the authors.
49 John Hill, *Ken Loach: The Politics of Film and Television*, London: BFI 2011, p. 116.
50 Leigh, *The Cinema of Ken Loach*, pp. 66–7.
51 Ibid., p. 72.
52 Loach quoted in Fuller, *Loach on Loach*, p. 42.

53 Barry Hines, Books for GCSE: *Kestrel for a Knave*, date unknown, BHP/Audio Recordings 12.
54 Barry Hines, 'Kestrel': Copy 1, Ken Loach Archive (BFI), KCL /6/1, p. 38.
55 Ibid., p. 32.
56 Garnett, interview with the authors.

2

The politics of hope in 1970s Britain

First Signs, *Speech Day*, *The Gamekeeper*,
Tom Kite, *The Price of Coal*

In this chapter, we focus on a period of extremely fruitful aesthetic production for Hines, in terms of the novels and screenplays that followed *A Kestrel for a Knave*. During the 1970s, Hines's political energies were directed towards considering the institutions and structures of life at a time of active struggle for workers' rights. Thus industrial action is apparent in *First Signs* (1972) on the part of its increasingly radicalised protagonist, who is a teacher, while class inequalities are anatomised further in relation to schooling in the 1973 Play for Today *Speech Day*, which uses Brechtian effects to this end. In the novel and screenplay of *The Gamekeeper*, published in 1975 and released in filmic form five years later, it is private land-ownership that is subject to scrutiny by means of what amounts to a realist allegory, and we explore here the ethical consequences of the change of medium from novel to film. Hines's 1976 screenplay *Tom Kite* was never filmed, but, as his surname implies, this drama was about an attempted flight on the part of the eponymous protagonist by means of footballing prowess, one that might take him away from Britain altogether. *The Price of Coal*, a two-part Play for Today, was broadcast in 1977 as a wry marking of that year's Queen's Silver Jubilee, in its portrayal of the effects of a royal visit to a South Yorkshire colliery, and the pit disaster that follows. The play's archival history shows the aesthetic effort Hines expended on weaving together documentary and narrative elements for this representation of a mining community, set at a critical period between the strikes of the early 1970s and that of 1984–85.

First Signs (1972)

Barry Hines's third novel, *First Signs*,[1] is probably his least known. Like *The Blinder, Unfinished Business, The Heart of It* and *Elvis over England*, it was not filmed, appearing between two of his most prominent works, *A Kestrel for a Knave* and *The Gamekeeper*. However, it is also undoubtedly his most politically explicit novel and develops the relationship between everyday lives in the South Yorkshire landscape that so underscored *A Kestrel for a Knave*, alongside a more sustained examination of the structures and institutions of class politics.

The novel concerns Tom Renshaw, a twenty-something who has left the South Yorkshire coal village of his youth, first for university and then to travel. When *First Signs* begins, Tom is living in London with Zelda, his journalist partner. He has made the decision to return North, and on the train home a passing comment by a fellow passenger triggers a flashback to Tom's post-university life in the Italian Riviera. During this period, the protagonist has an affair with a wealthy heiress and stays in her luxurious home. While in Italy, Tom discovers a mining site that prompts thoughts of his home life in the North of England. Hines then halts the flashback and has Tom return to the village of his youth. The rest of the novel is concerned with Tom's growing appreciation for the rural landscape near his home; his militant miner father's unsuccessful battle to keep his pit open; and Tom's own industrial struggle, as he leads a strike at the school where he works.

First Signs was published in the midst of the first miners' strike since the general strike of 1926, and Hines seems to anticipate the outcome of the struggle with remarkable foresight. Although the strike of 1972 was more successful than the one depicted in the novel, since the miners accepted an improved pay offer, reviewers at the time commented on Hines's timely (and in hindsight, prophetic) exploration of the theme of industrial tension in the North of England, as Ian Salisbury comments in the *Sheffield Morning Telegraph* by quoting from the dialogue: '"If our pit finishes," says Tom's father, "then this village finishes." This, surely, is what the current strike is about.'[2]

The novel therefore engages with immediate socioeconomic circumstances, yet its contemporaneity is counterbalanced by the sense of its connection to recurring, long-standing tropes of post-war

working-class writing. The scenario of a socially mobile graduate from a humble background re-engaging with the people and
places of his youth felt, to some, like a cliché in 1972. To return
to Ian Salisbury, an otherwise favourable review begins with a
note of caution: 'It seems as though every Northern proletarian novelist must sooner or later handle this theme. It's a kind of
compulsion.'[3] Of course, one way of understanding this theme in
working-class writing is to read it as a reflection on the author's own
background – Hines, for example, himself left Hoyland Common for
Loughborough University before working in London as a teacher,
just as Tom does, eventually returning to his home town. As Ian
Haywood notes, working-class writers such as Raymond Williams
(*Border Crossing* [1958]) and David Mercer (*Where the Difference
Begins* [1960]) also explore the theme in what he terms 'returning
native' narratives.[4] At this point it is useful to draw on Richard
Hoggart's work on the 'scholarship boy', and the sense that post-war
working-class 'returning natives' in fiction commonly experience
'a sense of loss' and, indeed, the melancholic stasis of being 'at the
friction point of two cultures'.[5] As Hoggart argues of the educated
working-class man (it is, of course, almost always a man): 'the test of
his real education lies in his ability, by about the age of twenty-five,
to smile at his father with his whole face and to respect his flighty
young sister and his slower brother.'[6] Again, the fault line for the
'returning native' narrative is often found in the family home, and
appears as the parents look upon their son with feelings of alienation
and regret, mourning a lost innocence and the memory of familial
harmony. In David Storey's *Pasmore*, published the same year as
First Signs, the 'returning native', Colin, a working-class university
lecturer, is scolded by his parents for cheating on his middle-class
wife, and the novel is centrally concerned with the protagonist's
sense of 'loss' and rootlessness as he is rejected by both of the classes
to which he is allied, in line with Hoggart's thesis. Yet in *First Signs*,
Hines defies the paradigm. For example, the relationship between
Tom and his father positions them as intellectual equals. Hines often
privileges the experiential political education of Sam Renshaw over
his son's theoretical one, gained from his degree in PPE:

> 'Listen Tom, my politics are born of necessity. It's not hard to be a
> socialist after a lifetime in the pits. But with you it's different, you've
> been to University, you've got an education behind you. You've

knocked around a bit and mixed with different classes of people. What I want to know is, how's all this affected you? Where do you stand now, Tom?' (101)

Sam has none of the insecurity of the Hoggartian patriarch, and Tom has none of the guilty intellectual authority of the scholarship boy. The narrator's description of the books in the Renshaws' home: 'the works of Marx and Engels, Lenin, Trotsky and H.G. Wells; all of which had formerly lived behind leaded glass in the china cabinet downstairs, but had gradually, through the years, been brought upstairs by Tom, to read in bed' (93), suggests that Tom's enquiring mind is as much the result of his home and community as it is his formal education. This positioning of the working-class home as a site of intellectual development also places Sam Renshaw alongside Sid Storey in *The Price of Coal* and Harry Rickards in *The Heart of It*: Hines's mining patriarchs, self-taught intellectuals and Marxist firebrands, reinforcing the author's deep interest in the relationship between education, experience and place.

Indeed, the spatial and cultural geographical construction of the working-class (often Northern) home is central to the 'returning native' narrative, and while it might appear that Tom's transition back into Northern, working-class life is almost idealistically easy, the narrator's description of his arrival suggests a willingness on Hines's part to register the problematic tendency towards a glorification of the impoverished, yet photogenic North, a space that has been constructed nostalgically through the gaze of its previously exiled resident. Tom listens with affection to the timetable announcer's accent: 'He smiled. He was home' (88). Later, when Tom boards a bus, he is overwhelmed by the 'pastoral landscape' (89) and feels compelled to share his wonder with a fellow passenger:

'There it is, missus.'
    Surprised, the woman looked across at him.
    'You what, love?'
    Tom nodded towards the panorama through the front window.
    'The North.'
    The woman looked, saw nothing, then observing that they were alone thought it best to humour him.
    'Yes, love. Very nice.' (89)

This notion of a generic, idealistically constructed 'Northern' space is, however, nuanced as the novel progresses, as Tom begins to re-engage with his environment, and the novel is rare among Hines's works for dealing with specific locations in South Yorkshire. When Helen, Tom's middle-class girlfriend, buys him a pocket watch for Christmas, Tom notices that it has been made by a (real) Sheffield firm, foreshadowing one of the novel's themes of industrial, working-class heritage, and initiating a narrative of place which is geographically precise: 'H.L. Brown. They've moved now. They're in Leopold Street opposite the Town Hall.' Helen observes that 'It's a small world …', but for Tom, 'it's never felt larger' (82). While the universal terms 'town' and 'city' are used to denote the urban space beyond the pastoral home (just as they are in *The Blinder* and *A Kestrel for a Knave*), we learn that Sam Renshaw works in a colliery at 'Staincross' (116), a real mining village near Barnsley, and Sam refers to the 'virgin seams' at 'Wharncliffe! Rockingham! Fitzwilliam!' (187). Again these are actual places in the coalfields between South and West Yorkshire, with Rockingham being Hines's local pit.[7] This regional specificity has the effect of sharpening the novel's political resonance while authenticating and making tangible Hines's now customarily poetic engagement with the semi-rural landscape of South Yorkshire.

However, for contemporary reviewers the novel's use of place still conforms to a rigid stereotype, as Clive Jordan remarked in the *New Statesman*: 'Barry Hines tends to locate his villains somewhere to the south',[8] and it is true that the opening depiction of a party in London and the brutal portrait of middle-class, expatriate life in Italy contrast sharply with the sympathetic treatment of the people and places of the North. Moreover, critics were united in their condemnation of the novel's prolonged Italian episode, with the commonly held view that, as Nina Bawden suggests, 'Tom's return home redeems not only himself but the novel as well'.[9]

However, Tom's experience of Italy does serve to reawaken his longing for home and gives rise to a renewal of his political consciousness, made explicit in his visit to a derelict mine:

> There was no pit-head winding gear or tall chimney, and the pattern of the buildings was unfamiliar. But he knew those stacks of rotting sleepers, and upturned tubs, the broken windows and the plants growing in the roof gutters. He knew those trodden, barren patches between the buildings that had been thick with dust in summer and thick with mud in winter. And although it was summer now and the sun was warm, and the mine had closed, it was still a miserable, chilling place to be in. Tom knew he was in a pit yard. (55)

This attempt at spatialising and historicising a shared, European working-class experience provides some justification for the Italian episode by temporarily challenging the reductive conflation of economic and cultural deficit with the Northern English region. Indeed, the ghostly description of the Italian mine foreshadows the elegiac tone that accompanies Hines's treatment of the mining community in England:

> They turned the corner at the crossroads, and walked in silence towards the row of shops. Tom watched his reflection in Crossland's drawn blind. It faded against the display of foodstuffs in Cooper's, then came back dark and clear in the drawn blind of Tunnecliffe's.
> 'Are they on holiday?'
> 'Who?'
> 'Crossland and Tunnecliffe.'
> 'They're shut.'
> 'What, all day? They've had the blinds down all day.'
> 'They've shut down.'
> Tom paused with his thumb on the sneck of the cobbler's door. The cobbler was still working inside.
> 'I didn't know that.' (140)

The evocation of a dying town of increasingly redundant workers and craftsmen underlines the social imperative of the miners' struggle in the novel and anticipates the post-industrial landscapes that Hines would go on to document in *Looks and Smiles* and *The Heart of It*. This mournful treatment of working-class community is reinforced by the scepticism with which Hines approaches markers of the new, such as the urban council flats that Tom visits in *First Signs*. As Tom arrives at the tower-block home of family friends Mrs Straw and her son, Roy, he is told: 'It's like a palace compared with what I was used to. But it's the flats I don't like. Well, I mean it's not natural living up in the air is it? … you just don't feel as though you belong anywhere' (207). We learn that she has moved to the flats after her husband was killed in a mining accident (213), and that he himself had originally moved from the 'declining Durham coalfield' in search of work. Just as he would in *Looks and Smiles*, then, Hines conflates post-war social housing with economic precariousness, the fragmentation of the family and a sense of geographical instability. Hines's suspicions of modern housing is apparent in his essay *This Artistic Life*, in which he reflects on Sheffield's tower blocks:

Next to these houses are four tower blocks of flats. Very neat, they
are. Nobody keeps pigeons in there. Or dogs or cats. Somebody might
keep a budgie in a cage. There's a paved area between the flats and a
circular ornamental pond. I bet the architect had heard all about the
destruction of the old communities and the building of shoe boxes.
… Sometimes boys play football in the square. But they spend a lot of
time fishing the ball out of the pond.[10]

This concern at a lack of open space for young working-class people
is equally apparent as Mrs Straw continues to describe to Tom her
frustrations with the flat:

> There's not much here for him either. Flats are no places to bring
> kids up in, kids need a bit of ground to move about on. I mean,
> what can they do? When they're outside they're too far away from
> their mothers. They can't play in the corridors. They can't even have
> pets. And back home our house used to be like Belle Vue. They were
> always bringing things home. If it wasn't newts or frogspawn, it was
> young birds or stray kittens. (207–8)

The sense of a nostalgic longing for 'back home' is reinforced by the
novel's contrasting poetic examination of the semi-rural landscape
around the Renshaws' older terraced house and the pit where Sam
works. Just as in *A Kestrel for a Knave*, long, meticulously detailed
passages describe the protagonist's loving encounters with the countryside, and again, just as in Hines's previous novel, the landscape
is never romanticised, with an earthy emphasis defying the expectation of an idealised, pictorial distance:

> He carried on, through nettles and brambles, willow herbs and
> bracken. He crossed a clearing where the grass was so lush that if he
> had picked a handful and wrung it, it would have produced a skin of
> moisture like a damp chamois leather. In this clearing, the grass, and
> the foliage of the surrounding trees were so green that the dew on
> them seemed to have run their colour, and tinged the very air of the
> clearing green. (120)

The land is later described as 'muscular and spare', as if reflecting
the stereotypical characteristics of its working, human inhabitants,
as the narrator tells us that 'the moor … was a daunting place,
and challenged life, even on a sunny summer morning' (125). Such
lingering treatments of space might be read as evidence of Rod
Nicholls's argument, that the novel's 'quality lies in the observation outside the narrative',[11] and the sheer frequency and sustained

nature of these sequences does indeed suspend temporarily the already sparse flow of story information. Yet, the pastoral descriptions do not function as mere lyrical decoration for the novel's core themes – as we have seen, the imagery provides a counterpoint to the novel's commentary on the rapidly changing working-class landscape and it also can be seen as the space which ignites both Tom's political re-orientation and the accompanying bond between him and his father. Indeed, Hines never allows the emphasis on the natural space to obscure the novel's socioeconomic interests. In persistently re-orienting his striking teacher and miner with their rural landscape, he seems to underline what they are fighting for, in effect politicising the more cerebral, contemplative spaces of their home life.

Hines's refusal to divorce his loving portrait of the rural spaces of working-class lives from their socioeconomic contexts generated much criticism from reviewers, many of whom argued that the literary quality of the nature writing was undermined by the explicitly political nature of the strike narratives. The author and Conservative politician Ferdinand Mount, writing for the *Financial Times*, celebrates the novel's lyrical emphasis on the natural realm:

> The mare and foal cropping in the field behind the pithead, the willow-herb sprouting through the cracked tarmac – the contrasts in the miner's landscape have rarely been more sensuously evoked than in *First Signs*. The feeling for place which was so well captured in *Kes*, the film made of one of Mr Hines' earlier novels, is here again as precise and affectionate as in the best D.H. Lawrence.[12]

However, Mount later goes on to describe the 'strike sequence' as 'containing all the realism of a serial in *Soviet Weekly*', suggesting that Hines 'lacks the large fairness of a major novelist'[13] for his prejudiced treatment of the middle classes. Similarly, Rod Nicholls argues that 'the trouble is that under the great superstructures which Hines imposes on his novels, there is a poet',[14] suggesting again that politics impedes or is distinct from poetry; while W. Price Turner writes of the novel that it 'contains some remarkably fine writing. If only [Hines] would boot the Socialist soap-box off stage, into the wings. He would stand taller without it'.[15] The overwhelming sense is that the working-class writer is perfectly entitled to describe artistically the working-class environment, but s/he must not explain the circumstances that exist within it.

The critics are right, however, to suggest that *First Signs* is a didactic, politically focused novel. Naturally for Hines, Tom's role as a teacher (and his leadership of the strike) enables the novelist to continue and make explicit his exploration of the education system as a symbol of class oppression that was initiated in *A Kestrel for a Knave*. In one of a number of political exchanges between father and son during their forays into the countryside, Tom discusses the narrow, stultifying nature of the school where he works:

> 'Do you know, we're not touching the majority of kids in our schools, we're not getting anywhere near them. All we're concerned with is the academic minority. The rest just trail along in their wake, following diluted academic syllabuses which are completely irrelevant to their lives.'

He placed the grass stalk in his mouth and chewed the sweet juice from the pale end.

> 'And the potential, Dad, the wasted potential. The talent that just withers through boredom and lack of care.'

He threw the grass dart fashion back into the field, where it vanished immediately amongst the other grasses. Sam Renshaw climbed the stile into the next field. At the top he turned round and looked down at Tom.

> 'Well, what did you expect? Education only reflects the society we live in, it doesn't change it. The whole system is geared to keep the power in the hands of the minority, where it's always been. Only when you've got a decent society will you get a decent education system, until then you're just fiddling.' (114)

This passage is significant for a number of reasons, since in one sense it illustrates our earlier argument that Hines positions natural spaces as points of stimulus for political thought and action. More broadly, however, Sam's connection of Tom's microanalysis of the school curriculum to a wider Marxist analytical framework serves to illuminate the alignment of the teachers' with the miners' strike within the broader parameters of class struggle. Such material is crucial to the plots of later works such as *Speech Day* and *Fun City*. Later, as Tom addresses the assembled parents of the schoolchildren, he makes a similar call for cross-class solidarity in the name of revolution:

> 'For we in schools do not change society, we merely reflect it. When you, the dockers and the miners, the car workers and the

steel workers are in control, then we, the teachers, will be in control, and not until. That will be the real victory, and that will be the culmination of what has happened here this morning.'

And Sam Renshaw, listening at the back of the crowd, nodded once, briefly, almost imperceptibly, then walked away, using the crowd as a shield so that Tom would not see him. (236–7)

This passage is typical of what Deborah Knight has termed 'critical naturalism'[16] in relation to Loach's film work, whereby class struggle is embodied within clear dialectical oppositions and made explicit in dialogue exchanges which favour the leftist position, through the privileging of an often politically articulate working-class protagonist, in this case Tom Renshaw, pitted against the cynical, middle-class other(s) – here, the school's head teacher, Mr Swinburne and his fellow blacklegs, and perhaps the dissenting middle-class reader, such as Mount.

The novel's didacticism reaches its peak towards the conclusion when Hines suspends the established balance between dialogue and description of place which so dominates the novel in favour of an almost journalistic, summative tone in a long, nine-page sequence. The content and form of the section marks a break from the dominant mode of realism and seeks, instead, to assert an atmosphere of revolutionary fervour:

For the first time many of the students saw that their teachers were not such a race apart and that their problems were their parents' problems. Concurrently many of the teachers came closer to the students than they had throughout their entire teaching careers. For the first time they realized the staggering potential of many of their students; those belligerent apathetic sloths who repeatedly baulked at their diluted academic syllabuses were suddenly informed and articulate about the questions involved, because these questions were relevant to their own lives, to the lives of their mates, and parents, and to the lives of all the people they knew on their estate.
[…]
Firehill would never be the same again. The spirit had stirred, and the struggle would now develop from the collective experience gained on that Friday afternoon. (225–6)

While it might be argued that the novel's Marxist emphasis is combined sensitively with, for example, its sustained exploration of landscape, this political content is more problematically integrated with other story elements. This is particularly the case in Hines's treatment of gender in *First Signs*. Indeed, as we have seen, political articulacy and action in the novel is focused firmly on father and son, and this privileging of the male perspective leads inevitably towards a marginalisation of female characters.

Of the three romantic relationships Tom is involved in, his affair with Helen is the most problematic. To this heiress who doesn't work, Tom says: 'What did you ever do to earn your money? Fuck all! You were born rich and you married rich. You've never had to lift a finger in your life!' (41). Tom's and Helen's sexual relationship is presented as a transaction which Tom reluctantly enters into; for example, before the couple begin a speed-boat race Helen tells him: 'If I win I want you to make love to me' (60). Indeed, Tom's hatred of the vacuous middle-class socialites he encounters in Italy is explicitly gendered: 'Tom marvelled at the meticulously preserved middle-aged women, some of whom he would have fucked given the opportunity. Then he realized that these women were the same age as his mother, and his aunties, and the mothers of his child-hood friends back in the village, and he compared their lives, and their condition, and he fumed' (46). This troubling conflation of class and sexuality is maintained on Tom's return to Britain, when a 15-year-old schoolgirl is described as 'already at her best. From now on, years of early mornings, and long monotonous hours in shops and factories would coarsen her, and she would be overblown even by the day of her white wedding' (166). When Tom visits Mrs Shaw, the narrator remarks that like Tom's mother 'and many of the women in the village, a lifetime of hard physical work, worry, and in her case tragedy, had aged her prematurely' (244). The sense here is that a life of unfulfilling work is all the more tragic in the case of women because it renders them less attractive. This unbalanced treatment of gender and, more broadly, sex and sexuality in the novel is an unfortunate mark against a work which is notable for being the first of Hines's novels to engage explicitly with coalmining, a subject to which he would repeatedly return, and for illustrating his continuing attempts to examine the ideologically bound discourses of education.[17]

Speech Day (1973)

The ambivalence evident in Hines's education-centred plays *Speech Day* and, written a decade later in 1983, *Fun City*, takes the form of an internal conflict of values. Education is meant to bring out the best in young people, yet takes place within a social context that demands their differentiation and obedience. By contrast for instance to *A Kestrel for a Knave*, these plays are distinctive in having the experience of education itself, alongside the individual characters, as their central focus, with the school as their institutional setting, in order to reveal broader elements of class- and work-related injustice. Like many of Hines's works, in which his analytic and ethical interest in questions of education and work is judged to be suitable for young audiences, *Speech Day* is a crossover text. It was directed by John Goldschmidt for the adult audience of the BBC's Play for Today, broadcast on 23 March 1973, and then in a second form for ITV's newly launched English Programme for schools in two parts on 3 and 10 October 1977.[18] The screenplay exists in print as an educational text, suitable for 'reading with older groups in secondary schools', according to Michael Marland's commentary on the script as published in the anthology *The Pressures of Life*, and in a shorter version 'adapted from the television play' for schools in the collection *Prompt Two*.[19]

Speech Day concerns the experiences of the teenage Ronnie Warboys (David Smith) at Attlee School on prize-giving day, and as a member of a working-class family living in an unidentified industrial city, as he contemplates his own future prospects in relation to the experience of his parents and brother. The school is named after the post-war Labour leader whose otherwise wide-ranging educational reforms did not include the introduction of comprehensive education.[20] As Alan Durband points out, although the play is set in the post-11+ era of comprehensive education, the supposed introduction of 'equality of educational opportunity', in place of the divisive grammar-school system, is qualified in the fictional school by the retention of 'the old divisions – based on academic ability'.[21] The screenplay makes understated hints that the action takes place in Sheffield. For instance, Mr Warboys, who is played in the film by Brian Glover, works in the smelting-shop at the plausibly but fictively named Brightside Steel, which is also the former workplace of George Purse in Hines's novel *The Gamekeeper*. Such hints take on visually identifiable form in the filmed version, whose locations include the Warboys's home in Hyde Park Flats, the streets near Sheffield United's Bramall Lane football ground, the varied Sheffield workplaces of the three adults, and Ronnie's grandfather's terraced house near the steel foundries.[22] As this variety of settings suggests, in *Speech Day* the realms of education and work are made to confront and shade into each other.

In *Speech Day*, the stratified form of education and its enforced priorities are revealed, in what constitutes an almost Foucauldian anatomy of school life, to prepare pupils to be members of a 'self-disciplining, self-regulating citizenry' under capitalism.[23] Thus one of the teachers, Mr Sanderson (Peter Wallis), need not give a reason for forbidding Ronnie's friend Robson (Glen Dalby) to wear his leather jacket into the school hall since it is the enforcement and internalisation of rules rather than their content that is important, as he unwittingly reveals: 'Yes, but your [jacket] is not acceptable and there the matter rests. Why can't you people be sensible about these matters?' (96). Similarly, the senior master Mr Douglas (Tony Caunter) issues a stream of conformity-enforcing commands as the pupils enter the school hall for the prize-giving ceremony: 'Move your feet not your tongues. Keep the noise down. Come here. Straighten your tie … Stop there', concluding with a rhetorical question to a pullover-wearing pupil, 'Vicky, why must you be different from everybody else?' (98). In the television play, a shot of the hall shows the mass of seated schoolchildren over an out-of-focus image of the large and shining trophies in the foreground, revealing that the prize-giving serves the purpose of division as much as reward. Indeed, a reproduction of a speech-day programme from Hines's *alma mater* Ecclesfield Grammar School appears in *This Artistic Life* as a signifier of class division that requires no commentary or caption.[24]

The play's anatomy of educational hierarchy and power is accomplished in a manner that is echoed by its form, as is hinted at in the title itself. In an obvious sense, speeches are the central event at the school's prize-giving ceremony, but they are also the mode by which the play's meaning is conveyed. The usual conventions of dramatic dialogue are extended to estranging effect in *Speech Day*. It is set on the 'day' of school prize-giving but is also a representation of the divergent voices 'of the day'.[25] These include clearly marked utterances expressing Marxist and, as we would now call them, neoliberal views on the part of Ronnie's grandfather and the local mayor respectively, while the headmaster quotes Martin Luther King's speech 'I have a dream' in a setting that immediately undercuts its call for equality. King's celebrated speech of the civil rights movement is juxtaposed with a scene in which Grandpa (Michael Atha) rails against religion's implication in class inequality, demanding, 'Whose side's God's on any road? He's got a terrible record as far as our side's concerned', so that the violence of the crosscutting subverts the headmaster's piety. The play's conclusion with a rendering of Hubert Parry's musical setting of Blake's poem 'Jerusalem' at the prize-giving ceremony draws on the poet's own disquiet about eighteenth-century class inequality. It also pays an intertextual debt to *The Loneliness of the Long Distance Runner* (Tony Richardson, 1962). In the film version of Alan Sillitoe's short story, the hymn 'Jerusalem' is matched with sharp incongruity to the violence accompanying the return of Stacey (Philip Martin), to the boys' reformatory from which he has tried to abscond. The political meaning of *Speech Day* is generated from the incompatible nature of these and other discourses, often acted out in frame-breaking speeches. Such self-conscious artistry is evident in the final text of the play and in its televisual form, while Hines's drafts show that even more extreme elements of this kind, by means of which characters stand clearly outside the world of the play to deliver impassioned addresses, were contemplated. The mixture in *Speech Day* of realism with political symbolism and disruptive devices makes it strikingly unusual in Hines's oeuvre.

Speech Day does not open at school but with scenes of Ronnie's home life that prepare us for the close connection between the worlds of work and education. In the first sequence, we see Mrs Warboys ironing in the living-room of a flat in a high-rise block. Narrative anticipation is generated by her hanging up an ironed white shirt and brushing down a blazer, while the national anthem plays on the television in the background. In the play's film version, Mrs Warboys's weary sigh at the music seems to be a response both to the tune and to the lateness of the hour. The national anthem, played by the BBC until 1997 to mark the end of the day's broadcasting, is matched in the following early-morning scene by the sound of an alarm clock that rings to waken Mr Warboys and his older son Danny (Andrew Beaumont) for work. We see Danny clock in, and the sound of the steel factory time clock continues over our first view of Ronnie, who is still in bed before school. The expectations raised by Mrs Warboys's careful preparation of Ronnie's school shirt and blazer go unfulfilled. We learn that he is in class 5G1, a member of a low stream at school, and not one of the prize-winners. As Ronnie puts it, 'a Dinky van'd be too big' for what he will be awarded (91).

The emphasis on marking official time and authority by means of the national anthem and the clocks becomes an element of the dialogue when these two opening scenes are followed by one in which Ronnie is late for school and encounters his English teacher, the sympathetic Miss Bedford (Denise Mockler), who is herself late:

> MISS BEDFORD: Good morning, Ronnie.
> RONNIE: Late again, Miss.
> MISS BEDFORD: You can talk, lad.
> RONNIE: Five minutes late. You'd have time stopped at our Danny's place for that.
> MISS BEDFORD: Time stopped?
> RONNIE: Yeh. They allow 'em three minutes a week. Anything over that they knock 'em half an hour's pay off. (86)

As we will see again in Hines's writing, for instance in *The Gamekeeper*, which was published two years after the broadcast of *Speech Day*, apparently different varieties of time-keeping all point irrevocably towards the 'time discipline' of an industrial work routine.[26] Equally, Ronnie's speech here is, like several of his other utterances, didactic in a way that is not concealed but foregrounded.

In *Speech Day*, the positive and transformative aspects of school are emphasised particularly in relation to literary and artistic activities, but these have to be abandoned on leaving school or, in the present case, for the sake of the speech day. Miss Bedford promises 5G1 'a treat' at the beginning of their English class, and gives out to the pupils what she considers to be 'one of the best sets of stories around today' (87). Hines's draft screenplays reveal that he changed his mind several times about whether or not to identify the stories. Although in the television play Miss Bedford never gets the chance to name the collection, the fact that it is Alan Sillitoe's *The Loneliness of the Long-Distance Runner and Other Stories* is clearly visible.[27] The stories' presence conveys a warning to the pupils about the nature of the institution, as well as registering Hines's intertextual debt. Not only does Sillitoe's title story, about the extreme authoritarian education of a Borstal, share concerns with Hines's work but so do others in the collection, about football ('The Match') and a negligent teacher ('Mr Raynor the Schoolteacher'), while Tony Richardson, the film's director, had been instrumental in gaining the funding to film *A Kestrel for a Knave*. Thus acknowledgement to both literary and filmic artistry is registered in this detail.

The decision not to mention Sillitoe's name in the broadcast version of *Speech Day*, or in either of the published scripts of Hines's play, emphasises the symbolic brevity of the pupils' encounter with literature. Instead of having the chance to read a work of fiction about elements of their own lives, including the worlds of education and work, which Hines describes as missing from all the novels he read at school,[28] the boys are themselves set to work. Miss Bedford's class is interrupted by Mr Douglas, whose nickname 'Dracula' is from a revealingly different literary source. He demands that the boys abandon their class to help George, the school handyman – played by Bill Dean, familiar as the grumpy fish and chip shop owner from *Kes* – to tidy up the grounds for the speech-day visitors. It is not just the summons to undertake what turns out to be point-less manual labour that prevents Miss Bedford from introducing the stories to her class. The boys are also shown to have interests, summed up by her as 'sex and soccer', that are not acknowledged within the 'moral orthopedics' of school life,[29] yet which also stand in the way of their being able to enjoy such activities as reading. Martin's yawning interrupts Miss Bedford just as she is about to tell her class 'something about the author' of the short stories, and his classmates claim that he is tired because 'he's out with his bird every night'. The failure of school to engage its pupils' interests is regretted here, as it is in Mrs Warboys's verdict, on Danny's account of sticking drawing-pins into the ceiling to mystify 'old McIntosh' during history lessons, that 'it's a pity you'd nowt else better to do' (99). It is tempting to link this anecdote to Mr Warboys's remark, in the family scene which acts as a pre-credit prologue to the film, that one of 'the only things' he can remember 'about history at school' is a maxim of Cromwell's, uttered 'when one of his officers told him that some of his men wanted to pray: "Let them pray if they like", he said, "but tell them to keep their powder dry"'. Mr Warboys's quoting of this summons by the republican Cromwell 'to blaze away at the proper time'[30] suggests that there is indeed a lesson to be gained from school, one which might conclude by destroying that very institution. The revolutionary implication of attending to the 'practicality' rather than the 'piety'[31] of Cromwell's utterance appears more explicitly in Ronnie's grandfather's irascible response to the appearance of Jehovah's Witnesses at his door: 'I'll give you spirit of God! What's God ever done for us? ... You want to chuck them Bibles away and get your bloody history books out' (100).

Miss Bedford's class on Sillitoe's short stories is finally cut short not by the pupils' inattention, but by Mr Douglas's insistence that 'some jobs want doing for this afternoon'. In place of Miss Bedford's agreement with a pupil that the anthology constitutes 'the best stories for the best class' (87), Mr Douglas's command is based on that class's lowly role in the school's hierarchy. As part of the tidying up he has been ordered to do, Ronnie disturbs a mathematics lesson by mowing the grass outside the classroom window, and is given a punishment of 100 lines for protesting that he doesn't like the work. The maths teacher exasperatedly informs his class, 'It's all right for him; he's nothing better to do with his time. I've got to get you lot through an examination at the end of the year' (91). Even the prospect of academic achievement is represented in the terms of its being a burden for the teachers.

Hines's writing that followed soon after *Speech Day* makes clear his bleak view of contemporary methods of schooling and its role in preparing individuals for a world in which work is scarce by means of demanding irrelevant 'qualifications'. In *The Price of Coal*, Tony Storey's proficiency in Latin enables his father Sid to translate the NCB motto 'Ex Tenebris Lux', but we learn that Tony had to give the subject up after a year, and that, according to Sid, 'you need seven GCEs to get a job sweeping up these days'. Not only does the stratification of intellectual life in this way quash young people's interest but such qualifications are the only recognised measure of aptitude. The maths lesson that Ronnie disturbs in *Speech Day* may be one for the pupils of a higher stream, but it is represented in terms of the teacher's gobbledygook: 'And therefore A and C is equal to ... and similarly ADO is congruent to ...' (90).

The very work to which the class of 5G1 are set is both unnecessary, since 'there's nowt to do', according to George, and superficial, as he adds: 'do the front – that's all that matters' (88). This anticipates the thoroughgoing treatment of this theme in 'Meet the People', the first of the pair of *The Price of Coal* plays, in which only those parts of the mine visible to Prince Charles are decorated for his visit. In *Speech Day* the realism is qualified as a means of showing the nature of work, so that the television play's *mise-en-scène* includes elements that are symbolic in a variety of ways. This sometimes takes the form of puns made visible. As the organising theme of the play's speech day reveals, Ronnie and his friends are destined not to be among the 'prize-winners' of life, while another pupil, Shirley, is shown to be Ronnie's female equivalent. The girls of the school's lower streams have been set to 'doing the eats' for the ceremony, and Ronnie persuades Shirley to give him one of the cream cakes meant for the dignitaries. This is a dramatisation of Ronnie's grandfather's explicitly Marxist conviction that 'Things are going to change':

> I agree with what Lenin said, when he said we ain't interested in size of crumbs, or even slices of cake. We want bakery, he said, so that we can determine the sort of cake that's to be baked. (104)

Ronnie's act of taking one of the 'butterfly buns' meant for others is thus one with a comically rendered revolutionary potential.

Soon after their gardening tasks are finished, the boys of 5G1 are summoned during a woodwork class to put out chairs for the prize-giving, interrupting a different kind of unvalorised activity: 'I want to get on with my table: I'll never get it finished!', as one pupil exclaims (92). The order by the woodwork master Mr Rees (Paul Copley) to his students, 'Aprons off, blazers on', reveals the interchangeability of the clothing judged appropriate for work and for education: the boys must wear their uniforms for the labour of moving furniture. The schoolchildren's work on show at the art exhibition provokes admiration in two teachers: 'That's terrific!', says Mr Rees of a painting of the Jarrow Crusade, the verdict combining appreciation of the artwork's aesthetic and political accomplishment (95). Yet the effort of labour is shown to rule out its own representation. In a draft version, the incompatibility of art and work is emphasised through the conceit of the tools of one trade turning into those of the other. Mr Rees wonders if the Jarrow artist will 'ever pick up a brush again when he leaves school?', to which the art teacher Mr Worrall (Bernard Wrigley) replies, 'Definitely. He'll pick up a sweeping brush at Leonard and Wolfe'.[32] This exchange was cut from the broadcast version, in which the fictitious steelmaking company of Leonard and Wolfe – a name registering a satirical mixture of the

names of the shipbuilders Harland and Wolff with that of Virginia
Woolf's husband – exerts telling influence over the pupils by means
of an essay prize named in their honour. Yet Ronnie tells George
that the company, his father's employer, is 'laying 'em off left right
and centre now'. The art exhibition conversation in the televised
play has been condensed into Mr Worrall's remark that he regarded
himself as 'Pablo's natural successor' until he 'took a holiday job on
a building site', with the result that he was always 'too shagged out'
to do any painting. The same point is thus expressed more directly
in the play's televised version.

Although *Speech Day* is not a drama-documentary in the manner
of *Threads*, its characters do act as the mouthpieces for clearly
identified non-fiction material, disrupting the realist surface to
almost Brechtian effect. Outside the football ground, Danny and
Ronnie detach themselves from the crowd to look in the window of
a shop selling motorbikes, in an instance of Hines's use of a symbol
that conveys here, as it does in *Looks and Smiles*, the possibility
of genuine intellectual engagement as well as that of mobility and
flight. Danny quotes officialese in explaining that he cannot afford
even a down payment for a bike despite following his school's
advice to enter an apprenticeship:

> You work for pocket money for five years and then you suddenly
> find that you're not guaranteed a job at the end of it. 'Owing to the
> fluctuating economic factors and the variable state of the Home and
> Foreign markets' – it's nowt but slave labour, that's what it is. (103)

In another scene, the documentary source is itself introduced into
the narrative when Ronnie and his friends travel back to school on
the top deck of a bus, and in the televised version it is also an object
in the *mise-en-scène*. Ronnie's school friend Wally (Kevin Jenkinson)
picks up the newspaper passed to him by Ronnie from his fish and
chips.[33] Ronnie points out the headline, '"School-leavers' plight":
that's us, isn't it?', and Wally reads aloud with perfect, perhaps
prize-winning, fluency the rest of the article, which asserts that
'Young people leaving school without qualifications tend to take
several jobs in quick succession, until at seventeen they are among
the long-term unemployed' (101).[34] The figure quoted in this semi-
documentary moment is still in the viewer's mind when the scene
abruptly returns to the school hall and we hear the headmaster
observe that 'Last year seventeen of the school's pupils gained

university degrees' (101). The same numbers in these two different contexts have opposed meanings. The academic success of the seventeen exceptions is described as if it were a rare personal achievement rather than acknowledged to be dependent upon the mass of those 17-year-olds who are consigned to 'mass unemployment'. This is the case not only because their schooling has failed them but because the existence of what Marx calls a 'redundant population of workers' is demanded by 'capitalistic accumulation itself'.[35]

Speech Day concludes with those speeches that are its subject as well as its discourse, alongside other self-consciously deployed elements of a prize-giving ceremony, including the school choir's singing. The mayor, Joe Brannigan (John Rolls), one of the dignitaries who addresses the school, is described by George as a class turncoat who has repudiated his background. Grandpa's insistence that 'Things are no better now than when I were a lad' is followed by a cut to the mayor saying the opposite: 'Nowadays with all the opportunities you've got almost anyone can get on provided he's prepared to work hard for it' (106). In one of the play's self-conscious abandonments of realist plausibility, we learn that the school handyman George knew Joe Brannigan in his youth as a fellow steelworker and 'hard as nails' union activist. In his guise as a Greek chorus figure who is necessarily on the margins of the action, visibly so during the prize-giving ceremony, George reports that Joe later became 'soft' and 'respectable', going for drinks with the managers after meetings 'as though it was one big game, pals together like' (106). He concludes, 'Well, you can't do that, Ronnie, it's war, lad'. This notion of class hierarchy, or life itself, as a 'game' is one that the play itself draws upon in using comedy for political ends. It seems that the mayor identifies the 'game' taking place in the wrong place, since it is, rather, the pupils at their maths lesson who are delighted by a 'diversion', and at the play's conclusion Ronnie's response to Brannigan's speech is an outburst of laughter that results in his ejection from the ceremony. As Foucault argues, being the focus of such scrutiny as that of Mr Douglas, who stands sentry at the back of the school hall, his surveillant gaze emphasised by horn-rimmed glasses, is meant to 'maintain the disciplined subject in his subjections', a role Ronnie rejects here.[36] The revolutionary potential of such subversive laughter, of which George drily observes, 'They wouldn't take kindly to that now, would they?', is acknowledged in these moments.

These roles and utterances are allegorical as much as realist. As the drafts show, Hines spent some time adjusting the precise balance of the two modes in *Speech Day*. In earlier versions of the script, Mr Warboys advises Danny to become a union official as a way of improving the workers' lot, while not only the mayor, Joe Brannigan, but also the other speech-day guest, Professor Jessup, embodies the role of a working-class man who has flourished by repudiating his own past. In the televised version and published script, Jessup's role is much reduced. Rather than another cautionary figure, he is simply a dullard in preference to whom Ronnie and his friends would rather hear a speech from Raquel Welch, George Best or even Mr Warboys. The school choir's songs were equally subject to revision in the process of Hines's drafting. The 'two modern folk songs' the choir sings in the televised version have an ironic effect, rather like the headmaster's recitation of the first few lines of Martin Luther King's speech 'I have a dream' (100). The last line the headmaster quotes, 'In a dark, confused world the spirit of God may reign supreme', includes the very phrase used by Grandpa in his scornful declamation, 'I'll give you spirit of God!'. The subtlety of the satire relies on its being directed against the headmaster's sanctimonious appropriation and not the utterance itself. Likewise, the choir sings a hymn that alludes to the traditional song 'Dives and Lazarus' from the New Testament story about a rich man refusing charity to the destitute Lazarus. This is followed by a twentieth-century folk song 'The Miracle' by the radical American singer Malvina Reynolds, which returns to the notion of 'spirit' but in a human-centred sense, as we hear: 'But give [man] room to move and grow,/But give his spirits play/And he can make a world of light/Out of the common clay' (103). More than anything else we hear in the play, these lyrics present an ideal for education.

The complex dialogic relationship of the songs to the world represented in the play makes their role an over-determined one. After each rendition, the staff and guests applaud a song although their behaviour conflicts with its lyrics. The drafts of *Speech Day* show that the play's concluding with 'Jerusalem' was a late decision made in preference to the much less ambivalent African-American civil rights song 'We Shall Overcome'. In *Speech Day*'s televised version, the lyrics of 'Jerusalem' are contrasted with particular scenes to equally satirical but more detailed effect. The choir's singing the phrase 'dark satanic mills' accompanies a shot of the dignitaries in the school hall; 'chariots of fire' is heard alongside a cut to smelting at Ronnie's father's steelworks; the 'bow of burning gold' as we see Mrs Warboys unhappily at work sewing in a textile factory. The final credits appear over a different kind of sound, in a scene where Danny is audibly and visibly at work, repeatedly 'inserting a steel bar into a machine' (107).

Alan Durband's apparently puzzling comment that 'Ronnie and his mates are docile in their ignorance' of the stratified educational system they inhabit makes sense if it is taken to refer to *Speech Day*'s inconclusive ending.[37] After the distressing spectacle of Danny's arduous and boring work, the credits close enigmatically on a school photograph of Ronnie. This conclusion is clearly quite unlike, for instance, the murderous insurrection on the part of the pupils that takes place on Founders' Day at the end of the public-school-set film *if....* (Lindsay Anderson 1968). However, the contrast between the songs and the visual montage of the Warboys adults' monotonous manual labour makes its significance more apparent than that of the various draft endings with which Hines experimented. An early draft has Ronnie and George walk out of the school together past 'the room where all the eats are set out ready', then 'the choir strikes up a complicated orchestration of "We Shall Overcome"'. All of this has been crossed out in the draft, and instead a handwritten addition appears: Ronnie 'walks out of school past cars (chauffeur asleep); staffroom [with] food laid out', while the last image is that of 'Danny at work'. This is the first hint that the world of school, including the signifiers of hierarchy and class in the image of the chauffeur and staffroom, will give way entirely to a representation of work in the last moments of the play. A transitional version of the script makes clear that 'we hear the singing of "Jerusalem" in the background'.[38] In place of what would therefore be three civil rights utterances – 'We Shall Overcome' as well as the two that remain in the final version, King's speech and Reynolds's song – Hines chose to conclude his play about twentieth-century malaise with imagery and soundtrack that draw on Blake's lament for industrial England's distance from the divine Jerusalem.[39]

The Gamekeeper (1975)

Barry Hines's novel *The Gamekeeper*, published in 1975, is inno-vative yet troubling to read in equal measure. This is evident in narrative and ethical terms, an effect that is redoubled in the film version (Ken Loach 1980), for which Hines wrote the screenplay. *The Gamekeeper* follows a nine-month period in the working life of George Purse, a former steelworker who has taken up the job of a gamekeeper on a ducal estate. We read of his efforts to raise pheas-ants, his battles with their natural and human predators, and the two shoots, of grouse in August and pheasant in November, which take place on the estate, as well as the effects of the gamekeeper's role on his wife and two young sons.

The novel of *The Gamekeeper* opens with what turns out to be a characteristically hybrid narrative style, not only combining factual with fictional discourse but also description with instruction:

> FEBRUARY. It was time to catch up the pheasants.[40]

The novel concludes in November of the same unspecified year, about which the narrator reports, 'In another month it would be Christmas, and the Season would be almost over. [George's] work would be easier then, for a few weeks; until February, when it would be time to catch up the pheasants again' (224). Such a temporality seems to contrast with the familiar Gregorian calendar, and with E.P. Thompson's notion of the 'time discipline' of industrial work routines.[41] Instead, it follows the birds' breeding season, since the pheasants are being 'caught up' by George at a particular time to begin the process of hand-rearing. Yet the 'Season', capitalised in the novel to ironic effect, represents a construction of time resting equally on class-based labour relations, as the repetitive nature of George's work reveals. Death is implicit in such labour, in actual terms for the birds and figuratively for those who undertake it. This seasonal pattern is one of killing as much as of animal husbandry. This is true not just for the pheasants, which George has to protect from predators and 'keep … alive for the official killers' (12), since, in John Berger's phrase, they are to be 'bred *and* sacrificed'.[42] It is also true for the birds designated as inimical to the pheasants, 'crows and magpies, jays and jackdaws' (54). For instance, we learn that in April, 'It was time to shoot a few [crows'] nests out before the foliage grew any thicker and concealed them' (53).

The novel's seasonal structure signals that a comparison between different kinds of work is certainly one of *The Gamekeeper*'s concerns. While George views his outdoor life with satisfaction by contrast to his previous employment in a steel foundry, for his wife Mary their situation is now worse. Her feeling 'fed up with looking at trees and fields all day' (67) is part of a more profound disenchantment with the family's circumstances. In place of the 'decent wage' from George's steelworking days, the Purses live in a cottage they neither rent nor own, without what Mary calls 'security', but dependent on their employers' goodwill: 'They seem to have us over a barrel, that's what gets me', as she puts it (66–7). The modern 'relic' of 'serfdom'[43] that their tied cottage represents is conveyed by the trope of a rotting window-frame at the Purses' home, about which George has to supplicate the estate manager in an unresolved quest to have it repaired. While the window is mentioned only briefly in the novel, in the film version the impossibility of having it mended is a theme threaded throughout the events of the gamekeeper's year. By this means, we are led to understand that it is not just George's labour, but George himself, who has been bought by the Duke.[44]

In a contemporary review, Robert Nye argues that the novel's 'moral' centres on the pointless nature of the gamekeeper's work, which is 'for nothing' since the birds, carefully reared by George, are all ultimately slaughtered 'for the peculiar pleasure of others'.[45] The Duke's wealth and leisure transform the dead animals from commodities into waste products, since they have no use-value to him beyond the act of killing. George voices this perception during the lunch break at the pheasant shoot: 'It makes you wonder what it's all about sometimes, doesn't it?' (212). In this sense George's move from steelworker to gamekeeper means that he 'changes his job but not his function',[46] undertaking repetitive work that benefits someone else, as he puts it of Brightside Steel: 'Eight hours of purgatory, week in, week out, until I was sixty-five' (66). While the job in a steelworks conforms to Marx's definition of 'productive' work, since it is labour that '*is directly transformed into capital*',[47] that of a gamekeeper functions rather to maintain the integrity of the privately owned land that underlies individual wealth creation. We learn that the steelmaker George Brown, a member of what the narrator calls 'the new aristocracy of businessmen' (175), has leased land to the Duke for the purpose of shooting, meaning that George

Purse is still working on the foundry's property. Neither kind of work offers a narrative with the possible resolution of escape or transcendence, as the novel's circular structure emphasises.

The killing of the birds and of the animals judged to be their predators makes *The Gamekeeper* disconcerting to read. In an unpublished review, John Berger describes the novel's representation of the grouse shoot as 'unforgettable', an epithet that registers the overlapping ethical and aesthetic effects of an almost 40-page sequence devoted to its narration.[48] In Loach's film version, the two shoots, of grouse and later of pheasants, are represented in relatively short sequences. In the cinematic pheasant shoot, rapid reverse cuts between the Duke (Willoughby Gray) taking aim and images of the flying birds in his eyeline make their deaths appear in abstract form, signified by the shapes of falling bodies.

In the novel, it is made clear that the Duke's pursuit of shooting is enabled by the possession of land, which includes the varied terrains of moors and woods suited respectively to grouse and pheasants; it is also necessitated by it, since the landed gentry must find a way to pass the time in the absence of a need to work. The birds' carcasses are sold at Smithfield or to the Savoy as a means of disposal, because the Duke does not need the money, or, in the case of the grouse, to celebrate the 'Glorious Twelfth', the date in August on which the shooting begins. This is another seasonal moment with markedly constructed origins. Its name is borrowed from the 'Glorious Revolution' of the Protestant William III's accession to the English throne in 1688, in the wake of which royal power was curtailed, but replaced by that of the 'landed class'.[49] In Hines's novel the piles of the birds' dead bodies constitute a symbol, one that takes a strikingly visual form in the film, of surplus in the sense of a superfluity that is valuable in signifying a landowner's dominion. Yet it is in the novel that we see a particularly fitting symbol of this kind, when two of the beaters lie down on the piles of bodies at the end of the pheasant shoot, as a joke with a real referent: they are on top of 'the furred and feathered dead', causing the Duke to 'bellow' and 'shake' with laughter (222). On the other hand, the birds exist wholly as use-values for the poachers, who wish only to eat them. Although George operates within an economy of exchange based on animals – he tries unsuccessfully to barter a ferret for some wood for the window-frame – his distaste for what might be called the 'shooting system' is expressed in his wish to opt out of it: we learn that 'if the [grouse] were not free, [George] would not have them' (176). It is not just the case that class-based exploitation underlies the practice of shooting game but that the animals' mass deaths are its most paradigmatic outcome as well as its symbolic expression.

The killing of the birds is made possible by George and his fellow gamekeepers, although the former is described as a 'functional killer' who 'never killed anything for fun' (133–4). By contrast, for the Duke and his friends the shoot is a deathly 'game', constituting not just a substitute for work but, it is implied, for any meaningful activity. As the narrator puts it, as if borrowing the Duke's own words, 'It was a full time job, travelling and shooting' (180). The grouse-shooting party includes not simply British aristocratic sportsmen but also European political figures, such as Count Mauriac, who, as the narrator puts it in phrasing that sounds tongue-in-cheek, 'flew over from France for every shoot', as if he were himself a bird; and Senhor Aveiro, a retired Portuguese diplomat, of whom we learn, in another term equally suited to wildlife, that he had 'settled' in England (162). This dramatises the comment made by George's fellow-drinkers in the local pub about the 'old Duke's' insistence on prosecuting the miners who worked in his pits when they were caught poaching: 'The Duke and the judges and such like, they're all in the same team, aren't they? Everybody knows that' (85). The precision about the hunting-party's members is significant on multiple levels, and these details, like those of the birds' lives and the distressing narration of their deaths, constitute the novel's painstakingly researched realist detail, including Hines shadowing a gamekeeper's work on the Wentworth estate near Barnsley, even as they act as synecdoches for injustice and exploitation. As Tony Garnett puts it of the bird in *A Kestrel for a Knave*, the animal metaphor here is also 'an inherent and necessary part of the action'.[50]

The novel's real focus on class through the activity of killing is revealed through its delineation of George's ambiguous role as facilitator or 'keeper' of the shoots. We are reminded by the narrator, once more in what sounds like free indirect discourse, that the gamekeeper 'had not spent the best part of a year raising [the pheasants] for anybody to shoot' (180), nor 'to provide food for hungry predators' (127), whether these 'predators' are animal or human. Since all the effort of George's work is to ensure that the birds only die at the hands of the 'official killers', any threat of the estate workers' withholding their labour has great significance. This is clear in relation to the impromptu beaters' strike on the morning of the pheasant shoot for the sake of a 50 pence rise to £3 per day. As George puts it, echoing and reversing Mary's phrase about their tied cottage, 'They've got [the Duke] over a barrel ... They could ask for a tenner this morning and they'd get it'(189).

In his review, Nye claims that, as in *A Kestrel for a Knave*, Hines 'is concerned essentially to capture something of the quiddity of the creatures he writes about', allowing the term 'creatures' to refer ambiguously to humans and animals. *The Gamekeeper* does explore the interiority, and thus the 'quiddity', of the animals whose lives and deaths it depicts, including that of George's dogs, a hare and a broody hen as well as the game birds. In a moment of sympathetic curiosity on his own part, George places himself in his terrier's position near a rabbit hole and tries to detect the same scents as the dog. This creates a division in the reader's identification, since the narrative is constructed to emphasise the fact that George's livelihood depends on the success of the hunt, yet also to make us regret and resist the inevitability of the animals' deaths. At the November shoot, a disquieting parallel is established between two sets of mothers and children having to hear the guns: 'Mary Purse and the boys could hear the beaters from the house', while the pheasants' 'foster mothers', the hens who had reared the chicks, 'were sitting in the hen house listening to the noise' (216–17). In place of the novel's focus on subjectivity, the film makes multiple transformations in the process of adaptation, most radically in relation to the animal deaths, but one that is also evident in the shift of the novel's free indirect discourse to filmic dialogue. An isolated moment from the novel in which George shouts obscenity-filled instructions to the beaters, to the Duke's mortification (198), becomes in the film an extended expression of the gamekeeper's suppressed anger about the birds' circumstances and his own. George's ambivalence about the killing, narrated in the novel, is acted out in the film. In the novel the escape of a lone bird, 'a young cock' who is missed by two sets of guns and flies away 'unharmed', provokes elation in George, who 'could not help punching it on its way with a clenched fist' (194). In the film, the viewer is prompted to interpret a fleeting moment in which George's upward glance follows the path of a bird flying over the Guns' heads and out of sight, his response enigmatic. The pheasant's flight conveys the possibility of evading terrible odds, its 'will-to-live' offsetting the gamekeeper's practical fatalism as well as what Berger describes as the novel's 'near-despair' at its sense of 'historical hopelessness'.[51] Luke Spencer appears to take the same stance in observing that 'the world belongs to organized hunters, not free-flying individuals'; yet a third possibility exists, at least if the birds are viewed as metaphorical, that of 'collective action'.[52] Indeed, the novel's construction of a reader who must decipher the significance of the extreme detail of bird-rearing and slaughter can be seen to constitute a view that counters such 'pessimism'.[53]

Hines's late decision about the title of his novel, which meant discarding the alternatives *Vermin* and *Enemies of Game*, entailed the abandonment of any overtly allegorical likening of class hierarchies to those of species.[54] Instead, the conflation of animal and human implicit in the phrasing of the discarded titles is enacted within the world of the novel. Thus we see that the birds are not allegorical stand-ins for workers, as it might seem at first, but representative of industrialised work-relations more widely. The narrator of *The Gamekeeper* is an idiosyncratic construct which sometimes speaks in what sounds like a personalised voice, for instance in breaching its customary deadpan account by commenting directly on the cruelty of badger-digging or the poverty that led to the Jarrow Crusade (132, 153). An instance of free indirect discourse, in an unusual appearance of the technique in Hines's writing, uses one of these phrases in its showing of George's view of animals divided up into classes: 'He was not interested in lapwings … Lapwings were not enemies of game' (8). The binary of 'enemies' and 'game' transcends that of human and animal, and George speaks of the local people as if they too were on its wrong side. George's exasperation with a local poacher extends to his verdict on the man's children: 'They all ought to be gassed in their beds like they do rabbits' (22).

The uncertainty about whose voice we are hearing preserves the ambiguity of George's persona as it appears in the novel, or, more precisely, as he responds to the contradictions of the gamekeeping role. These are contradictions of class expressed in terms of species. George argues with Mary over what Ian's schoolteacher calls the 'cruelty' of his work, claiming instead that the real harm is that of industrial labour: 'If she'd worked in some of the places I've worked in she wouldn't be so bloody fussy about killing a few rooks' (66). Yet the elaborate trapping and shooting of birds and mammals that George undertakes, described in equally elaborate detail, shows that this is a defensive understatement. George acts according to an animal hierarchy which in part follows Berger's analysis of animals, post-Descartes, being considered to be either 'companions' or 'machines',[55] yet includes the other relational categories of 'enemies' and 'game'. Despite his shooting rabbits and birds, and setting traps which catch hedgehogs, foxes and even domestic animals, George is aghast at someone leaving a dog in a car with the windows closed – 'the poor little bugger was panting its heart out in there' (78), as he puts it – and stays outside all night when his terrier is trapped underground. The gamekeeper's system reveals that dogs are companions and co-workers, by contrast to the pheasants and even his own sons, who are underlings. Jacob Leigh describes George's reactions in the film to trespassers and poachers, whom he threatens with non-existent penalties, as 'unconscious coping strategies',[56] and indeed paradoxes are evident in his vigilance: while he sternly forbids little girls to pick flowers because they are trespassing on the Duke's property, George 'always let them keep the bluebells'. His living out the contradictions of the gamekeeper's role is expressed at a variety of textual levels. George's surname being synonymous with that of the 'purse' rabbit trap mentioned in the screenplay,[57] as well as his refrain, 'I've got a job to do', when questioned about the implications of his work, are expressions of his being trapped as well as doing the trapping. The challenge to the reader to interpret George's behaviour becomes an element of the plot when we learn that the beaters 'could not determine his attitude' on the occasion of their strike. However, the narrator implies that, given the 'early experiences and loyalties' of George and his fellow-gamekeepers, it should be obvious 'which side they were on' (187–8). This phrase is another intertextual glance forward, this time to Loach's documentary anthology film *Which Side Are You On?* (1984) about the miners' strike,[58] its title invoking the political divisions that a picket line, like a grouse shoot, makes manifest.

The film adaptation of *The Gamekeeper* draws on the novel's crossover of human and animal, yet at the same time the change of medium reinforces the impassable gulf between the two. References to the class-related meaning of hunting elsewhere in Hines's fiction take pictorial form. In *Unfinished Business*, Lucy's eye is drawn to a hunting print at the parental home of her lover Dave, in which she sees that the 'servant girl' bringing drink to the huntsmen 'was the only person on the ground. Just her and the dogs', its implications made clear when we learn that Dave's father has been involved in Lonhro asset-stripping. In a draft version of the screenplay for *The Price of Coal*, Mr Forbes's secretary Sheila recommends putting a framed thank-you letter from Prince Charles for his visit to the pit on the wall beside some hunting prints, as she puts it, 'They sort of go together, don't they?'[59] The appearance of hunting takes a different form in Loach's film of *The Gamekeeper*. The killing of individual animals on film, sometimes shown in close-up, as well as the shooting of birds en masse, constitutes a shift from the novel's ambiguous symbolism to extreme filmic realism.[60] Loach's preliminary notes on Hines's novel reveal the process by which he envisaged the adaptation of the animal metaphor into its visual version. For instance, he was attentive to George's double role as rearer of pheasant chicks and of his young sons. As the novel's blurb has it, the birds are his 'progeny'; yet their fate implies that rearing necessarily entails killing. This is evident in Loach's response to the novel's blurring of pronouns, as we see in his summary of a scene of George and his sons at work: 'The boys clean the mown grass off the rearing field. The eggs hatch … The gamekeeper picks one up: he kills those with obvious deformities.'[61]

As we argued of *A Kestrel for a Knave*, Hines's novel is already cinematic in its use of visual symbols. The politics of land takes priority over landscape, so that locations are named only as the narrative requires, or to convey a relational significance. Thus we learn that 'The gamekeeper's cottage faced outwards across arable land. Three fields away was the main road, which marked the boundary of the Duke's estate, and across the road stood the flats and maisonettes of a new council estate' (11). Class relations are laid out topographically here, as suggested by the use of 'estate' to mean both privately owned land and rented public housing. In the film, the main road appears in the *mise-en-scène* as the line signifying in visual terms the boundary of the Duke's domain, marked out by 'No Trespassing' signs. Thus we see George's younger son Ian run from school across the road back home carrying the kitten he wants to adopt. As Leigh argues, 'the long shot of Ian crossing the road' from the public to the private realm in this sequence is 'emblematic' of the film's concern with the intersection of 'social and physical environment'.[62] But the kitten cannot easily be taken from one world to the other in this way, and Ian has to return it to school. The siting of the gamekeeper's cottage within the ducal estate, from which he works to exclude 'people like himself',[63] that is, his former work-mates and the fathers of his children's fellow-pupils, shows his compromised situation. In the novel, none of these locations is named. The Duke's home is known simply as the Big House, while the location of George's former workplace in the nearby city is identified only in terms of a fleeting hint, since it is called Brightside Steel. Minimalist site-specific signifiers appear, such as the names of Lord Dronfield, the aristocrat for whom George loads during the grouse shoot and whose title is taken from that of a Derbyshire town seven miles from Sheffield; and that of the Dame Edith Sitwell school which local children attend, named after the writer and occupant of Derbyshire's Renishaw Hall on the outskirts of Sheffield, who was one of a family of ironmasters and landowners.

The film of *The Gamekeeper* offers a visual equivalent to the novel's prioritising of land over landscape, so that although it is clearly filmed in South Yorkshire, it is not about that specific region. (See Figure 2.) The filming schedule makes clear what the attentive

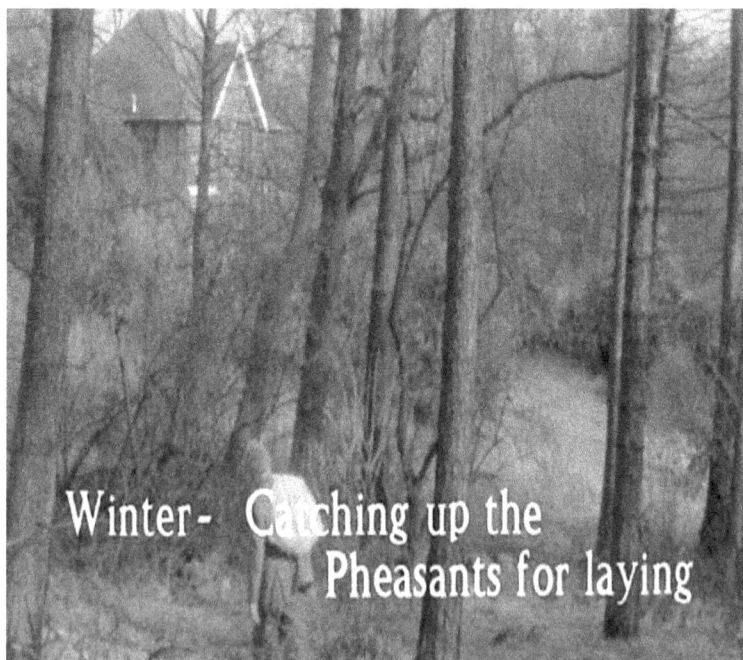

2 The opening of *The Gamekeeper*

spectator will be able to identify: Wortley Hall stands in as the Duke's stately home and Wortley as its estate village, while George's former workplace is located in Sheffield's industrial suburb of Attercliffe, just south of Brightside, and the shoot was filmed on Hallam Moor.[64] The film's soundscape of local accents equally allows for the identification of South Yorkshire. Hines took pains in interviews about the filming not to identify the specific locations in acknowledgement of the imaginary nature even of the visual geography.[65] In the novel, George and the gamekeepers travel from the Duke's estate to the grouse moors via the city's industrial area, an unlikely route in terms of the film's locations. The appearance of a literal geography in the service of symbolic meaning has led critics of the film to identify it as a hybrid of documentary and drama, just as Loach's *Cathy Come Home* (1966) and the Hines-scripted *Threads* (1984) use documentary tropes for fictional plots.[66] The film of *The Gamekeeper* follows the fiction's discourse in this respect, as it does with its use of intertitles to mark out George's seasonal work. This is a cinematic version of the novel's offsetting the individuality of the gamekeeper and his family by adopting a generalising documentary narration. It is not just a stylistic device but, as John Berger argues, a profound connection of narration to subject: George 'gives himself over – as the writing gives itself over – to all the practical tasks at hand'.[67] Thus George is often simply referred to by the narrator as 'the gamekeeper', his activities conveyed in the present tense suited to a livestock manual ('Gamekeepers use various feeding methods …' (13), 'a brail is a leather fastener' (17), and passages are quoted verbatim from non-fiction sources such as publications by the RSPB and League Against Cruel Sports.

However, the film version of *The Gamekeeper* is not a harmonious blend of documentary and drama but one characterised by aesthetic and actual violence. As with the novel, this is made manifest in relation to genre.[68] As was invariably the practice in his collaborations with Hines, Loach cast non-professional actors to take the roles of the film's children, and also those of the Guns, 'first-rate Hoorays', as he puts it, 'who were clearly more keen on getting the fowl out of the air than they were in making the film'.[69] In this instance, neo-realist casting and filming have an extremely realist outcome. Although the number of visible deaths at the two bird shoots is small, making the unquestioning cruelty of class relations take form in this way is a goal the film cannot attain without repeating that cruelty. The animal deaths 'punctuate' fictional with documentary space, as Vivian Sobchack puts it in an analysis of the 'massacre' of rabbits in Jean Renoir's film *La Règle du jeu* (1939).[70] Sobchack records her distress on subsequent viewings of the film at the death of an individual rabbit, 'every time I see it being sacrificed for my narrative pleasure', and just such a killing also takes place in *The Gamekeeper* at George's hands.[71] In both films, the 'sacrifice' could equally be described as one made for the sake of political satire, directed against the war in Renoir's film, class exploitation in that of *The Gamekeeper*. However, it might seem that such a goal is fatally compromised by the onscreen deaths that are meant to convey it. As Jonathan Burt argues, clear distinctions between diegetic and extradiegetic realms are 'ruptured' where animals appear onscreen at all,[72] even more so when they are killed. In *The Gamekeeper* filming and hunting entail each other. This is suggested in the very title of Loach's 'Shooting Schedule', and in Anthony Hayward's ambiguous description of the need to mount 'four separate shoots' for the film over the course of a year.[73] Such a link between filming and hunting reappears even more clearly in an entry made by Loach during filming for the grouse shoot: 'Plus extra shots of pheasants',[74] in which the use of the same word for units of filmic signification and blasts from a gun reveals the fact that the imagery sought is specifically that of the birds' deaths. This intertwining of the two acts does not rest simply on an accidental pun but rather on the homology between camera and gun, as a note about filming the 'grouse drive' shows: 'Could all crew wear sombre-coloured clothes so the grouse don't get frightened off.'[75] This instruction differs subtly from that of a more workaday instance, in which a warning is issued not to park 'crew vehicles' in shot 'when we are filming exteriors at Wortley Hall'.[76] In the note about clothing, it is made clear that the film crew are part of the shoot in every sense. They are not simply recording a hunt that would have taken place anyway in order to reveal its brutality but ensuring that it happens.

The detail of the novel and the documentary sources that Hines consulted, as well as Loach's summary of those parts of the novel about shooting and his comments in interview about the film, confirm the fact that their views on hunting are akin to those of Jean Renoir, who hated it.[77] Yet despite its profound concern with the 'paternalism and social inequalities' that are presented as 'the natural order of things', and thus shown to be as 'immutable' as species difference (188), the film of *The Gamekeeper* runs the risk of enacting what it otherwise so exhilaratingly exposes, by transforming the novel's literary signifiers into those of the real.

The Price of Coal (1977)

The relationship between the film and novel of *The Price of Coal* is unlike that of any of Hines's other works, apart from *Looks and Smiles*, since the novel was written after the screenplay. In his preface to a reprint of the novel, which was first published in 1979, Hines describes this text as having been 'developed' from the pair of Play for Today television dramas directed by Ken Loach and broadcast in 1977.[78] Hines expended much of his aesthetic energy on the screenplay of *The Price of Coal*, in terms of working out its precise narrative form and the specificities of dialogue and situation, as the existence of several full draft versions attests. This makes it possible to trace Hines's working methods in a particularly detailed way, in relation to his use of historical material as well as his compositional and editorial practices. The drama consists of two connected parts, the first, 'Meet the People', a wryly comic story about the preparations for the visit of Prince Charles to the fictional Milton Colliery, the second, 'Back to Reality', about a pit explosion that kills five men.

While the novel is a retro-adaptation of the final screenplay, it has its own status within Hines's oeuvre, and critics approaching his novels assess this work too.[79] The screenplay and novel are symbiotic, since the fiction is able to reinstate some details discarded from the screenplay drafts, yet cannot include others. This is the case for instance of the dialogue improvised in the film by those actors drawn from the Northern club circuit, including Jackie Shinn, who plays the manager Mr Forbes, Stan Richards, whose role as the miner Albert Rhodes led to his being cast as the long-standing character Seth Armstrong in *Emmerdale*, and Bobby Knutt, as the miner Sid Storey. The novel and television play use their generic techniques to slightly different effect. The novel signals the varieties of strategic and mocking reverence in its capitalised references to Prince Charles when Forbes's committee members hear about 'the Visit': 'One of the men asked if He was looking for a job. Another replied that He could have his' (8). However, the film's reliance on dialect, including the use of second person singular pronouns, is not fully reproduced in its written version, as we see in the novel's version of a scene in which the miner Harry (Ted Beyer) admonishes the apprentice Pete (Peter Black), who is engaged in planting trees for the royal visit: 'Nay, lad, plant the thing right if you're going to. We'll still be here you know when the Visit's over. We might as well get some benefit out of it as well' (18). The process of drafting and refining the television play's script and that of the novel not only offers insights into Hines's compositional methodology but has wide-ranging generic and political implications for the precise meaning of *The Price of Coal* in both its forms.

The success of the two *Price of Coal* television plays and their distinctive mingling of verbal and visual material was clearly still clear in the minds of some of the novel's reviewers, who greeted it ambivalently. One review regretted the absence of 'freshness', no doubt in part because of the story's familiarity, while another from the *Financial Times* seems unwittingly to act out the very social divisions that Hines's narrative represents by describing it as an expression of 'fashionably liverish spleen'.[80] While these verdicts are extreme, it is true that in compositional terms the novel is subsidiary to the television play. Although much of the artistic effort Hines spent in shaping *The Price of Coal* took place in relation to the screenplay, he did experiment with alternatives to linear narration for the novel. In relation to the first play, 'Meet the People', about Prince Charles's visit to Milton Colliery, Hines used a collection of material from different sources for his screenplay. He wove into it elements of the Queen's real-life visit to Silverwood Colliery in July 1975, drawn from newspapers as well as National Coal Board publicity. Hines also used details from a description by students from the Cranfield Institute of Technology concerning a visit to their institution by Prince Philip.[81] Versions of these details, including a rumour that lamp-posts would be painted only on the side visible from the road by which Philip would travel, and the continuous watering of the Vice Chancellor's lawn for six weeks beforehand, have their mine-related equivalents in Hines's play. Thus we learn that, rather than repairing a broken window, the brick holding it open is to be painted white, to the astonishment of the men working inside, and the muckstack is seeded with grass so that it will, according to Mr Forbes, make the Prince think he is in the Peak District.

While some material discarded from the screenplay as it was filmed made its way back into the novel, other instances of action and dialogue from the plays were omitted from the fiction. For instance, the dialogue in a scene where a downpour forces a group of men to use a giant garden parasol in place of an umbrella to get home from the local Working Men's Club appears in neither the screenplay nor the novel in the precise form it takes in the film, and the same is true of one in which two fitters watch a group of pit managers crouching down, their behinds in the air, to inspect what Forbes calls the 'green haze' of the grass seedlings growing on the muckstack. The film represents the fitters' dialogue with effective concision:

FIRST FITTER: What're they doing?
SECOND FITTER: I don't know. They look like a team of bloody ostriches getting ready for a race.
FIRST FITTER: Silly pillocks! Shout 'off'! (*both laughing*)
SECOND FITTER: Off!

In the novel, the dialogue is much more expansive yet less concrete. 'I think they're getting down to their marks to have a race' (34) is all that remains of the absurd yet precise image of the ostrich, with its suggestion that the managers' heads are buried in the sand in every sense.

Conversely, unscripted incidents from the film, such as the concluding moment to the first play 'Meet the People' in which an NCB area manager's toupée is blown off when the royal helicopter lands, do not appear in the screenplay but were written up by Hines for the novel.[82] The production history of *The Price of Coal* television dramas gives evidence of another facet of the collaboration between Hines, Ken Loach and Tony Garnett. While Hines's final script includes much – although, as we have already seen, not all – of the visual detail of the broadcast dramas, it was the producer and director who suggested its final form as a pair of Plays for Today rather than a single one.

The Price of Coal was originally conceived by Hines as an individual play to focus on the preparations for a royal visit to a pit, filtered through the experience of a miner, Sid Storey, and his family. The appeal of a play whose ethos was 'education by entertainment' is clear.[83] Extremes of class and work are brought into juxtaposition by means of a comedy that relies on both realism and the absurd, and these modes are often interwoven. This is evident for instance in Albert Rhodes's suggestion that, instead of bringing an Elsan chemical toilet, as used in wartime Lancaster bombers, into the pit for the Prince's convenience, he could stand on the winding-gear, since he is 'the highest peer in the land'. This moment also continues a thread of spatial symbolism, in which the dark world of the mine, filmed in an especially constructed pit at the disused Thorpe Hesley mine, is contrasted with the sunny landscape above, and indeed Prince Charles is never seen underground. The suggestion by Garnett and Loach for a second drama to 'counterbalance'[84] the comedy of the first alters the nature of the original play, as is made clear in the plays' descriptive draft names of 'The Visit' and 'The Disaster'. The broadcast title of the first play, 'Meet the People', repeats both the phrase used for Prince Charles's visits to local communities but also, with an extra-diegetic significance, allows the viewer to 'meet' the characters in preparation for the jeopardy and suspense of part two. In particular, the second play leaves the fate of the central character Sid in the pit accident uncertain until the drama's end. The second play's title, 'Back to Reality', likewise quotes the words of a character to ironic effect, in this case those of the pit manager Mr Forbes as uttered in part one. Having scolded a pair of apprentice miners, Forbes returns to plans for the royal visit, including the laying of a red carpet in the pit yard, with the remark to a group of managers, 'Now, we'll try to get back to reality, eh?'. While here Forbes means the 'reality' of the royal visit, in the second play the term has the opposite significance: that of a return to everyday life and the 'filthy, dangerous work' of mining, in Hines's phrase from the novel's preface (v). The 'price' of this work is revealed by the detail of the plot, in which the pressures of production targets mean that an apprentice miner is left to complete a repair by himself, causing a fatal explosion.

The two plays together possess a significance that either taken alone would not have. This includes the implication that while expenditure for a royal visit is unquestioningly authorised – itself a hotly debated topic between the miners in the first play – the same is not true of safety measures in the pit, given that the priority is profit. Indeed, this is the kernel of *The Price of Coal*'s political meaning. It is conveyed in the rival importance of the visit and the disaster, to cite the plays' original titles, and the fact that, in a society 'that's based on class and inherited wealth and privilege', as Sid puts it, pomp takes precedence over lives. The continuities of this kind between parts one and two are evident in the *mise-en-scène* of 'Back to Reality', in which the winding-gear that looms over the action of the explosion's aftermath is still noticeably white after its repainting for Prince Charles's visit. In the novel, more is made of this irony, including Forbes's receiving a telegram of thanks from the Prince after the explosion has occurred, and miners having to enter the NCB offices for news of their colleagues' fates past the hanging baskets and geranium tubs put out as a royal welcome. These small novelistic details were removed from the final screenplay, and thus the film, for the sake of narrative streamlining. In their place, the essential connection between the plays is made clear in the concluding utterances of a pair of dramatised sequences. In 'Meet the People', the area manager Ron Atkinson (Robbie Platts) reads aloud from a newspaper report of a disaster that took place in 1912 at Cadeby Main pit on the same day as the visit to a nearby colliery by Queen Mary and King George. The existence of the second play makes Forbes's decision to leave this out of the Prince's souvenir album of cuttings seem full of premonition. The same is true of Atkinson's conclusion about this episode in which we learn that '86 men and lads were killed':

ATKINSON: That was bad luck. (*Pause*)
FORBES: What do you mean?
ATKINSON: The accident happening on the same day as the visit.

In 'Back to Reality', by contrast to Atkinson's priorities, which are shown here to consist of sparing royalty any inconvenience, the connection drawn by the NUM official, Brian Ackroyd (Max Smith), between the visit and the accident is one characterised by black irony: 'That's two disasters in a row, then', as he puts it. The notions of 'luck' and 'disaster' are scrutinised here, as they are more concretely in the second play in relation to the accident's origins. The question of responsibility or blame for the explosion is subject to several instances of dramatised debate, in Hines's trademark manner, just as the significance of Prince Charles's visit was in 'Meet the People'. In 'Back to Reality', the terminology of 'an act of God' is discussed in relation to the pit explosion. Those affected see such phraseology as an attempt to shrug off responsibility for what are the acts of men: 'More like somebody's slipped up somewhere', as one miner puts it. Forbes reminds Carter that, as managers, they are responsible for understanding what caused the event: 'of course we should know: that's what we're here for.' Yet it seems, particularly by reason of Ackroyd's passionate rejection of the notion of contingency implicit in referring to the explosion as an 'accident', that the real culprit is both invisible and omnipresent. It is the institution of late-capitalist industrialisation and the class structure that supports and enables it which underlies the chain of events leading up to the accident.

Such a conception of causality has implications for the second play's own plottedness, including its reliance on the device of withheld knowledge and suspense. In the novel and play, the blast in the mine has a shockingly disruptive function akin to the atomic explosion in *Threads*, and the screenplay stage direction to *The Price of Coal* shows how closely it resembles that event: 'Then there is a blue flash and a blast of air so strong that it knocks men flying.'[85] Indeed, the detonation in *Threads* is a giant example of the escalation we see in the earlier play: as in 'Back to Reality', a chain of events, the origins of which lie in mistaken priorities remote from people's everyday lives, has a terrible outcome. In *The Price of Coal*, the fates of the men who go missing are revealed gradually and belatedly. In particular, we only learn what has happened to Sid, who is severely injured but still alive, through Kath's reported speech in the closing moments of the film, and do not see him again. An early draft of the novel avoids such radical disruption of narrative expectation. This version of *The Price of Coal*, entitled 'Getting Better', opens with Sid recovering in hospital from the injuries he sustained in the blast. It is not impossible to imagine that a filmic version might have presented both the royal visit and the explosion in the form of an extended flashback from such a vantage-point,[86] although that is not how the screenplay is structured. 'Meet the People' in its final version unfolds chronologically in present time. The opening of the film plunges us straight into a consultative committee meeting at which Forbes tells his staff about the royal visit. Forbes's proposing a motion to cancel the rest of the meeting's agenda is followed by Sid's counter-proposal to cancel the royal visit. In earlier drafts of this opening, the viewer learns of the visit before the 'people' do, when Forbes is informed of it over the telephone, in a way that loses the film's immediate dramatic conflict.

What might seem to be an abundance of detail for the sake of character construction within the realist project, as we see it in 'Meet the People', is, rather, in 'Back to Reality' a collection of factors crucial to the threads of the plot. This is the case for Sid's wearing his son's Tony's green football socks, which allows him to be identified after the blast by the rescue team and by us as viewers; and for the characterisation we are given of Frank Morris and Steve Oates, the fitter and apprentice charged with repairing the pit motor, which results in the explosion. The underground darkness in which they are seen in the film version of 'Back to Reality', so that it is even hard to detect that Frank is played by the Hines/Loach regular Phil Askham, is appropriate to their all-important yet tellingly minor role in the narrative.

Such concealment of who has fallen victim to the pit blast in the final version of screenplay and novel is not simply a narrative device but also a political one. We learn that two unnamed miners, one of whom is dead, can only be identified by their clothing. The deputy Phil Beatson (Bert Oxley) asks Mrs King (Christie Gee) if her husband, the young miner Ronnie (Philip Firth), was wearing a signet ring or 'green football socks' for the day's shift, relying on the fact that the viewer knows the latter are Sid's: he joked that they signified his 'come-back' in an earlier scene. Only in retrospect does it become clear that the socks were the sign of life, the signet ring of death, as the sole way to identify one of the corpses. Denying the viewer any superior knowledge conveys the fact that industrial fatalities are both omnipresent and arbitrary, so that hoping for the safety of one miner entails the death of another. The careful construction of the narrative detail of the football socks makes them a way to reveal Sid's character and familial role before the explosion, yet they also become narrative clues. Hines took equally great pains in drafting the moments where the news of death is revealed. The stage direction for the scene in which Phil asks Mrs King about her husband Ronnie's clothing was minutely amended in several different drafts of the screenplay, and also for the novel. In a late version of the screenplay, a scenario of sudden grief is directly represented when Mrs King's answers to Phil's questions lead him to say he has 'bad news' for her: 'There is a moment as she realizes what the bad news is. Then she buckles at the knees and starts to cry. Beatson gets hold of her and leads her back up the corridor to Carter's office.' In the final screenplay, Phil explains that he will take her to Carter's office, and we do not see Mrs King's tears onscreen.[87]

The conclusion of 'Back to Reality' consists of a final withheld revelation, since it ends in both film and novel with the union official Alf Meakin and the deputy Geoff Carter arriving at Albert

3 Long take of street at the conclusion to
The Price of Coal: Back to Reality

Rhodes's house to deliver the news of his death to his wife. In the novel, the narrator describes Alf removing his cap at the door 'when he heard the bolts being withdrawn on the other side' (173). We are left as if in a moment of unresolved and perpetual delivery of bad news. The filmic equivalent is a static long shot of a street of terraced housing. (See Figure 3.) A car enters the frame at an angle, driving slowly away from the spectator so that its occupants, Alf and Geoff, can get out at the door of Albert Rhodes's house. The credits roll over their distant figures, as they wait for the door to be opened. There is a marked withdrawal of the camera from the kind of visual and emotional close-up that characterised the imme-diately preceding scene in the Storeys' living-room, in which Kath tells Janet and Mark that their father is alive but badly injured. The effect is one of making impersonal this intensely personal narrative, once more implying that this is a story with a general relevance.

With a different effect, Hines's drafts show the development of small episodes in 'Meet the People' from very minor origins into self-contained comic narratives. These include the conversation between Sheila and her fellow-secretary Linda in which they marvel at the size of Prince Charles's pit boots; and that of Dick Hemsley's snap-tin, noticed during a bomb squad inspection to be lying suspiciously out in the open in its army bag. Tracing the detail of this process of augmentation gives us an insight into Hines's compositional methods, since it is clear that these vignettes were not initially conceptualised in a fully-formed state but were expanded upon over time. Their significance for the screenplay as a whole becomes clear by means of the very process of editing, either through the fleshing out of small sequences or the condensing of longer ones.[88] Expansion takes place in the case of the pit boots scene, a rare instance in *The Price of Coal* where women talk together without the company of men. Originally this scene featured Sheila alone, reverently musing to herself that the Prince's boots are 'the same size as our Derek's', but now concludes with an innuendo that mystifies Linda: 'You know what they say about men with big feet …'. Thus it is made comically clear that Prince Charles's effect is felt throughout the mining community in its varied ways. On the other hand, the episode of Dick Hemsley's snap-tin is reduced by removing an utterance of the opposite kind, one in which he speaks wryly in this all-male setting of his wife, playing up to the implication that his bag might have contained a bomb in place of the sandwiches she has made for him: 'Listen, if my missus wanted to get rid of me she wouldn't bother with no bombs. It'd be the bread knife, straight in the back' (88). This dialogue from a draft screenplay has been restored to the novel, in contrast to the film, where the episode concludes with less detail by making Dick laconic in the face of the bomb squad's excessive vigilance. 'Alright, no bother', are his final words. The process of paring down in this way itself generates an effect of greater and more absurdist realism. This is also clear in the removal of just those narrative threads of causality in smaller instances which are so crucial to anticipating and explaining the pit explosion. In 'Meet the People', Mark's wish to go fishing instead of greeting the royal visitor is over-explained in a draft screenplay, in a way that offers mundane practical reasons for a preference that is left, in the final version, as an unexplained confluence of the son's political views with those of his father.[89] In 'Back to Reality', complicated detail is given to explain Mark's taking refuge in the chicken-run on his father's allotment when Sid goes missing. Thus in the draft screenplay Kath insists that he feed the chickens because Sid will 'play hell up if we forget'.[90] By contrast, the novel centres the meaning of this action on the boy's interiority, since Mark thinks it 'a good idea' to go to the chicken-run (144), making the scene echo one from *First Signs*, in which Tom seeks refuge in his father's allotment at a time when he is organising a teachers' strike. Thus in the television play *The Price of Coal*, emphasis lies rather on a succinct visual expression of Mark's fears for his father's safety as he plays a predicting game with the eggs, reciting, 'Yes. No.' for each one he gathers.

In its early versions, the pit accident in 'Back to Reality' was caused by a faulty fan, following the detail of a real-life explosion that took place in Houghton Main pit near Barnsley in June 1975, at which five men were killed and another seriously injured.[91] As well as newspaper accounts of the incident, Hines relied for the detail of his play on the NUM report, written by Arthur Scargill. Scargill was the president of the Yorkshire NUM at the time and had been its compensation agent until 1971. Elements of both these official roles underlie Scargill's representation in the text, although several references by Forbes and the managers to suspicions that the NUM will mount compensation claims in the wake of the accident were dropped from the final screenplay. Some of the details from the Houghton Main disaster are altered in both film and novel so that in place of the fan, we learn that the cowl on a motor has been damaged by falling debris and needs to be replaced. This apparently small change is in part generic, emphasising the script's increasingly fictional nature. The removal of the fan detail fortuitously allows us see the defect in the machinery also as the motor of the plot itself. The script is constructed so that the faulty motor is a topic in the dialogue from the outset, giving the plot a 'fatalistic' appearance of a kind that is, as we will see, rejected by another of Hines's characters, Lucy in *Unfinished Business*, in relation to Thomas Hardy's fiction. Any such sense of inevitability is by contrast absent from 'Meet the People', where the conclusion to the preparations for Prince Charles's visit is deliberately low-key, without any kind of narrative revelation or mishap. In the film, the Prince's eventual arrival is viewed from afar and is not followed by a zoom or close-up. Such a cursory concluding moment thus offers a formal equivalent

4 Mark fishing in *The Price of Coal: Meet the People*

to the play's implication that the effort exceeds the event. Indeed, 'Meet the People' ends finally not with the royal arrival but with a sequence showing Mark fishing in the local reservoir while the credits roll. (See Figure 4.) In visual terms, this represents a gesture of opting-out on Mark's part. In metaphorical terms it offers an embodiment of the image Sid used to convey to his son why he considers the visit 'daft', as Mark phrases it. Sid uses the metaphor of a pond stocked with fish for the sake of an important visitor, when, in his view, 'I think that them fish should be there for them who fish there regular. They're the ones who've the right to them' (80).

Perhaps the most intriguing excision from the drafts of *The Price of Coal* screenplay is that of the figure of Arthur Scargill. A cameo part for the then-president of the Yorkshire National Union of Mineworkers was included in 'Back to Reality', constituting a counterpart to Prince Charles's role as a different kind of public figure in 'Meet the People'.[92] The film production team had 'excellent relations' with Scargill and the miners' union during the period in which his inclusion in the drama was planned. However, negotiations with the National Coal Board to film on their land, particularly the location shooting at the disused Thorpe Hesley colliery near Rotherham, would not have been possible if he had been included. In the terms of Tony Garnett's account, the idea of Scargill's appearance was to the NCB 'a red rag to a bull', and he therefore does not appear in the final version.[93]

The references to Scargill which remain in the script make *The Price of Coal* as a whole seem ominously proleptic of the effects of the miners' strike less than a decade later, when he was president of the NUM. A theatre version of *The Price of Coal* was staged at the Nottingham Playhouse in May 1984, in which Duggie Brown, the film's Geoff Carter, took the role of Sid Storey. Although the director, Kenneth Alan Taylor, who had also presented *Kes* on stage, had chosen to dramatise *The Price of Coal* before 'the situation in the coal fields of Great Britain' changed so greatly with the calling of the strike, the play's meaning alters in such an extreme historical context.[94] John Kirk describes such a change as a shift to pathos or even trauma in the post-industrial era, but it is Luke Spencer's account of the audience's awareness of the television drama's revelation of a 'spoiled capacity for change' in the light of pit closures that seems most fitting.[95] Scargill embodies such a will 'for change' in the draft screenplay for the pre-miners' strike era.

However, although it would be fascinating to have the filmic record of his role that the drafts of *The Price of Coal* promise, Scargill's appearance would have caused generic disruption to the drama. Even if we imagine that he was playing himself, the documentary effect would have exceeded that of the historical events on which the plays are based, the details of which Hines deliberately altered and fictionalised. In the draft in which he appears, the real-life specificity of the faulty fan, before Hines altered it to be a faulty motor, remains in close proximity to the figure of Scargill, redoubling the documentary effect: two miners report to him their sighting of 'sparks' flying out of the fan, following the precise detail of events that took place before the Houghton Main explosion.[96] None of this material remains in the final screenplay, nor does Hines's plan to show, 'behind the credits' for 'Back to Reality', film footage of Scargill giving a speech at the 1975 Scarborough NUM conference, in which he defended demands for a miner's weekly wage of £100 'by quoting a series of recent pit disasters'.[97] As we will see, this material has instead been diffused into the fictional characters' dialogue.

Scargill thus functions as the focus of a much more documentary and polemical element in the draft screenplay, one which did not come to fruition. In a political sense, he crystallises a tendency in *The Price of Coal* for what Spencer calls a 'potentially transformative collective feeling', portrayed in general terms as well as those of particular political developments. Spencer argues that 'we can be absolutely certain' how miners like those in Hines's narrative would have responded to 'Scargill's call' to 'defend their jobs and communities in 1984'.[98] Indeed, this is borne out by an excised passage from the draft screenplay, in which a miner indignantly declares that the press have made Scargill 'the most hated man in Britain' when 'all he's ever tried to do is get a decent wage for the lads'.[99] Scargill's playing a part as himself in the television drama would have symbolised the uncanny effect of the fictive or proleptic real. The role of Scargill's character in the draft is not that of an agent in the plot but rather one of an onlooker or witness, and a public spokesperson. As he actually did at Houghton Main, the fictional Scargill accompanies the rescue team down the pit, but his words give him the role of a chorus figure, limited as they are to his asking such questions as, 'How far's the ripping edge from here?' Scargill's public utterances in the world of Hines's play include his issuing a press statement about his intention to call for a public inquiry into the disaster. Such minimalism seems designed to leave room for improvisation and for the visual and generic impact of Scargill's appearing at all. It also means that removing Scargill's role as a character was straightforward. In the final screenplay, scenes often appear just as they were planned, including one in which Forbes shows the deputies and union officials a map of the mine to locate the missing men, but without Scargill's presence, while dialogue attributed to him, for instance a speech about the 'capitalist press' and its prejudicial reports on the mining industry, is simply toned down and transferred to the NUM official Brian Ackroyd. The idea of a public inquiry, which alludes to the actual report issued under Scargill's name about the Houghton Main disaster, is diverted instead into a dialogue of resigned anticipation between Forbes and Carter in the final screenplay.

In the filmed version of the screenplay, Scargill's presence does not take the form of a figure in the drama as it does in the early draft but a series of verbal traces, some of which are visually rendered. In 'Meet the People', Forbes's arrival at the pit on the day of the royal visit is disrupted by his catching sight of a slogan daubed in giant white letters on a wall. In early drafts the graffiti reads, 'This way for the Royal Circus!', but, in substitution for Scargill's appearance as a character, in the final version his name appears instead, in the legend 'Scargill Rules! OK!' Forbes's fear that the graffiti could make the management 'the bloody laughing-stock of the bloody pit!', is in clear contrast to the delight of the apprentices ordered to repaint the wall, who want it to be left as it is. Forbes threatens elaborate punishment for the 'hooligan' responsible: 'I'll string him up from the pithead by his bloody knackers!', as he puts it. Material from draft versions of the screenplay that could seem to imply Sid was that 'hooligan' has been excised. In an early draft, Sid paints the motto 'Royal Coach' on the paddy-train that is to take Prince Charles to the coal face,[100] in an apparent prefiguring of that draft's 'Royal Circus' graffiti. Since the identification of the culprit is neither possible nor necessary, the Scargill slogan seems more fittingly in the final screenplay to represent a communal utterance. This irruption of the voice of organised labour into the play substitutes for the figure of Scargill himself, and continues more explicitly in 'Back to Reality'. Not only are the successful strikes of 1972 and 1974 invoked by both Sid and Kath but contemporary campaigns for improved conditions are debated in the context of the explosion. Mrs Dobson, awaiting news of her son Alan, claims that '£1000 a week is not worth it', let alone the £100 the union is demanding, while Ackroyd, the NUM official, reminds the men in the canteen that the next campaign will be for 'industrial democracy'. 'If we were responsible for the everyday running of things', as one miner puts it, 'safety and production would go hand-in-glove.' Scargill's name is transferred to the dialogue in this instance now that he does not appear in person. When the local MP Eric Johnson arrives, Alf says of him to Brian Ackroyd, 'Scargill's mate, that, isn't it?', in a line that has been altered from the original, 'Your mate, Brian?' In the filmed screenplay, Brian responds, 'He's no mate of Arthur's'.[101]

In a review of the television drama, Peter Kemp argues that the two parts of *The Price of Coal* constitute a farce followed by a tragedy. Yet the generic differences between the two plays are apparently elided by their shared intertitles. 'Two films set in South Yorkshire' appears over the opening sequence of each, beneath it an extra subtitle, 'A film for the Silver Jubilee', which makes *The Price of Coal* historically and politically specific, while also more generally symbolic.[102] However, it seems rather that the pair of plays encapsulates in their dual format the opposing facets of Hines's ambivalent feelings about the mining industry. 'Meet the People' draws on the positive aspects of the mining village's communitarian cohesion and linguistic inventiveness, in which class is not just the source but the target of its comedy. It seems more accurate to describe the first play as carnivalesque, in contrast to Kemp's notion of farce. Elements of hierarchy-subverting mockery and reversal take place throughout, and the pit as embellished for Prince Charles's visit itself takes on a carnivalesque look. The curtained commemorative plaque is likened to a Punch and Judy show, the paddy-train to a miniature 'pleasure-gardens' engine, and the painted pit-head to Blackpool Tower. The reference to Blackpool represents what could be described as the carnivalisation of a tragic motif by means of editorial practice. Forbes's concern, ironic in view of what happens in his own pit, about the lax safety practices of 'outside contractors' who usually work on the Blackpool Tower and do not use 'painters' harnesses' on the winding-gear, has also been excised.[103] But the very process of paring down has generated a joke about the pit-head's resemblance to a pleasure beach by means of what remains. It is perhaps this element of 'Meet the People', its surface comedy integral to a sharp critique, that makes it more successful, and more typical of Hines's best work, than the tendency to tragic monologism of 'Back to Reality'.

'Back to Reality' focuses on the equally class-based threat to the same mining community as part one in its tragic plot. The significance of the second play is summed up in a comment, deleted from the final screenplay, from Annie, who works in the pit canteen: 'There'll only be safe pits when there's nobody down them.'[104] As we have argued, all the threads of dialogue and detail in the second play set up the disaster which is its central concern. Only the play's opening cricket match between Tony and Mark seems, as a reviewer put it, fully to continue part one's mode of subversive writing in an apparently comic observational guise, yet 'then the plot intervenes' and disaster overtakes the everyday.[105] However, despite his keen sense of the onerous and life-threatening nature of mining, a job he soon renounced, Hines naturally campaigned alongside the striking miners in 1984–85, including Women Against Pit Closures, and his views of the significance of mining for South Yorkshire are always evident in his writings about that conflict.

Tom Kite (*Injury Time/Man of the Match*)

Between 1976 and 1978, Barry Hines was engaged in writing the screenplay for a project which would never come to fruition. This was a feature film about a talented, maverick footballer who is hounded out of Britain following a failed big-money move to a successful club in the North of England; the protagonist, Tom, ends up playing out the last days of his career in the rapidly expanding North American Soccer League. While the film was never made, exploration of its content as it progressed and the context of its development offers significant insights into how Hines's thematic interests clashed within the commercial demands of feature-film making.

The *Tom Kite* project (a title abandoned after Hines discovered that Tom Kite was the name of an American golfer) was initially conceived by Scott Marshall, a London-based talent agent, and one of his clients, Christopher King, a young television director.[106] Both had spent time in the United States (Marshall is American by birth and King had studied film in the USA), and, having observed the boom in interest in 'soccer' following the Warner-Entertainment-backed New York Cosmos's acquisition of Pelé in 1975, they began to develop a feature-film concept based on the game in the USA. Marshall had just read *The Gamekeeper* and saw a writer who would 'show the warts'[107] of a story, so Hines was approached as the project's screenwriter. Although the drama had initially been rejected for development funding by the National Film Finance Corporation in early 1977, Marshall and King were successful later that year in receiving seed finance from the BBC. Roy Baird, who had worked with Ken Russell as the producer on *Lisztomania* (1975) and *Mahler* (1974) and who would go on to produce *Quadrophenia* (Franc Roddam, 1979), was included, and it was with Baird's Picture Palace Productions that Hines signed an agreement to act as the screenwriter for *Tom Kite* in June 1977.[108]

By 1978, Hines had left the project, having responded to the commission with a bleak, temporally complex screenplay. Reflecting on the project in an interview for this book, Marshall noted that Hines's script lacked 'simplicity' and that the ending particularly was missing the required 'positive' note.[109] King had apparently 'fallen out of love with Barry's writing',[110] and the script was therefore edited in such a way that effectively ended Hines's involvement. The commercial rationale for the project was obvious. As mentioned, the sport was in receipt of substantial investment in the USA and, given that many of the football teams were backed by entertainment companies, a feature-film tie-in made business sense. In early 1977, Marshall and King had held positive talks with the rock star Rod Stewart, who expressed an interest in playing the starring role, and they subsequently outlined their plans for financing the film in a letter to Hines:

> Our present plan, when the screenplay is completed and a contractual arrangement has been reached with Rod Stewart, is to approach Warner Brothers whose interest would be twofold: 1) Warner Brothers Records release Rod Stewart's records in the United States 2) Warner Brothers parent company, Warner Communication, own the New York Cosmos, for whom Pele plays, and have heavily invested in establishing professional soccer in the United States .
> [...]
> We feel that the commercial appeal of the project is based jointly on the world wide popularity of Rod Stewart and of soccer but we would also like to make the point that the release of the film could coincide with the World Cup tournament in 1978, where there will be a tremendous upsurge of interest in the game.[111]

The producers were relying on the increasing commercialisation of the North American Soccer League, and Stewart as their bankable asset. Later that year, however, King and Marshall had shifted their focus to Robert Powell for the lead, who was described as 'very much in the ascendancy', following the success of the Emmy-nominated *Jesus of Nazareth* miniseries. Marshall and King were therefore understandably working to position the proposed film to take advantage of market trends. However, as the financing process wore on and the 1978 World Cup was over, the expansion of the North American Soccer League failed to grow in line with the huge investment that it had received. Audiences were static until 1981, before dropping rapidly as franchises folded and the television broadcasters pulled out. Ultimately, then, the *Tom Kite* project fell victim to this precarious commercial climate: conceived in response to the hoped-for linking of the capitalist efficiency of Hollywood with the global reach and heritage of 'soccer', the proposed film was acutely susceptible to market forces. Moreover, the project was headed up by an unproven director in King (he would go on to have a consistent career in UK television, directing episodes of *The Bill* and *Casualty*) which might have counted against its viability. Indeed, one of Hines's agents, Richard Odgers, cast doubt on *Tom Kite* for that very reason: 'it's naturally a toss-up whether finance would be made available for a film to cost more than 2 million with an untried director.'[112] The economic uncertainties and artistic compromises of the film industry put Hines in uncharted territory. He set about writing *Tom Kite* having just completed his most politically articulate work for the screen yet, *The Price of Coal*, collaborating with Ken Loach and Tony Garnett, as committed socialists working within the known parameters of public service broadcasting and the Play for Today tradition. The *Tom Kite* project, with its commercial strategy and links to pop stars, demanded that Hines adapt significantly his approach to writing – there is little evidence that he was willing or able to do so.

In helping him to prepare for the screenplay, Scott Marshall sent Hines a range of articles detailing the rise of 'soccer' in America. Many of the articles justify the potential economic viability of the project, with, for example, a piece in the *New York Magazine* comparing the New York Cosmos to Warner's other prized assets: 'the movie *The Exorcist*, singers like Linda Ronstadt, Frank Sinatra, rock groups like the Rolling Stones, electronic pinball, Bugs Bunny, Superman, cable television'.[113] Another prophetically suggests the limitations of the sport's repositioning as an entertainment product, and Cosmos director Jay Emmett complains that 'we can't control soccer like our other businesses'.[114] Marshall also provided his screenwriter with articles identifying a trend of successful sports films in the wake of *Rocky* (John Avildsen, 1976), perhaps anticipating that Hines would be inspired to write a similarly unambiguous underdog story, but, as we will see, he was not. Also amongst the research material, however, were pieces by thoughtful commentators such as the novelist Brian Glanville reflecting on the changing socioeconomic conditions of the game, specifically the trappings of the 'nouveau riche' footballer: 'working-class boys with fat upper-middle class incomes'.[115] Glanville also noted the emergence of players such as Liverpool's Steve Heighway, who studied for a degree in economics at Warwick before beginning his professional career at Liverpool at the age of 22, suggesting that such examples challenged the 'unhealthy and exploitative ... myth' that there was only 'one way for footballers to be produced'.[116] These explorations of the relationship between football, class and education strongly reflected Hines's own interests in the game, and it was from these familiar themes that he would take the inspiration for *Tom Kite*.

Indeed, upon reading the screenplay it is abundantly clear that Hines rejected the established trends of the sports film: there is no uplifting narrative of redemption with Tom escaping the conservative confines of the game in the UK to achieve autonomy in its exciting new territory of the USA. Hines instead used Marshall and King's scenario to return to the thematic territory of 'Flight of the Hawk' and *The Blinder* – ambiguous narratives which registered the pleasures and liberating joys of football, but also its tendency towards exploitation and its complex relationship with the structures and codes of working-class life. Hines's vision for the project was therefore rooted in his artistic philosophy and political values, and was bound inextricably to his experience of life in South Yorkshire as a schoolboy footballer and later a teacher. In short, Hines ignored (consciously or otherwise) the commercial expectations that had been placed upon him as the screenwriter of a potential feature film. The source of Hines's excellence here became a liability.

Before going into the detail of the screenplay, it is important to register that Hines was well qualified to write a football film. As we have discussed, his background as a player and his time at Loughborough positioned him as a 'student of the game', with the personal connections to draw on a number of qualified insights for his own research on the topic of football in the USA. Indeed, material in the Hines archive suggests that he was in correspondence with Allen Wade, a fellow Loughborough alumnus, who was at the time technical director at the English Football Association.[117] Wade wrote a number of influential coaching manuals, and, like Hines, brought an intellectually focused, academic rigour to his understanding of the game. Wade contacted Rodney Marsh on Hines's behalf in order to set up a meeting between Marsh, Hines and George Best. Wade assured Marsh that Hines was a 'serious author and not a journalist' and that he was a 'fair footballer'.[118] While it is not clear whether the meeting took place, it is obvious that Hines drew inspiration from both men for his titular protagonist in the *Tom Kite* screenplay. Best and Marsh were both mercurially gifted flair players who left Britain for the USA after falling foul of the football establishment. Similarly, when Tom is forced to depart his hometown club for 'City' (Leeds United in Hines's early drafts), he is unable to adapt to his manager, Vickers, whose traditional, 'safety-first' approach to the game is at odds with Tom's philosophy, 'to win with a bit of style'.[119] Tom's despair on the pitch has a catalogue of disciplinary consequences, the breakdown of his marriage and problems with alcohol, all factors contributing to his departure to America.

Thus, Hines's starting point for the screenplay's Tom Quinn character was to position him not as a plucky everyman but as a depressed and jaded individual for whom the move to the USA is not about self-discovery and frontier-building but exile and desperation. This is reflected by the film's fragmented temporal structure: Hines begins the screenplay with a melancholic, reflective Tom in his American beachfront home, where the sea and sand trigger another flashback to pre-season training at the English seaside when Tom was playing for 'The Town'; we then return to the present day, before another flashback to Tom's previous life in England, followed by a conversation with his American girlfriend about his son, which precipitates a memory of his own youth, playing football happily as a 15-year-old. Hines therefore uses Tom's passive, ultimately unsatisfying experience of life in the USA as a means to explore the key episodes that led to his present situation – covering his hopeful early career and, most extensively, the breakdown of his relationship with Vickers at 'City'. The screenplay ends ambiguously with Tom lining up for the national anthem before a game in the USA, with Hines suggesting that 'we slowly pull away and reveal him in England kit lined up for the international match at Wembley. Over this shot we continue to hear the American National Anthem until it ends' (94). Hines therefore disrupts spatial and temporal continuity as Tom looks 'into the crowd' although 'we don't see who he is looking for, but he finds someone he knows, and we close with him standing there, ball at his feet, arm raised and smiling' (94).

The inconclusive ending, with the subject of Tom's gaze never revealed, combined with the deliberately disjointed temporal and narrative structure, gives the impression that Hines was writing what was in effect an art film, rather than a commercially viable sports narrative in the vein of *Rocky*. Indeed, the screenplay's dispersed focus on Tom's psychological, subjective realm recalls David Bordwell's analysis of 'the biography of the individual' common in

European art cinema, rather than the 'classical filmmaking' that for Bruce Babington is 'typical of the great majority of sports films'.[120] Long descriptive stage directions of Tom's on-field activity that occur throughout the screenplay are further evidence of Hines's distinctive authorial and thus art-cinematic vision for the film – indeed, this was clearly an approach he was used to, having worked with relative artistic freedom in his collaborations with Loach and Garnett. When reviewing Hines's early drafts, Sheila Lemon made the point that the specific nature of his stage directions risked, at the very least, second-guessing King's direction, suggesting that 'a lot of the important information you give us in the stage directions was not "translated" into script terms. I know it is the director's job to make sure the audience understands what is happening in the course of the game … but I do think we ought to see more of the pressures and frustrations he is undergoing outside rather than merely the evidence of them on-field'.[121] Hines was, of course, writing football filmically in the same way that he had aspired towards a literary approach to the game in 'Flight of the Hawk' and *The Blinder*, situating the pitch as a site of affective meaning.

In this sense, Tom Quinn's 'safety last' (36), cavalier footballing style and philosophy is markedly similar to Lennie Hawk's, as is his relationship with his parents: his father, like Lennie's, is delighted when he signs with the local side that he and his son support, while his mother expresses caution:

> MRS QUINN: I still think he shouldn't be joining any club yet. Mr. Parkin said the same when I went up to parents' evening. He said he's university material our Tom. He said he could get to Oxford or Cambridge if he worked hard.
> MR QUINN: Oxford or Cambridge. He'll be able to buy 'em when he's been in the game a few years. (11)

Hines explores once more the relationship between footballing and academic excellence, and makes this an issue of gender with the 'two sides' represented by mother and father, just as they are in 'Flight of the Hawk', *The Blinder* and his later television play *Born Kicking* (1992). In *Tom Kite*, Hines is able to expand further the theme, connecting to his protagonist's sense of political articulacy and rebellion. Indeed, Tom's outspokenness and willingness to challenge authority is interpreted as a sign of uncharacteristic and dangerous intelligence for a footballer. In a scene during his early days at 'City', Tom refers to the 'Dreyfus affair' (28), which results in bemused responses from his teammates:

> LES: What's he doing, swotting up for Mastermind? What did he say to the boss, biggest miscarriage since who?
> GEORGE: Miscarriage of justice, you thick sod.
> SAMMY: Since Dreyfus, he said.
> LES: Who's he anyway?
> GEORGE: Plays midfield for Derby don't he? (28)

This allusion to a nineteenth-century French political scandal marks Tom out as a misunderstood, complex individual, distinct from the collective presence of his teammates. Later, towards the end of his time at the club, Tom gives an indiscreet interview to a reporter which results in another fiery exchange with his manager:

> TOM: I didn't shoot my mouth off. I expressed my own thoughts on what I thought was wrong with the game.
> VICKERS: Fuck your thoughts! Who do you think you are, Chairman Mao? We'll do the thinking here, me and Johnny and the coaching staff. (61)

Here Hines explicitly positions the 'thinking' Tom against an establishment that seeks to regulate its dissenters at every opportunity. Vickers's Maoist slur results from Tom's consistent questioning of (capitalist) authority, at one point suggesting that the directors 'should stick to selling scrap metal and pork pies' and that all 'they're after is success at any price' (40). Tom's awareness of his status as a commodity is even more apparent in the scenes in the USA, with Hines clearly using the North American Soccer League's embrace of the entertainment industry as a mechanism for critiquing prophetically the increasing commercialism of the game across the world. For example, when Tom is asked to wear a uniform during a pre-match 'meet and greet' exercise with fans, he responds that he is a 'footballer' and 'not a tailor's dummy' (40), while he tells Kate: 'I don't like having to sell myself all the time. I'm a footballer, not a salesman' (48). Moreover, while Tom is critical of the small-time businessmen who run football in Britain, he is even more sceptical of the North American owner of The Gladiators:

> Al doesn't love the game. He doesn't even understand it properly. He understands selling though, and if he can sell the club to the public he'll stick with it. If he can't, he'll bale out, it's as simple as that. (68)

The suggestion that the success of football in America was almost entirely dependent on the owners' desire for profit rather than their feeling and passion for the game was ultimately borne out with the league's demise, but the thinly veiled criticism of the commercialisation of 'soccer' was another example of the visibility of Hines's political inclinations. It is telling, for example, that Scott Marshall had attracted interest in the film from George Strawbridge,[122] the owner of the Tampa Bay Rowdies and precisely the kind of investor that Tom criticises. It is inconceivable that Strawbridge would have supported a feature film which challenged the success and growth narrative of the National American Soccer League that the franchise owners were so reliant upon.

Thus Hines's football screenplay was manifestly not appropriate as a vehicle for the promotion of the sport in America, in fact quite the opposite. As Garry Whannel argues, the conventional sports film relies on sport's 'implicit narrative structure', the 'rule-governed contest which results in a winner'.[123] Hines defies this convention in two ways: firstly, disrupting the linear expectation of a final 'showdown'[124] which enables the hero to achieve some kind of long-sought-for success, by contrast to which Hines's fragmented temporal structure seems consciously to deny suspense; and secondly, centring the film on a sporting protagonist for whom winning is not everything. To return to Whannel's argument, 'the inherent narrativity' of 'competitive individualism' which makes sport (and sports films) a 'metaphor' for 'lived experience under capitalism'[125] is deconstructed in Hines's vision for *Tom Kite*.

The failure of the *Tom Kite* project tells us much about Hines as a screenwriter. While we are not suggesting that the film would have been made had Hines compromised and produced a commercially favourable screenplay, there can be no question that he was unable or unwilling to depart from the formal and thematic features that had characterised his work up to 1976. Thus, as we have argued, the screenplay bears a direct relationship to Hines's first work, *The Blinder*. The latter is bound by an episodic, non-linear realist structure found in many of his novels and screenplays, and is once more a narrative which is reliant on a fixed evocation of Northern place and a focus on working-class cultures, and displays persistent criticism of the market and institutional bodies of authority. Hines's authorial signature in these different media was increasingly distinctive and consistent.

Notes

1 Barry Hines, *First Signs*, London: Michael Joseph, 1972. All page references in text.

2 Salisbury, 'The clear eyed prodigal', *Sheffield Daily Telegraph*, date unknown, BHP/FIS 5.

3 Ibid.

4 Ian Haywood, *Working Class Fiction: From Chartism to Trainspotting*, London: Routledge 1996, p. 111.

5 Richard Hoggart, *The Uses of Literacy: Aspects of Working-Class Life*, London: Penguin 2009 [1957], p. 263.

6 Ibid.

7 The mines are also named after aristocratic families whose wealth was drawn from coal and steel.

8 Clive Jordan, 'Room mates', *New Statesman* 25 Feb 1972, BHP/FIS 5.

9 Nina Bawden, review, *The Daily Telegraph* 30 March 1972, BHP/FIS 5.

10 Barry Hines, *This Artistic Life*, Hebden Bridge: Pomona Books 2009, p. 2.

11 Rod Nicholls, 'All's Peaceful up at the Mill', *Age* 26 June 1972, BHP/FIS 5.

12 Ferdinand Mount, 'Yokels and nannies', *Financial Times* 24 Feb 1972, BHP/FIS 5.

13 Ibid.

14 Nicholls, 'All's Peaceful up at the Mill'.

15 W. Price Turner, untitled, *The Yorkshire Post* 24 Feburary 1972, BHP/FIS 5.

16 Deborah Knight, 'Naturalism, Narration and Critical Perspective: Ken Loach and the Experimental Method', in George McKnight, ed., *Agent of Challenge and Defiance: The Films of Ken Loach*, Connecticut: Greenwood Press 1997, p. 61.

17 Specifically, Hines approaches these themes in a more progressive manner in *The Gamekeeper* and *Unfinished Business*.

18 See 'Even State Schools Go Independent with Television', *Education and Training*, 19 (10) 1977, pp. 315–16.

19 Barry Hines, *Speech Day*, in Michael Marland, ed., *The Pressures of Life: Four Television Plays*, Harlow: Longman 1977, p. 172; all further references in the text are to this edition. Alan Durband, ed., *Prompt Two: Five Short Plays*, London: Hutchinson 1976, p. 17. The version of the script published in *Prompt Two* has been quite radically 'adapted': the whole of the play's action is set in the school, meaning that none of the Warboys family appears, nor are any of the locations

outside the school included. Significant dialogue from characters who have been excised in this way has been transferred to those who remain, for instance from Grandpa to George.

20 The school's name appears on a board in the televised version, but is anonymous in the script. The introduction of comprehensive education took place instead in 1965 under Harold Wilson's Labour government.

21 Durband, ed., *Prompt Two*, p. 7.

22 The Sheffield locations include the factory James Neill Tools in Napier Street where Ronnie's brother Danny works, Mr Warboys's workplace at Brown Bayleys steelworks in Attercliffe and Mrs Warboys's clothing factory, referred to as Laidlaws in the script (itself the name of a Sheffield steel company), but filmed on the premises of S.R. Gent clothiers in Heeley. The scenes in Grandpa's house were filmed in Amberley Street, Darnall.

23 Nick Peim, 'The History of the Present: Towards a Contemporary Phenomenology of the School', *History of Education* 30 (2) 2001, pp. 170–90: 181.

24 Hines, *This Artistic Life*, p. 113.

25 Mikhail Bakhtin, 'Discourse in the Novel', *The Dialogic Imagination*, trans. and ed. Michael Holquist, Austin: University of Texas Press, 1981, p. 277.

26 E.P. Thompson, 'Time, Work-Discipline and Industrial Capitalism', *Past and Present* 38 1967, pp. 56–97.

27 Alan Sillitoe, *The Loneliness of the Long Distance Runner and Other Stories*, London: W.H. Allen 1959.

28 Barry Hines, *This Artistic Life*, p. 68.

29 Michel Foucault, *Discipline and Punish: The Birth of the Prison*, trans. Alan Sheridan, New York: Vintage 1979, p. 10.

30 William Safire, 'Keeping your powder dry', *New York Times* 23 February 1997.

31 The two epithets are linked in this verdict by the lexicographer Bergen Evans on Cromwell's saying (quoted in Safire, 'Keeping your powder dry'), but seen as being at odds by Grandpa.

32 BHP/SPE 1.

33 This detail is omitted from the television version, where the newspaper is simply one picked up from a seat on the bus.

34 In draft form, the extract that Wally reads is much longer and focuses specifically on the north-east of England, making its emphasis perhaps too specific. In the same draft, another boy thinks that Ronnie is drawing their attention instead to an article titled 'Judge does his own love tests in sports car' (BHP/SPE 1), one which was excised here but reappears more significantly in *The Gamekeeper*. The nature of this

article reveals Hines's view of newspapers' priorities, which for the most part favour trivia over any record of the reality of their readers' lives.

35 Karl Marx, *Capital: Volume 1*, trans. Ben Fowkes, Harmondsworth: Penguin: 1976 [1867], p. 630.

36 Foucault, *Discipline and Punish*, p. 187.

37 Durband, ed., *Prompt Two*, p. 8.

38 BHP/SPE 3.

39 'We Shall Overcome' appeared for the first time in the September 1948 edition of the *People's Songs Bulletin*, the journal of an organisation directed by the musician Pete Seeger, a collaborator of Malvina Reynolds.

40 Barry Hines, *The Gamekeeper*, Harmondsworth: Penguin 1979 [1975], p. 7. All further page references in the text.

41 Thompson, 'Time, Work-Discipline and Industrial Capitalism'.

42 John Berger, 'Why Look at Animals?', *About Looking*, London: Vintage 1992 [1977], p. 7.

43 Tom Brass, *Labour Regime Change in the Twenty-first Century: Unfreedom, Capitalism and Primitive Accumulation*, Leiden: Brill 2011, p. 210.

44 See the use of this phrase in a House of Commons debate on the Abolition of Tied Cottages Bill put forward by the MP Bob Cryer, in which a Kent agricultural worker, evicted from his cottage when the farm changed hands, is quoted as saying, 'I was bought', *HC Deb 19 June 1974 vol 875 cc489–92*.

45 Robert Nye, review, the *Guardian* BHP/GAM 5.

46 Bert Cardullo, *Loach and Leigh, Ltd: The Cinema of Social Conscience*, Newcastle: Cambridge Scholars Publishing 2010, p. 72.

47 Karl Marx, *Capital* volume 1V, 1, p. 393, italics in original.

48 John Berger, unpublished review for *New Society*, BHP/GAM 5. The accompanying letter to Hines is dated 6 November 1975, just two years before the publication of what Jonathan Burt describes as Berger's 'extraordinarily influential' essay 'Why Look at Animals?', also in *New Society*, suggesting a continuity of ideas (Burt, 'John Berger's "Why Look at Animals?": A Close Reading', *Worldviews* 9 (2) pp. 203–18: 204).

49 Eric Evans, 'Landownership and the Exercise of Power in an Industrializing Society: Lancashire and Cheshire in the Nineteenth Century', in Ralph Gibson and Martin Blinkhorn, eds, *Landownership and Power in Modern Europe*, London: HarperCollins 1991, p. 145. On the term 'glorious', first recorded in a sermon of 1716, which coupled the discovery of the Gunpowder Plot with the Glorious Revolution as examples of divine intervention, and its use in relation

to hunting from the late nineteenth century onwards, see Elizabeth Knowles, *The Oxford Dictionary of Phrase and Fable* 2006.
50 Garnett, interview with the authors.
51 Berger, review.
52 Luke Spencer, 'British Working-Class Fiction: The Sense of Loss and the Potential for Transformation', *Socialist Register* 24 1988, pp. 366–86: 378.
53 Burt, 'A Close Reading', p. 217.
54 BHP/PRC 2. See also Philip Ridley's 2015 play *Radiant Vermin*, in which the eponymous victims of slaughter are not represented allegorically as animals but are members of the 'precariat' and the homeless. Thanks to Poppy Corbett for this reference.
55 Berger, 'Why Look at Animals?', p. 11.
56 Jacob Leigh, *The Cinema of Ken Loach: Art in the Service of the People*, London: Wallflower 2002, p. 129.
57 Screenplay, BFI Ken Loach archive, KCL-9–3, p. 24.
58 The film was banned in 1984 by the South Bank Show, which had commissioned it, and screened later that year by Channel Four.
59 Hines, *Unfinished Business*, p. 186; 'Getting Better' BHP/OTHER, p. 47. In both the film and novel of *The Price of Coal*, there are horse-racing prints in Forbes's office in place of the hunting ones (p. 56).
60 Although Burt cautions against the dangers of 'valorising the linguistic over the visible animal', as Berger and other critics do in the case of zoos, *The Gamekeeper* does offer a 'spectacle of slaughter' to different effect in both mediums, 'A Close Reading', p. 214.
61 'Breakdown of novel', BFI Ken Loach archive, KCL-9–3, p. 102.
62 Leigh, *The Cinema of Ken Loach*, p. 129.
63 Ibid., p. 126.
64 Shooting schedule, November 1978, BFI Ken Loach archive, KCL-9–3. Hayward describes the filming as taking place at Wentworth, but this is an error that seems to arise from the fact that Trevor Jones, the gamekeeper on whom Hines based his character, worked at that country house (*Which Side Are You On?*, pp. 155–6).
65 Mark Hanna, 'Playwright for Today: Barry Hines', *The Cherwell*, Friday 3 February 1978, p. 7.
66 See Jacob Leigh's discussion of the film's production by ATV's documentary department and its preparing the way for Loach's documentaries of the 1980s, *The Cinema of Ken Loach*, p. 115.
67 Berger, review.
68 The success of such generic ambiguity is evident in the film's citation on the website called 'The Hunting Life: Your No 1 Source for Fieldsports': http://www.thehuntinglife.com/forums/topic/287452-the-gamekeeper-by-ken-loach/

69 Quoted in Hayward, *Which Side Are You On?*, p. 156.
70 Vivian Sobchack, *Carnal Thoughts: Embodiment and Moving Image Culture*, Oakland, CA: University of California Press, p. 245.
71 Ibid., p. 268
72 Jonathan Burt, *Animals in Film*, London: Reaktion 2002, p. 11.
73 Hayward, *Which Side Are You On?*, p. 156.
74 Shooting schedule, 22 November 1978, BFI Ken Loach Archive, KCL-9–3. Although the detail is specific to its own filming context, such an intertwining of animals and film is not particular to *The Gamekeeper*; see Laura McMahon, 'Screen animals dossier: An introduction', *Screen* 56 (1) spring 2015, pp. 81–7.
75 Shooting schedule, 16 November 1978. On the notion of camera and gun performing the same function, see Linda Kalof and Amy Fitzgerald, 'Reading the Trophy: Exploring the Display of Dead Animals in Hunting Magazines', *Visual Studies* 18 (2) 2003, pp. 112–22: 115.
76 Shooting schedule, 15 November 1978.
77 In his summary of Hines's novel, Loach's distaste for the expression of class privilege through shooting seems apparent in his omitting any detailed summary of the November pheasant shoot: 'Description of pheasants being shot etc', 'Description of shooting etc' ('Summary of novel', 196, 213). On the other hand, the 'etc' could suggest simply that such detail will be fleshed out during the filming process and is not needed in the script.
78 Barry Hines, *The Price of Coal*, Hebden Bridge: Pomona 2005 [1979], p. v, all further page references in the text; and *The Price of Coal* (Ken Loach, 1977), broadcast on 29 March and 5 April 1977.
79 See for instance John Kirk, 'Figuring the Landscape: Writing the Topographies of Community and Place', *Literature and History* 15 (1) pp. 1–17; Spencer, 'British Working-Class Fiction', pp. 366–86.
80 Anonymous review, *The Scotsman*, 7 May 1979; *Financial Times*, 7 April 1979. The latter review expresses its own unfashionable 'spleen' in adding that *The Price of Coal* is a 'bilious and boringly contrived little tract for our times', while *Kes* is an 'overrated work by the same writer now inflicted on innumerable schoolchildren'.
81 Letter, September 1977, BHP/PRC 11.
82 Anthony Hayward ascribes the incident to Loach's visual fascination with toupées and wigs, although it has a narrative role as well, embodying the discomfiture that can be brought by royalty even on the pit managers, *Which Side Are You On?*, pp. 142–3.
83 Hines quoted in ibid., p. 156.
84 Ibid., p. 141
85 BHP/PRC 9.
86 'Getting Better', BHP/OTHER 89.

87 BHP/PRC 7&10.

88 Whole elements of the screenplay were cut from 'Meet the People', including a visit to the pit by a group of school-leavers, their dialogue drawn from Hines's collection of NCB recruitment leaflets; a debate in the miners' canteen about nationalisation that takes place in the pupils' hearing; and scenes at the local bowling-green. From 'Back to Reality', sequences in a local dance-hall and the appearance of a vicar offering unwanted support have been removed. All these episodes repeat from different angles the burden of the argument between Sid and Alf about whether the royal visit should have been sanctioned by the union, which takes place during a game of snooker in 'Meet the People', as well as concerns about working conditions.

89 Mark claims he has not been able to go fishing recently due to being taken into Sheffield to buy new shoes by his mother the weekend before, and that he is going on a 'club trip' the following one.

90 BHP/PRC 12.

91 In an apposite prefiguring of Hines's play title, the then Energy Minister Tony Benn's verdict on the explosion was that 'there is still a very high price in human life to be paid, for the coal we get in this country' (quoted in 'The human price paid for nation's coal', anonymous article, *Yorkshire Post* 18 March 2014, http://www.yorkshirepost.co.uk/news/community/nostalgia/the-human-price-paid-for-nation-s-coal-1-6505238, visited 3 August 2016).

92 Prince Charles, played by the ironically named David King, is represented silently and from a distance so that only his gestures and general appearance are needed for the fiction. By contrast, there was never any suggestion that Scargill's role should be taken by an actor: he is named in Loach's casting list under the heading 'NUM', along with the other actors, BFI Ken Loach Archive, KCL-9–3.

93 Garnett, personal communication, 3 November 2015.

94 Programme notes, BHP/PRC 18.

95 Kirk, 'Figuring the Landscape', pp. 7, 5; Spencer, 'British Working-Class Fiction', p. 368.

96 BHP/PRC 12.

97 BHP/PRC 6.

98 Spencer, 'British Working-Class Fiction', p. 381. He focuses only on Hines's novel, not the television dramas or the screenplays.

99 BHP/PRC 6.

100 BHP/PRC 1; this detail has been reinstated in the novel, *The Price of Coal*, p. 26.

101 None of this dialogue appears in the novel. Most references to Scargill have been removed, marking the fiction's distance from the history of the screenplay.

102 In keeping with the spirit of *The Price of Coal*, Loach turned down
     a nomination to be awarded a Silver Jubilee OBE in the year of the
     plays' release; Hayward, *Which Side Are You On*, p. 143.
103 BHP/PRC 5.
104 BHP/PRC 7.
105 Anonymous, *Scotsman* review.
106 The project was also known at various points as *Injury Time* and *Man
     of the Match*.
107 Scott Marshall, interview with the authors, 9 November 2015.
108 BHP/TOM 3.
109 Marshall, interview with authors.
110 Ibid.
111 BHP/TOM 3.
112 BHP/TOM 3.
113 Peter Bodo, untitled, *New York Magazine* 7 May 1977, BHP/TOM 2.
114 Ibid.
115 Brian Glanville, 'The money game', *Sunday Times* 4 June 1978, BHP/
     TOM 2.
116 Ibid.
117 BHP/TOM 3.
118 Ibid.
119 Barry Hines, 'Tom Kite', unproduced screenplay, p. 17; all further
     page references in text, BHP/TOM 1.
120 David Bordwell, *Narration in the Fiction Film*, Wisconsin: University
     of Wisconsin Press 1985, p. 207; Bruce Babington, *The Sports Film:
     Games People Play*, New York: Wallflower Press 2014, p. 2.
121 BHP/TOM 3.
122 Marshall, interview with the authors.
123 Garry Whannel, 'Winning and Losing Respect: Narratives of Identity
     in Sport Films', *Sport in Society: Cultures, Commerce, Media, Politics*,
     11:2–3, 2008, pp. 195–208: 197.
124 Ibid., p. 198.
125 Ibid.

3

Thatcherism and South Yorkshire

Looks and Smiles, Unfinished Business, Fun City, Threads

In this chapter, we trace the aesthetic and political effects of the early years of Margaret Thatcher's Conservative government on Hines's writing. His screenplay for the 1981 film *Looks and Smiles* takes an art-cinematic form to explore the pressures of the era's unemployment on young people, in his fourth and final collaboration with Ken Loach. By contrast, Hines's novel *Unfinished Business* (1983) examines the possibilities of social freedom, in this narrative about the class-related and existential implications for a 29-year-old woman of going to university. Hines's unfilmed screenplay *Fun City* (1983) returns to his concern with secondary education, in the form of a bleakly comic fable about the bureaucratic and commercial pressures on schools. Finally, Hines's script for the 1984 film *Threads* uses social realism in a Cold War-era setting to horrifying effect in its portrayal of what an atomic attack might look like. The archival history of *Threads*' drafts and production reveals how its mingling of documentary and dramatic tropes took shape, as well as the nature of its symbolic and factual relation to British politics in this era.

Looks and Smiles (1981)

Looks and Smiles marked the end of Barry Hines's career-defining collaboration with Ken Loach. Released some twelve years after their first film together, it returns to the themes of *Kes*, updating them for the changing economic and political climate of the early 1980s. As Loach explained:

> The thing about the boy in *Kes* was that he was a lad with all kinds of possibilities, and yet society had planned that he would be a manual

worker, and that's all he was ever going to be, whoever he was. The interesting thing, a decade later, was that the problem facing a lad like him wouldn't be that he was going to do a job that he wasn't suitable for – but that he wouldn't have a job at all. That just seemed like an interesting thing to explore.[1]

The film's focus on the bleak prospects of three recent school-leavers in Sheffield is therefore underpinned by a sense of fatalism, whereas in the previous decade, in plays like *The Price of Coal* and Hines's novel *First Signs*, resistance to an established order and the imagination of alternatives are still conspicuous markers of Hines's authorial and political outlook.

Hines had initially intended to 'write a love story', but 'the theme of unemployment took over'.[2] The title, *Looks and Smiles*, derived from a reference from Tolstoy's *War and Peace* about courting, alludes to this initial focus, but Hines was clearly interested in the integration of a romantic and more broadly familial narrative within a wider political context. In handwritten notes on the film, Hines wrote of the way in which 'marriages, relationships between parents and children are influenced by social conditions', and it is absolutely the case that the film uses the central romance between Karen (Carolyn Nicholson) and Mick (Graham Green) as a structuring device for the film's contemporary themes. Anthony Hayward, however, argues that 'this topicality was never projected enough to make *Looks and Smiles* a strong political voice against Thatcherism', a point which fits, as we will discuss, with other criticisms of the film's apparent lack of political force and clarity. However, it is important to recognise that *Looks and Smiles* can be viewed retrospectively as a document of the effects of early Thatcherism and is a text which subtly captures the human costs of the increasingly bleak economic situation – like *The Gamekeeper*, it eschews outright didacticism but maintains a clear political focus. Hines's archive reveals that as early as 1977 he was researching the problem of youth unemployment, with a particular focus on the perceived inefficacy of Callaghan's Labour government's Work Experience scheme, which had been initiated in 1976.[3] In one of his research documents, an article by Keith Harper, the labour correspondent at the *Guardian*, Hines underlines a description of the scheme as 'a device for pushing people higher up the queue in line for jobs which do not exist'.[4] This indicates that one of the underlying tenets of *Looks and Smiles*' institutional critique – the prevalence of short term 'schemes' over meaningful and secure employment opportunities for the young – was a long-standing interest of Hines's that can be read as part of his sustained engagement with education, rather than being seen as purely a reactive position against the government of the day.

Evidence of the research for the film also, therefore, reveals that its gestation was unusually long, with Hines beginning the screenplay for *Looks and Smiles* in July 1978, still some three years before its premiere. As a result, the screenplay, as we will show, took on a number of forms and, as the film's press release states, 'when it appeared that finance for the film was not forthcoming' Hines wrote a novel, an adaptation of his own screenplay 'in case' the film 'should never see the light of day'.[5] This was an early sign of the increasing difficulty that both Hines and Loach would find in pursuing their chosen projects during the 1980s. The book was published in September 1981,[6] four months after the film version shared the prize for contemporary cinema at the Cannes Film Festival (alongside Juliet Berto and Jean-Henri Roger's *Neige*) having beaten the official British selection, *Chariots of Fire* (Hugh Hudson). However, its release schedule in the UK was fragmented, to say the least. Having been screened at the London Film Festival, the film was then broadcast on television (ATV) on 19 May 1982 before being given a limited theatrical distribution in December of the same year.

Looks and Smiles is therefore difficult to categorise. It is a feature film which was effectively delivered as a TV play, and exists, too, as a novel, with the novelisation taking place alongside the protracted development of the screenplay rather than as a post-hoc adaptation. These features make an assessment of the film's – and, to some extent, the novel's – authorship complicated. As we will see, auteurist analyses of *Looks and Smiles* which naturally position it as a 'Loach film' have underplayed, tacitly or otherwise, Hines's role in the text, as has occurred in similar scholarship on *Kes*. Indeed, critical appreciation of *Looks and Smiles* is scarce, yet, taken in the context of Hines's work, the novel and film mark the mid-point of Hines's most consistent and radical period, ranging from *The Gamekeeper* through to *Threads*, in which issues and representations of labour politics, landscape and the practice of everyday life were finding increasing synergy. As we have intimated, *Looks and Smiles* is notable particularly for its identification and

exploration of the increasingly precarious post-industrial conditions of working-class experience: prophetically hinted at in *Billy's
Last Stand*, and developed more thoroughly in *First Signs*, the focus
on employment in *Looks and Smiles* brings these issues to the
centre of Hines's writing. Using his own experience of Sheffield as
a starting point – in handwritten notes, Hines describes the reasons
for shooting in Sheffield as both practical, as he puts it, 'I live here',
and thematically meaningful: 'Industrial areas: mining, steel: no
need to go anywhere else: unemployment developed rapidly since
I started the script …'[7] – Hines's interest in location in *Looks and
Smiles* is deeply political. The film (and novel) is concerned fundamentally with the notion that its working-class characters are
unable to negotiate and maintain a secure and meaningful sense of
identity in their own communities. Mick can find no work as an
apprentice mechanic or in the more traditional sites of industry in
Sheffield, while his father (Phil Askham) is increasingly insecure in
his own employment in the steelworks; his best friend Alan (Tony
Pitts) is forced into dangerous – and in the film's ethical world,
dubious – labour as a soldier in Northern Ireland; Karen, along
with her mother (Cilla Mason), has already left her home city
of Newcastle for Sheffield in the fruitless search for more fulfilling employment; and Karen's father (Arthur David) is an exiled
Geordie lorry driver raising a second family in Bristol. *Look and
Smiles* therefore dramatises an unstable economic geography of
the North, which finds individuals at the mercy of an increasingly
unforgiving, Darwinian labour market: one that demands that its
constituents are mobile and willing to sacrifice career aspirations,
community bonds, family and relationships. In *Looks and Smiles*
the emotional threads and networks of identity that once defined
and shaped a cherished sense of place are shown as increasingly
precarious.

Thus to view *Looks and Smiles* as primarily 'a Ken Loach film'
is somewhat problematic. For example, John Hill's otherwise thor-
ough monograph on Loach devotes very little attention to *Looks
and Smiles* and, with only one mention of the screenwriter, when
the film is described as 'scripted by Barry Hines',[8] with no reference
to the novelisation. Hill is understandably governed here by the
director's own retrospective ambivalence towards the film, drawing
on Loach's view that it marked an 'end of an era' in his work, and
'missed creating the outrage in the audience that should have been

there'.[9] Indeed, in an interview with Graham Fuller, Loach expands on his own misgivings about the project:

> I was aware that we'd got a bit self-indulgent momentarily. It should have been a funnier film than it was. I think I just wasn't tough enough in the shooting and in the cutting, and I think it should have just been a bit sharper and tighter and a quarter of an hour quicker. It's too lethargic and gently paced and when I think about it now I want to give it a kick up the arse.[10]

Loach's view on the film's apparent 'self-indulgence' can almost certainly be seen to stem from its austere formal and structural qualities that, both for Loach and the film's critics, might be seen to obscure its political themes. Shot entirely in black and white, the role of the cinematographer Chris Menges is particularly conspicuous in constructing an aesthetic which Jacob Leigh describes as akin to 'stark photojournalism'.[11] This is established almost immediately in the film's title sequence where five static, sustained (varying between 16 and 13 seconds) long shots foreground Sheffield's (post-)industrial landscape. This meditative, observational style is present throughout the film and is a component of, for Leigh, the film's 'loose, open-ended quality' that generates a sense that 'it could end anywhere.'[12] As Leigh goes on:

> *Looks and Smiles* reveals the depression that people felt in the industrial North of England during the early 1980s; but it is as depressing as Mick's life. Its aimlessness may come from a decision to have the film reproduce the aimlessness of the characters.
> [...]
> ... in *Looks and Smiles* a lot of the dourness of the film comes from the dourness of the three leads and the gloomy character of depression-hit Sheffield, rendered sharply in black and white.[13] (131)

Leigh is right that the film possesses an episodic quality more akin to art cinema than the linear structure of Loach's later works. For example, when Mick and Karen attend a football match together, they have an argument and Karen dumps him on the spot. This rupture abruptly suspends the romantic component of the narrative for over a quarter of the film, before Mick, with little exposition, decides to attempt reconciliation in the final act. This might be understood as one of the 'causal gaps' typical of the 'episodic'[14] art film, and such disruptions here fragment the continuity and coherence of character development, adding to the film's sense of 'aimlessness', albeit one that we might argue is motivated by the attempt to capture the experience of an empty existence of the dole rather than by the demands of narrative spectacle. Leigh's final point, a subtle criticism of the performance of the three teenage leads, all of whom were, in line with Loach's customary practice, non-professionals with little or no training, is reflected in some contemporary criticism of the film. Hilary Kingsley, for example, bemoans 'the mumbling and twitching'[15] of the young actors as 'too much hard work to watch', and it is true that the raw performances combined with the film's stark formalism and sparse structure contribute to what Sean Day-Lewis describes a sense of 'gloom rather than the anger Mr Loach wants',[16] almost exactly anticipating the director's own criticisms of the film.

Looks and Smiles is therefore popularly regarded as a noteworthy but flawed film that signalled a break in Loach's career before the shift in style and approach which marked his 1990s renaissance. As suggested earlier, such a reading undermines the importance of *Looks and Smiles* within an analysis of Hines's own career, and ignores his work in writing the novel and multiple versions of the screenplay. With this in mind, it is important, too, to register that while the film was little seen, it was well received by a number of critics, with many celebrating precisely the aspects that have been deemed problematic in scholarly accounts of Loach's work. Ahead of the film's theatrical release in December 1982, Alan Brien, writing in the *Sunday Times*, praised its use of non-professional actors as enabling a seemingly elusive verisimilitude: 'They are simply "*there*" – the most difficult achievement in the cinema".'[17] He is equally praising of Menges' cinematography, 'which seems at once unsparingly realistic and yet as graphically vivid as etchings by Doré or Piranesi – the factories and furnaces in the background like mediaeval castles, the subways and backstreets like tunnels into nightmare'.[18] Similarly, Nancy Banks-Smith, reviewing the film for its television broadcast, was drawn to its neo-realist qualities, its combination of the authentic and the painterly:

> The young principals were absolute amateurs and the memorably named Graham Green who played Mick has considerable, natural, stumpy power. And they had Sheffield working for them. The sheet metal, the plate glass, the flats, the flyovers, the acres of faces. Cecil B. de Mille in all his glory could not call on sets and extras like that. Wherever you struck it, it rang true.[19]

Both critics identify aspects of *Looks and Smiles* for praise which are also visible in Hines's, Loach's and Menges's other collaborations, *Kes* and *The Gamekeeper* – this shared commitment to a poetic-realist approach characterised by lingering treatments of space and place might therefore be one way of identifying the strains of Hines's authorship within *Looks and Smiles*.

For example, in all his screenplays (not just his collaborations with Loach), Hines's stage directions are indicative of a prescriptive treatment of the characters' relationship with their environments, and *Looks and Smiles* is no exception,[20] reflecting a similar interest apparent in his novels. For example, after the film's title sequence discussed earlier, Loach cuts to an area of wasteland in which Mick and his friends ride a motorbike (later revealed to be stolen) and evade the police. In the screenplay, Hines describes the space vividly:

> There is a stretch of waste land on the edge of a Mick's estate which the council is clearing for new housing. It looks like a bomb site with parts of the old terraced houses still standing and heaps of rubble everywhere.
>
> Local youths ride their motor cycles here, and a track has been established over the hillocks of packed earth and across the rough flat sections. (4)

And while the filmed location lacks the desperate quality of Hines' imagined space, Loach and Menges portray the environment in a way which invites a poetic engagement. The scene lasts around two minutes, and is composed of five long shots with the boys' voices only audible when narratively significant dialogue, for instance about the motorcycle, is heard ('it's been nicked!'[6]). This places greater emphasis on the wasteland's location and its relationship with the estate in the background (where Mick and Alan live) and the vast panorama of the city in the foreground, with the wasteland's raised position making use of Sheffield's hilly landscapes to foreground spatially the characters' collective sense of alienation. (See Figure 5.) One of Loach's criticisms of the film was that it lacked 'a central image', such as 'the bird … in *Kes* … or the countryside in *The Gamekeeper*',[21] but viewed more broadly, 'the wasteland' does enable a number of the film's themes to cohere. For example, in the novel, Hines provides a fuller account of the space's significance:

> Two weeks later, when they had just left school, Mick and Alan and two of their friends were playing on a motor-cycle on a piece of

5 The local wasteland in *Looks and Smiles*

wasteland on the council estate where they all lived. The Council had
started to clear the site for new houses by knocking down a terrace
of old ones, but they had been forced to suspend work because of
government cuts in public expenditure. (5)

The site therefore draws together the end of Mick and Alan's child-
hoods and their coming-of-age within a depressed, malfunctioning
economy, a realisation made visible within the landscape itself.
Indeed, this is made explicit later in the film when Mick, who is so
often reflective of the socioeconomic circumstances he finds himself
in, rather than actively engaged in understanding them, uses another
unsatisfying meeting with a job centre worker as the platform for a
political speech which returns us to the wasteland:

MRS REID: Well, it's the economic situation ...
MICK: It's stupid. There's loads of jobs want doing. There's a piece of
    spare land near us where they've knocked some old houses down
    to build some new ones, and it's been left like that for ages now. My
    dad says they can't afford to build them now because of expendi-
    ture cuts. It's daft. What about all the money they're paying out on

the dole, and to send people on these courses and work experience schemes? Why don't they give you that money to be in a proper job? Just think of all the apprentices they'd need if they started building houses at the end of our street. It doesn't make sense. (87)

Hines justified 'the didactic nature of his speech because Mick is not just theorising, his analysis comes from his own personal experience of the dole'.[22] This therefore returns us to one of the central themes of the writer's critique of education that is visible throughout his work. Here, Mick's experiential analysis of the politics of unemployment is conveyed both explicitly through the screenplay and through reference to the cinematic (and literary) image of the lyrically rendered urban landscape.

Therefore, one way of reappraising *Looks and Smiles* from the perspective of Hines's authorship is to connect its aesthetic and thematic components to his other works. For example, we have discussed how the elegiac tone of *First Signs* is derived partly from its near-romantic treatment of the semi-rural pit village which contrasts with the novel's negative depiction of modern, high-rise, urban housing. In *Looks and Smiles'* filmic treatment of Sheffield, these themes are developed and made more visible. It is significant that Mick's traditional working-class family, of mother and father and son and daughter – with both parents working, albeit precariously, in steel and confectionery, two traditionally Sheffield industries – live in a 1930s house with a shed and garden, while Karen's fraught relationship with her single mother is played out in a council flat, specifically one in Sheffield's now demolished, Brutalist, Kelvin Flats development.

When Mick visits Karen to rekindle their romance, Hines's description of Karen's home in the novel is striking in its evocation of high-rise misery, describing 'streets in the sky … that remained chilly on even the warmest days' (203), 'the stink' in the lift, and the sight of two boys 'dropping a television set over the wall' (204). In the film, the scene is less chaotic and thus avoids an explicit criticism of the environment; however, the four-shot sequence in which Mick rides to and then arrives at Karen's home is filmed in a way which suggests that the space should be read as not merely narratively significant but, like the wasteland, as possessing poetic value. Handwritten annotations to Loach's shooting script describe how the first shot, in the film a 15-second panning long shot, should use a 'long lens'; that the next, another 15-second take of Mick as he arrives on his motorbike, should enable us to 'see the architecture'; and then what is described as a 'still pause' should see Mick in the distance walking along the bridge from one block of flats to another, which results in another long take of 14 seconds.[23] The sustained, distanced and repetitive nature of the compositions draws attention to the nature of the flats and their placement within the landscape, echoing the static frames in the film's title sequence. Again, these images might be seen to reflect Hines's own treatment of the space as conveyed in the novel, since he uses the flats' elevated position to reflect on the changing nature of the city's landscape; the contrast between the cold modernity of the high-rise and Sheffield's steel heritage; and the atmospheric experience of an increasingly dormant industrial landscape:

> The sky was brightening a little and a break in the clouds released a slanting shaft of sunlight. It illuminated the cathedral, vacant office blocks and in the distance, the jagged silhouettes of the steel mills. The air was so clear over the industrial side of the city, that it was more like Sunday than Monday afternoon. (204)

In these ways then the film's 'observational' aesthetic, as it emerges from a lyrical engagement with the urban landscape, might be seen as indicative of the poetic-realist approach that characterises Hines's earlier collaborations with Loach, reflecting, as we have argued, Hines's primary, literary engagement with location.

As we suggested earlier, the film's art-cinema register has been seen by Loach as the source of its alleged lethargy, with a feeling that he 'wasn't tough enough in the shooting or the cutting'.[24] This comment might also be worth considering in light of the novel and the early versions of the screenplay. For example, while Loach suggests that *Looks and Smiles* was too long, an examination of the film's development suggests that the elliptical nature of the final version came about, at least partly, as a result of substantial edits to and departures from the narrative as it was originally conceived.

For example, Jacob Leigh's analysis of the film provides as an instance of Loach's and Menges's distanced but 'sympathetic observation',[25] a scene where Mick and his friends congregate at a shopping centre:[26]

> The camera has followed Mick as he walks towards the other boys and chats, though we do not hear what they say. The policemen

approach the group and talk: again, we do not hear what they discuss. Loach and Menges film this action in a single long shot. The lighting is dim; the concrete shopping centre encloses the group; shoppers persistently criss-cross the space between the camera and the boys: the narrative meaning of the shot/scene is obscure, yet nothing motivates this obscurity except the aspiration to record objectively rather than organise a dramatic structure or involve the audience with the characters.[27]

The potential thematic and narrative significance of this interaction – the threatening presence of the police; the apathy of unemployed youth; and the exploration of institutional discipline – is implicit rather than clearly foregrounded. The scene is, in line with those sequences that we have already discussed, deliberately open-ended and reflects rather than seeks to analyse Mick's experience. However, in the novel and screenplay the presence of the police is much more conspicuous, as is the analysis of the childlike boredom of Mick and his friends on the dole. For example, in both the novel and in drafts of the screenplay, the wasteland scene mentioned earlier is integrated into a more tightly organised cause-and-effect system that makes clearer the relationship between crime and unemployment. In these versions, following the pursuit by the police, an officer arrives at the Walsh family home to question Mick about the stolen motorbike, in a scene which enables Hines to develop further Mr Walsh as a voice of left-wing, working-class morality in the narrative. Mick's attempts to get a job are sarcastically remarked on by the officer: 'You should apply to the police force. Plenty of vacancies there for fine upstanding lads' (20), to which, in an 'equally sarcastic manner', Mr Walsh replies 'You what? I bet they're getting trampled to the death in the rush to get in after the pay rise that you've just had' (21).

Indeed, there is an attempt to explore the sociology of crime in the film, as Mick and his friends break into their local working-men's club and the proceeds fund Mick's longed-for motorbike, but, in line with the film's realist, episodic structure, there are no consequences of this transgression. By contrast, in earlier versions of the screenplay, Mick and Karen are arrested for driving without a licence or insurance, and a scene with Mick in court finds Hines developing his examination of the structural relationship between Mick's lack of economic agency and the hierarchical power structures of the society in which he finds himself. It is Mr Walsh who first hints at this at when he learns of Mick's misdemeanour: 'It's only a matter of time before they start setting some examples. They'll try to stop all this mischief with harsher sentences instead of providing jobs,'[28] before the political and economic analysis of crime is further developed in the court scene. Here Mick is let off with a fine, since he shows remorse, is joined by his family in court and is in employment (in this version, Mick accepts a job stacking shelves in a supermarket), before the magistrate in his summative statement deploys a proto-Thatcherite analysis of the plight of Mick, and others like him:

> I am fully aware of the old adage about the Devil finding work for idle hands. However, the economic situation cannot take the entire blame for individual acts of culpability. It would be entirely irresponsible of us, and a shirking of our moral duty to lay the blame for criminality at the feet of something as abstract as, 'the state of society'. ... Moral values do not shift according to the prevailing industrial climate; right is right and wrong is wrong, regardless of economics.[29]

This is further evidence of *Looks and Smiles* being conceived as initially a more politically overt work, with a clearer examination of the institutional organisation of power, ideology and class. Similarly, in earlier versions of the screenplay, Alan is killed by a booby-trap in Ireland and the proposed film concludes with his funeral, although in some versions, by way of a postscript, we see Mick embodying prophetically Norman Tebbit's 1981 'on your bike' speech, as he decides to move to Birmingham in search of work in the wake of his friend's death. The political significance of Alan's death is made explicit in the draft screenplays through the vicar who presides over the funeral, and who in one draft decries 'another futile death in a conflict which legislation appears incapable of bringing to an end. Which indeed it cannot end',[30] and by Alan's father: 'He should have never been in Ireland. What's our Alan got to do with Northern Ireland? It's not his fight. (*Pause*) He's been killed for nothing. Wasted. A life just thrown away.'[31] The emphasis on the tragic needlessness of Alan's death connects more conspicuously to the eventual film's thematic concern with the structural problems of youth employment, positioning Alan as a victim of both a futile war and, symbolically, an economy which fails to provide fulfilling work for its constituents. More broadly, Alan's death reinforces the film's implicit criticism of the police and, by extension, the military, as complicit in the suppression of the working class in times of economic hardship: in addition to the scenes involving the police that we have already mentioned, in the film Mick's father warns against his son joining the military on account of his prediction that the army would soon be involved in 'strike-breaking'.

The decision to cut Alan's death clearly took place at an advanced stage of the film's production, with Loach's notes revealing a 'to-do list' for the funeral scene, extensive evidence in Hines's archive of material relating to the war in Ireland, and records of meetings between himself, Loach and ex-servicemen who were involved in the 'troops out' movement. The eventual ending, a freeze-frame of Mick in the dole queue – intertextually evoking cinematic iconographies of youthful disenchantment in films such as Truffaut's *400 Blows* (1959) – is enigmatic and captures a sense of the film's open-endedness, and the irrevocable, extra-textual continuities of its social themes and concerns. (See Figure 6.) Therefore, while the art-cinematic ambiguity of the closing shot might be seen to confirm criticisms of the film's sparseness, it can also be viewed as

6 Mick in the dole queue in *Looks and Smiles*

a haunting vignette of the relentlessly mundane cycle of misery that comes with unemployment, as opposed to what would have been the almost cathartic, conclusive tragedy of Alan's death.

It is clear that drawing on the screenplay's development enables a broader, more holistic view of this complex, multi-dimensional film to emerge. Similarly, further examination of the novel reveals the extent of *Looks and Smiles*' status as a text directly engaged in the lived experience and socioeconomic context of everyday life in a recession-hit working-class city. Hines's adaptation of his own screenplay makes explicit aspects of the film's political commentary (as apparent in the *mise-en-scène*) which are otherwise implicit. For example, on Mick's first visit to the careers office he arrives at 'a new office block in the city centre' where 'TO LET signs were displayed in windows on every floor and on the top floor, a final sign read: 30,000 SQ.FT OF FLOOR SPACE TO LET' (9). This sense of disused or temporary space in place of the markers of industrial heritage and, by extension, job security, is developed as Mick and Alan do the rounds of the factories and mills in the city's industrial sector and find 'windowless tin factories that ... looked temporary and insubstantial, as if they could be removed overnight leaving nothing but a concrete floor to greet the workforce next morning' (32). Later, Mick sees the older steel mills, and finds 'nothing temporary about the companies here. Many of them had been established in the nineteenth century and their blackened brick buildings stretched for miles along the river banks and filled all the roads and streets' (32). However, we are soon told that none of the 'firms ... either nationalised or privately owned, wanted any more apprentices. Despite the permanence of their premises and their established reputations, they were no more certain of the future than the ephemeral firms on the Trading Estate' (32). Viewed alongside the visual text, this pessimistic portrayal of the city's once-thriving industrial landscape has its visual equivalent in the film's title sequence. The first shot of the series – showing a factory, a train track and a river – is particularly illustrative of the sense of industrial decay that the narrator describes here. Its photographic stasis, all the more apparent in black and white, has the effect of making a contemporary image appear as a period composition; so that the present-tense industrial landscape appears haunted by its past, and the memories of its inhabitants.

Later in the film and the novel, Mick and Alan sit on a pair of swings as Alan weighs up the option of a career in the army. The composition is particularly powerful in capturing the threshold between childhood and adulthood that both characters occupy. Without work, the school leavers return to the spaces of their youth, but the swings can no longer contain them, since they are men now: but men shorn of agency and hope. The novel brings these themes of desolation to the surface: 'They were tired and dispirited. They had no money, no jobs and no prospects. Even the weather and the sun on their faces did not comfort them. It made them feel worse' (39). Hines therefore uses the literary form to develop an examination of the emotional and psychological effects of unemployment that are otherwise absent in the film. For example, as Mick returns from another fruitless job search, he notices 'sheets of newspaper on the pavement', with headlines that read, 'WAR DECLARED ON SCROUNGERS' (73), and seems overwhelmed by this corrosive discourse (all too visible in contemporary narratives of unemployment):

> He could not face traipsing round all the firms again and seeing the same NO VACANCIES signs on board after board, or meeting gate-keepers and receptionists who, with a supercilious look and smug shake of the head, seemed to revel in his misfortune. It was humiliating. It made him feel ashamed: like a beggar. (73)

Where Graham Green's restrained, almost passively naturalistic performance in the film embodies something of the boredom and frustrations of youth unemployment, Hines here conveys its shame. Later, we are told that Mick 'hated being in the house in the afternoon; watching horse-racing on the television and going to sleep on the settee' (79), and the sense is clear that the 'revolutionary gesture'[32] that some critics called for is impossible for a character (and a generation) so overwhelmed by the debilitating melancholy of life on the dole.

Given the novel's secondary status, its presence in relation to the film of *Looks and Smiles* has been understandably underplayed. Yet the book version has received some scholarly attention. Both John Kirk and Luke Spencer praise its prescient political focus, and connect the novel to Hines's wider oeuvre. Kirk identifies 'the increasing sense of personal hopelessness of young working-class people in the very different context (no work), to that of *The Price of Coal*'.[33] Significantly, both Kirk and Spencer draw attention to the same arresting passage towards the end of the novel, as Mick and Karen travel down to Bristol to see Karen's estranged father:

They travelled on the motorways. This is what they passed: Squashed
birds. A smoking van on the hard shoulder. Police cars lurking in
lay-bys. A derelict coal-mine. Slag heaps. A deserted village. Dead elm
trees. Tractors grubbing up hedgerows. Broiler houses. Strips of lorry
tyres like cast off snake skins. JESUS LIVES scrawled on a bridge.
New housing estates in the wilds. Long vehicles. A coachload of senior
citizens on a mystery tour. A vintage car. Company cars. Cars with
leopardskin seat covers. Cars with dogs nodding and hands waving
in their windows. A motel. A two mile tail-back going the other way.
A GET-IN-LANE-NOW sign. Major roadworks for mile after mile.
A crash surrounded by police cars and ambulances with flashing blue
lights. An abandoned dog running fearfully and exhausted along the
central reservation. A rusty mudguard. A buckled crash barrier. A
burnt out car down an embankment. Broken windscreen glass. Blood
on the road. A kestrel hovering over a scorched bank. A slimy canal.
New trading estates with FACTORY UNIT TO LET signs. Silent factories. Empty council houses. Overgrown allotments. A stinking river.
Acres of new, unsold cars. A busy golf course. Scrapyards. A flock
of gulls on a rubbish-tip. Polythene flapping on a barbed wire fence.
Litter: in fields, in woods, in streets. A convoy of army trucks. (222–3)

Kirk sees in this passage 'personal despair framed by public squalor',
and identifies Hines's 'cinematic' approach in constructing a 'meto-
nymic collocation' of 'fragments' which 'signal' a 'general decay', as
Mick and Karen observe 'the detritus of a market economy in crisis',
suggesting that 'human life, when there is no hope, will become part
of that same waste',[34] while Spencer also reads the sequence as symbolic of the 'youngsters' personal hopelessness', and generating a
'vivid image of the 1980s'. Both critics also note the presence of the
police and the military in Hines's bleak, state-of-the nation vignette.
For Spencer the haunting presence of the trucks 'hints unmistakably
at the coercive power with which the State, responsible for such
waste, will increasingly defend itself',[35] while Kirk notes the images'
'retrospective significance in relation to developments in the 1980s
and the policing of the 1984–85 Miners' Strike'.[36] To build on
these links to Hines's other works, the sense of forced geographical
displacement; the destruction of nature, so often a source of hope
in earlier texts; the lost innocence of youth and the seeming impossibility of happiness through romance; and the pervasive presence
of state authority, twinned with apocalyptic imagery, connect the
passage to Hines's allegorical treatment of post-industrial Sheffield
in *Threads*. Moreover, Kirk is right to identify the 'cinematic',

montage-like tone of the prose, but this filmic register differs radically from the reflective aesthetic found in Loach's film of *Looks and Smiles*. In this scene, Hines departs from his (and Loach's) poetic realist style in a manner similar to the final moments of *Kestrel for a Knave*, eschewing sustained, descriptive treatments of the landscape in favour of a fragmented collage aesthetic, characterised by short sentences and list-like prose. To continue the cinematic allegory, the fragments are 'edited' so that quotidian observations ('Cars with leopardskin seat covers. Cars with dogs nodding and hands waving in their windows') clash disconcertingly with dystopian imagery ('an abandoned dog running fearfully and exhausted along the central reservation', … 'Broken windscreen glass. Blood on the road'), making conspicuous the text's analysis of the ideological forces that determine the increasingly precarious and fragmented experience of everyday, working-class life.

In both broadening out the analysis of Hines's authorship across mediums, and drawing on the thematic continuities in his oeuvre, we suggest that, while *Looks and Smiles* marked the end of a chapter for Loach, it can be reclaimed for Hines as a central text, as a radical and prophetic examination of the rapidly changing condition of working-class life in the North as Britain experienced the first throes of deindustrialization.

Unfinished Business (1983)

In a change of political emphasis from that in *Looks and Smiles*, Hines's novel *Unfinished Business* of 1983 centres on the figure of Lucy Downs, a married woman with two young children, whose decision to enrol for a university degree in English Literature at the age of 29 alters the nature of her life and that of her family. Lucy's encounter with new ideas and different lifestyles, as well as an affair with one of her tutors, prompts her to question and then abandon her conventional life as a suburban housewife. Although the location is not named, so that the novel's meaning should not be tied too specifically to a place, the fact that its setting is based on the city of Sheffield seems quite clear. The university that Lucy attends possesses a 1960s concrete high-rise block, here named the Schweitzer Tower, after the Nobel Peace Prize-winning Albert Schweitzer, modelled on the University of Sheffield's Brutalist Arts Tower where Hines himself had an office.[37] The details of her courses and life as a mature student, as shown by the research material gathered by Hines, represent an amalgamation of that institution with Sheffield Hallam University,[38] although the focus on Lucy's inner world also makes this setting symbolic. *Unfinished Business* is unusual in Hines's oeuvre in having a female protagonist through whose eyes we see events. However, Lucy's experience and history is, rather than an entirely new departure, a developed and extended version of elements evident in Hines's earlier works, and leads in turn to his play *Born Kicking* (1992) about a female footballer.

The story of Lucy reveals the effects of particular life choices and constraints of one family member on all the others, as is more usually the case in Hines's works in relation to working men, such as George Purse in *The Gamekeeper*, Sid Storey in *The Price of Coal* and, as we will see, Dick Hayes in the novel's intertext, *Two Men from Derby*. In Lucy's case, the kinds of small-scale questioning or rebellion on the part of women, which appear elsewhere in Hines's writing but do not change the existing conditions, become central to the plot. Although *The Gamekeeper* constitutes a precursor to the overt gender awareness of *Unfinished Business* in some respects, its focus is on the routine of Mary Purse's husband George, and we see her household duties only when he does. While there are necessarily scenes in *The Price of Coal*'s second play, 'Back to Reality', where Kath and her activities are represented on their own account after Sid goes missing in the pit explosion, further moments were excised from early drafts of the screenplay in order to ensure that its emphasis remained on her husband. For instance, at the beginning of a draft version of 'Back to Reality', Kath and her friend Edna see the miner Cliff cycle past at top speed on 'his son's brightly coloured Chopper bicycle', the fact that they are unaware he has been summoned to take part in the pit rescue evident in Kath's comment, 'Soft as brushes, aren't they, men? They never grow up, do they?'[39] This early instance of dramatic irony is replaced in the film by a version in which Cliff's wife is aghast that he has to abandon cutting the grass outside their house in order to take part in the rescue, as she declares: 'As soon as you start, there's something happens at the pit!'. In both cases, comedy is derived from women's misrecognition of the importance of men's work. It is only in *Unfinished Business* that a consideration of women's role within industrial capitalism constitutes the narrative itself. In this novel it is by contrast the detail of a man's occupation that forms the background, and we learn only in passing that Lucy's husband Phil's job at Bowes Engineering has become one of 'uncertainty and unremitting stress' in the wake of its takeover by a global conglomerate.[40] The hints at the pressured working conditions, which do not give Phil 'time to check the quality of the work produced' (72), are the kind of narrative seeds which, in a different text, might have provided a plot device about safety cuts leading to disaster, akin to that in 'Back to Reality'.[41]

Just as the class formations in Hines's other works have retained their relevance even if their contexts in the steel and mining industries no longer exist, *Unfinished Business* emphasizes for a twenty-first-century reader how much patriarchy's links to capitalism remain in place, even if circumstantial details in relation to gender have altered.[42] Reviews describe the novel as representing a pressing 'contemporary predicament', seen as 'one of the most interesting problems in contemporary life', while the critic Hanna Behrend claims that it offers a 'skilful' analysis of 'topical conflicts' relating to Lucy's social and personal circumstances as a 'respectable working man's non-earning wife'.[43] Other reviews register the urgency of the novel's message in a direct address to the reader. By including *Unfinished Business* in her 'Christmas Book Choice' for 1983, Fay Weldon urges a female readership to action: 'Read this one, pass it on, be warned – and go ahead!', while Netta Martin assumes interest in the novel on the part of both men and women, encouraging 'any wife who feels that her husband takes her for granted' to read Hines's novel. However, it is revealingly unclear whether Weldon is exhorting women readers to go to university or leave the family home, while Martin's warning to 'neglectful husbands' that it will provide 'food for thought!' is to ignore the novel's examination of gendered education and work as well as personal relationships.[44]

Despite this acknowledgement of the topicality of *Unfinished Business* on its publication in the early 1980s, for readers in the present era of fourth-wave feminism the lineaments of gender relations are less typically summed up by Lucy's experience. The blurb describes the novel's centring on 'one of the most difficult dilemmas facing modern relationships',[45] a 'dilemma' which is of course not simply about women's education, although this offers a new twist on Hines's usual concern with the school experience of teenage boys. Rather, it is about the 'unfinished' nature of self-determination and 'problematic emancipation'[46] in the face of social expectations

and conventional roles. As Gloria Steinem argues, 'every economics course ought to start not with production but with reproduction', an insight that governs Hines's novel.[47] Lucy's awareness of
the difficulty of changing her circumstances makes her attuned to
the details of what would now be described as 'everyday sexism',
including the professor who 'glances at her legs' during her interview (25), alongside institutional elements of gender imbalance. Her
misreading the surname of the lecturer Dave Pybus as that of the
cookware 'Pyrex' is a slip that brings home to Lucy the absence of
women lecturers (23). Later she sits in on an innuendo-laden debate
between male and female students about the practice of mixed
football, the terms of which not only seem little different to twenty-
first-century debates of this kind but also give voice to essentialist
arguments for gender division in relation to a sport which Hines
presented as an exclusively masculine world until his composition
of *Born Kicking*.[48]

Unfinished Business is set during a time of debate about the
nature of a relationship between Marxism and feminism, elements
of which are dramatised in the novel.[49] It opens with a scene representing social change, as Lucy's husband Phil witnesses the demolition of the 'sooty' inner-city terraced houses of his childhood home
in Morley Street, to which he contrasts the 'modern detached houses
and dormer bungalows' of his present life in suburban Linnet Close
(5). As is often the case in Hines's writing, the notices and names
of everyday signs, such as the 'No Trespassing' injunctions in *The
Gamekeeper* and the plethora of warning notices in *The Price
of Coal*, is a significant means of interpellating working people.
In this instance, Phil has moved from an inner-city street named
after a former textile town to one that advertises the bird life of its
suburban location, in a way that Lucy at first loves then comes to
question. Phil's view of the demolition appears unambiguously positive as a symbol of his improved circumstances in a skilled role as
a welder, prompting him to exclaim 'Thank God for progress' (5).

Although *Unfinished Business* was never adapted into filmic
form, perhaps because of its apparently close resemblance to Willy
Russell's play *Educating Rita*, which was released as a film in 1983,
the opening demolition scene constitutes a literary establishing
shot. It also prefigures the novel's concluding with another disman-
tling, that of Phil's marriage.[50] Phil's return home at the novel's
opening appears unexceptional, since 'Lucy was standing at the

sink peeling potatoes' (6). However, since this is also the day on which Lucy receives her A-level results, it is clear that her distance from a role of this kind precedes and prompts her decision to go to university. Thus when the letter offering her a university interview arrives, Lucy attempts to distract Phil with an 'impressive display of domestic devotion' (20). In this way she deploys what Judith Butler would call an 'imitation of [gender's] own naturalized idealization', enacted here as an imitation of its social roles.[51]

The kind of ambivalence that we saw in relation to how George Purse in *The Gamekeeper* is represented takes enhanced form in Lucy's case, in a way that some reviewers experienced as the novel's 'token' effort to represent every point of view,[52] but which is related by complex narrative means for polyphonic ends. Even if the 'sympathy' of the implied author with Lucy is apparent throughout,[53] the novel presents different responses to its protagonist's circumstances. In a sustained version of the dramatised debates about land in *The Gamekeeper*, the royal family in *The Price of Coal* or disarmament in *Threads*, Phil's failure to turn into Lucy's patriarchal antagonist, despite his early threats 'not to allow' his wife to go to university, is matched by her being shown to increasingly less sympathetic effect as she appears to follow in single-minded fashion her friend Tanya's advice to 'look after herself for a change' (111). Thus, as one in a series of what might have been cuts between ironically contrasting scenes in a cinematic version of *Unfinished Business*, we see Phil called from work to take their son Mathew to hospital because Lucy is studying in the library and cannot be found. As this example of incompatible aspirations shows, the novel's tokenism is strategic, as a way of making clear that the dilemmas it represents are not those of an individual's pathology but, as in George Purse's case, personifications of what it means to live out ideological contradictions. Phil's coming to take pleasure in the kinds of task he assumes in Lucy's absence, such as cooking the children's meals and reading *The Water Babies* to his daughter Tracey, makes his 'the real emancipatory success of the novel', in Behrend's phrase, as 'a man freed from the need of a woman's subordination'.[54] However, in terms of the plot, Phil's transformation is less successfully rendered. This is not only because, as Behrend argues, Hines presents the case for 'a complete divorce of women's progress from men's', so that the former can only take place outside a working-class household,[55] but also because the novel's narrative threads are allowed to drift in a way that is fittingly open-ended, although overall perhaps too 'unfinished'. There is no denouement to the marital rift, and Lucy just slips out of the door at the novel's conclusion.

Likewise, the narrative allows for no confrontation between Lucy and her lover, the lecturer Dave, and indeed she conceals her concerns about his often casual and thoughtless behaviour with the result that significant elements of the plot simply vanish.[56] Lucy's affair, with a man one reviewer describes as 'the faculty minotaur',[57] is represented not just as a challenge to the reader's conception of the kind of 'business' she must pursue, nor, as the novel's paperback cover implies, simply a romantic choice between two suitors. Indeed, even where Hines's writings have what could be described as a romantic plot, as in the case of *Looks and Smiles*, this is simply a means of incarnating other forces of a social and political kind. For the most part, it is an already established marriage that appears in his novels and screenplays, revealing, although not, until the present novel, explicitly critiquing, the fact that even 'a freely chosen marriage' conceals an 'underlying economic compulsion'.[58] The same is true of the depictions of courtship in Hines's writing, against which parents warn their children because it foreshadows not just the risks of pleasure but of entry into the adult world of work. In *Unfinished Business*, Dave embodies both intellectual and personal freedom, in contrast to Lucy's relationship with Phil. The latter's relief in finding the word 'metallurgy' in the dictionary when searching for 'metaphysical' in an effort to understand his wife's poetry essay underscores his association with 'productive' rather than intellectual labour (45). Intimacy itself supports the conventional pattern of their marriage, where sexual relations form part of a psychological system of offering reassurance on her part, reward on his (31, 104).

Yet the contrasting sense of 'sex as spontaneous gratification' associated with Dave entails a freedom that also excludes, if we see him, as Behrend does, as a 'sexual and political philanderer ... incapable of personal or social commitment'.[59] Lucy ponders the difference between 'negative and positive freedom' for a university politics seminar, concluding on neither side of these freedoms' definitions as 'absence of personal restraint' or 'restraint for the greater good' (112).[60] This dilemma is relevant to Lucy's situation in general and specifically in relation, respectively, to her affair and to her marriage. Such a distinction between different kinds of freedom is most strikingly dramatised when Dave persuades Lucy to join him for a tryst in the 'props store' at a student play where Phil is in the audience. Bringing the alternatives offered by the two men into such uncomfortably close proximity emphasises the moral and emotional unsuitability of the alternative represented by Dave. His response to the episode in the props cupboard is an immediate repudiation of his relationship with Lucy: 'I'm not sure what we ought to do about it though ... the complications could be hideous' (162). Such uncertainty is shared by the novel's plot, an inconclusivity that produces a sense of Lucy acquiescing in this relationship in place of her marriage.

The episode in which Phil attends the student play marks one of the moments of the reader's greatest distance from Lucy, whose rebellion against married life on this occasion takes the form of horror at Phil's best suit with its 'old-fashioned' baggy trousers, and, after some celebratory wine, dismissal of a babysitting neighbour: 'Let Judith babysit for ever! ... That was all she was good for anyway' (153, 159). The shifting between different viewpoints is apparent here to the point of self-consciousness, as is also the case in an episode from which Lucy, and her polarising viewpoint, is absent. The threat represented by a wife who might no longer be available to support her working husband is subject to debate at the engineering works where Phil is a welder. Here he defends his wife against his workmates: 'You can't expect her to do everything at home now that she's studying as well.' The discussion of the implications of Lucy's 'studying', which Phil's workmates take to mean that 'you have to cut your own snap now', is interrupted by Roy's paying attention instead to a page three newspaper photograph of a partially clad woman, of whom he declares 'I wouldn't mind studying her' (46). This transformation of the intransitive verb 'study' into its transitive form, returning a woman safely into being its object, also has an extradiegetic reference. It glances back at a moment from the film of *The Price of Coal*, in which the need to 'shift' a Pirelli-style calendar 'off the wall' is an acknowledgement of the whitewashing that will have to take place for a royal visit to the pit, rather than a critique of the imagery.[61] A similar use of a trope of gender subordination to stand in for another injustice occurs in an unsettling pub conversation in *The Gamekeeper*. We learn that the judge in a case of rape, which was said to have taken place in a sports car, had to try out the car 'with another girl' to see if such an action were 'physically possible' (81). The gender implications of these incidents from two of Hines's earlier novels constitute their 'blind spot', in Luce Irigaray's phrase,[62] and take second place to a concern with class privilege and the ruling classes' distance from working men's lives. *Unfinished Business* implicitly revisits and reviews these moments of 'blindness'.

Even more self-reflexively than these small reconsiderations of moments from his writings, *Unfinished Business* returns in more sustained fashion to an earlier work of Hines's. As we have seen, Lucy's joining the student drama society enables both artistic and romantic self-expression. She takes part in staging a play which, although nameless in the novel, is clearly modelled on Hines's *Two Men from Derby*, broadcast in 1976 as a television drama and later that year on the radio.[63] The play is often described as one 'based on [Hines's] grandfather's experiences',[64] since the latter worked as a miner throughout his life despite being invited for football trials at Leicester City. However, such a summary overlooks the play's unusual structure, which places all the dramatic emphasis on the female character. In *Two Men from Derby*, a pair of talent scouts from Derby County football club call on Freda Hayes for an appointment with her husband Dick, a miner who, in Godot-like fashion, never arrives. Freda sends Stanley, the boy next door, to search for her husband in all the local pubs, but it becomes clear that he has deliberately missed the meeting. The play's action is set in the 1930s on washday and consists of Freda, who is visibly pregnant, undertaking such heavy household work as soaking, boiling, washing and putting through a mangle all the household linen as well as her husband's work and football clothing, stoking the fire for the boiler, making bread and her husband's dinner. During their conversation with her, the talent scouts, George and Joe, outline what life as a footballer would mean for Dick, whose work is not represented, and for Freda, all of whose activity is shown on stage. Freda learns that her husband would earn twice what he does as a miner, and live in a house provided by the club, complete with a bathroom. However, for all the danger and discomfort of Dick's job, it appears, as Peter Shepherd puts it in his introduction to the published script, that 'he has much more to lose than [his wife] in risking the football trials and life in Derby', not least forfeiting the game as a source of relaxation.[65] In a contrasting twist, in *Unfinished Business* it is his wife's domestic tasks that become leisure activities for Lucy's husband Phil.

As the stage directions for *Two Men from Derby* put it, 'it is important that Freda should be seen to be working hard throughout', but that the two men do not attempt to assist her even with the 'heavy jobs', since 'the nature of her work is taken for granted by them' (3). However, although it is described with as much attention to technical detail as the gamekeeping and mining in Hines's other writings, Freda's work is not the generator but the casualty of the plot: any change of circumstance depends only on her husband. In *The Gamekeeper* we learn that George likewise watches Mary doing the washing-up, yet he 'never considered helping his wife with the pots ... There was rigid demarcation in the Purse household' (25). Indeed, the provision of a rent-free house with which the scouts tempt Freda is a glamorised version of the Purses' tied cottage. It is only in *Unfinished Business* that such a division of labour constitutes a sufficiently significant plot device on its own account that the status quo is altered. In *Two Men from Derby*, the topic of women's versus men's work is debated outright by Freda and Joe, the more voluble of the two scouts and himself a former miner. When Freda sees the possibility of her husband becoming a professional footballer as an escape from being trapped at home doing household chores, Joe retorts that Dick is the more disadvantaged: 'You're better off filling washing tubs than coal tubs, believe me' (15). Although this dialogue is not cited in *Unfinished Business*'s account of its staging, Lucy responds to the play in the novel as if she is supporting Freda's position: 'I know what it's like to be stuck at home all day like that. It's like being in prison' (140). Yet when Tanya valorises gender over class, declaring Freda's husband to be 'a bastard ... out drinking all the time while his wife is stuck at home', Lucy defends him by recourse to the nature of his work: 'Isn't he a slave as well?' (82–3). The complex polyphony of these varied positions, within and about the play, is amplified by Tanya's act of misreading, since, as Lucy indicates, it is never made clear that Dick is out drinking, although the second scout, George Hirst, voices such a suspicion. The implication is that Freda's class identity can no more be ignored than that of the middle-class feminist Tanya, who does not know what Freda's washing-dolly is, but offers a mystified Lucy some organic honey with which to sweeten her ground coffee.

Unlike the eponymous 'two men' or *The Gamekeeper*'s George Purse, as his defence of Lucy to his workmates shows, in *Unfinished*

Business Phil does start to cross the line from one kind of work
to another. His purchase of a recipe book, *Great Dishes of the
World*, turns out to be for his own use, not a heavy hint to Lucy,
as she initially suspects. Yet the novel's shifting, polyphonic representation of his viewpoint and Lucy's makes Phil's conversion not
only ambiguous but also to enact debates about the less obvious
differences between men's and women's work. Thus the apparent
movement in narratorial sympathy to Phil is just as qualified as the
initial identification with Lucy. Reviewers admired the 'imagery of
the child/man' used to convey Phil's engagement with household
tasks,[66] including his claiming now to 'enjoy the kids much more
than I ever did before' (197), and his enthusiasm for ironing shirts,
of which we learn that 'he quite enjoyed nosing and gliding between
the buttons. It was like riding on the dodgem cars at the fair' (137).
On another occasion, Lucy becomes 'increasingly irritated' by Phil's
'absorption' in what was to her 'the irksome task' of cleaning the
children's shoes (193). It is as if his taking pleasure in what was to
her unpaid and unacknowledged labour implies that, in the terms
of the well-known debate, women's work in the home runs the risk
of being classified as a leisure activity.[67] For Phil, by contrast, it is
a novelty, as the repeated description of his 'enjoying' it reveals.
Indeed, it is the spectacle of Phil's absorption that prompts Lucy
to declare that she is leaving, implying that this is the only way to
evade the binaries of marriage.

The unnamed version of *Two Men from Derby* which appears in
Unfinished Business is an image of that play rather than a reproduction. Thus Freda is now Alice, her miner husband a steelworker, and
the scouts are from Tottenham Hotspur rather than Derby.[68] As an
art work it has also altered. Since no stage directions are offered
to explain why Freda is afraid that the men at the door might be
bringing bad news from the pit (85), Lucy has to interpret this for
the other students, yet in the real-world version of *Two Men from
Derby* such a fear is made clear in the dialogue (5). Ian Sainsbury
claims that the play's absent husband offers a 'mirror image' of
Lucy's story in the novel, since they are both in danger of aban-
doning ambition 'through lack of nerve'.[69] However, it seems that
Lucy's circumstances prompt the reader to reflect on Freda's life
rather than Dick's. The words of the former about her husband –
'it's easier to think that you could have made it, rather than to know
that you didn't' (23) – convey a state of mind that is the opposite

to Lucy's daring. While Freda's ability to change her situation is extremely restricted in *Two Men from Derby*, its revisitation as a play-within-the-novel in *Unfinished Business* is part of the process that allows the female protagonist to alter everything.

The full significance of Freda's predicament in *Two Men from Derby* only emerges when it is framed by Lucy's in *Unfinished Business*. This is made plain when Lucy is prompted by Tanya's remark on the trap represented by modern household improvements on Freda's mangle and boiling tub to wonder whether 'they [had] just been bought off with gadgets' (154). This enfolded structure encourages a temporal relativity in relation to the historical vantage-point from which it is read. Lucy's reference to the play's author, whose sympathies she claims to be obviously with Freda despite the fact that he is a man (83), is a hint at the relationship between the two works – Hines's drama about his grandfather, as revealed by its appearance in a later novel, turns out rather to be one about his grandmother – and a metafictional comment on the novel itself, in which a polyphonic structure has replaced a clear sense of narratorial judgement.

The ending of the play, in which Freda, after the football scouts have departed, throws Dick's dinner into the fire and only at the last minute saves his football boots from the same fate, is debated between Tanya and Lucy. The detail of the play's ending as it appears in the novel diverges from that of the television drama, *Two Men from Derby*, since the version in *Unfinished Business* follows instead the script of the radio adaptation. The television play ends with action rather than dialogue. Freda retrieves the boots from the fire, as the stage direction has it: '*There is no damage done, so she puts them back into the bottom cupboard and closes the door*' (27). By contrast, at the conclusion of the radio play and the version in the novel, action is translated into dialogue. Freda's gesture of resignation in closing the cupboard door on the boots is transformed into an expression of overt dissatisfaction at her lot while carrying on with her manual labour. Having rescued the football boots, Freda declares, 'Well, this is not going to buy the baby a bonnet, standing here doing nothing. (*She takes a shirt out of the tub and puts it through the mangle.*) God, what a life ...' (156).[70] The novel's drawing on the radio adaptation of *Two Men from Derby* rather than the original television play means that it benefits from the radio version's more explicit representation of

Freda's disappointment, in its necessary reliance on dialogue and sound by contrast to the television play's ending with silent action. The version used in the novel is thus expressive of a view that Tanya calls 'fatalistic' and 'defeatist', since Freda's discontent is uttered as she continues to use the symbolic mangle onstage: as Tanya puts it, she 'has no choice but to accept a life of drudgery and subjugation' (83).

At her university admissions interview, Lucy had expressed distaste for *Tess of the D'Urbervilles*, describing Hardy's novel as 'too fatalistic. There was no hope in it' (28). She does not agree with Tanya's verdict on the play, and it is as if the gendered fatalism that characterizes its plot and that of *Tess* is most aptly contradicted by her own trajectory, in which she sets off alone into an unknown future. At the novel's end, Lucy decides not to keep the door key to her family home as she leaves, but 'drops it through the letterbox' (208), a marked contrast to Freda's action of resignedly closing a different kind of door.

Fun City (1983)

Fun City is a short one-act play set in a single location – a school headmaster's office – where the action takes place in real time. The play's mode is one of satirical farce, in comparison to Hines's earlier education-centred play *Speech Day* (1973), with its realist allegory of class difference. *Fun City*, which Hines completed a decade after *Speech Day* in late 1983, was commissioned for a series of six half-hour plays by a mixture of new and established writers to be produced by Quintet Films. However, Quintet was not able to raise the finances for filming, with the result that Hines's *Fun City* exists in the public realm only in the form of a published stage-play script intended for schools.[71] The play concerns the fate of Tony Kyle, a pupil at Wordsworth School, who is brought by the PE teacher, Mr Shearer, to the office of the headmaster, Mr Travis, on suspicion of having stolen a five-pound note from another boy in the sports changing-room. Travis manages to get Kyle to admit to the theft by threatening to detain him during the lunch break, and we learn that Kyle stole the money so that he could play a nuclear-war video game at the eponymous Fun City, a local arcade. Travis then breaks the promise that he and Mr Shearer made not to report the boy to the police.[72]

The entirety of *Fun City* takes place in Mr Travis's study, making it seem at first that the drama's viewpoint is that of the headmaster on whom the play opens. In *Fun City*, the restricted setting places great emphasis on the interaction between Travis and Kyle. Apart from the arrival at Travis's office of various adults, including Mr Shearer, Travis's secretary and some other teachers, school life is shown through a pair of protagonists who are located at the opposite ends of the school's hierarchy: the headmaster and a reluctant pupil with a police record. Other events that take place outside the confines of Travis's study are made known by a variety of dramatic devices, including telephone calls, conversations held in the corridor outside the room, and by means of the headmaster's binoculars as he looks out of his office window. As Hines puts it, by this method many central events are not shown but known by their sound or by report.[73] The play's mode is thus what Hines calls a 'bizarre and comic' version of 'the familiar'.[74]

The audience's first sight of Travis takes the form of his 'doing press-ups in his shirt sleeves in the middle of the room' (61), and his obsessive fitness regime continues throughout the play. It constitutes the topic of his exchanges with both Mr Shearer, to whom he loses in an arm-wrestling match at the play's end, and Kyle himself, who instantly adds up the total calories in a plate of biscuits before the headmaster can do so. Travis's habit of taking any opportunity to do another exercise, even during his interrogation of Kyle, is an expression of his belief in the principle of 'survival of the fittest', tellingly foreshadowing the use of this phrase in *Threads*, and equally of his taking part in a 'School Aid' fund-raising effort. As he claims, the school's finances are so parlous that it has to rely on 'gimmicks and the begging bowl'. Thus Travis has to contend with, yet is also an embodiment of, the effects of contemporary political priorities on schooling.

Hines undertook his customary research into the likely kinds of issue to be faced in an 'inner-city school' such as Travis's in the early 1980s, as shown by his relying on the detail from a real-life 'Deputy Head's Schedule'. This document, which outlines the Deputy's work for one day, includes details of pupils' misdeeds, such as several instances of shoplifting and other kinds of theft, truancy, drinking and glue-sniffing, accidents and illness, as well as pupils threatened by violence at home. In several cases, distressing incidents from this catalogue are transformed by Hines into ludicrous or comic elements in the play, so that education-related satire is balanced against the farcicality necessitated by the one-act format. The Deputy Head's notes on 'a group of girls waiting to be reprimanded for hair colour' seems likely to be the origin of Kyle's rebelliously 'extravagant hairstyle', consisting of his 'completely shaven head' adorned with a 'coloured strip of hair down the centre' (64), revealed when Travis demands that he remove his woollen hat. The documented case of a girl who has recently lost her father and for whom arrangements must be made for her to go on a school trip, is transformed into the play's blackly comic incident in which a teacher mishears that a dog, rather than a dad, has died. Inappropriate sexual activity on the part of a male pupil in class, taken from the real-life schedule, becomes a fictional incident related fragmentarily by Travis over the telephone:

> TRAVIS: Yes ... They were doing what ...? In RE? Good Lord, what were they studying, Genesis? (65)

Another of the play's details combines the elements of two incidents, a theft and a schoolgirl pregnancy, from the Deputy's list, and we hear Mr Travis's half of a telephone conversation as he gradually realises the reason for a pupil's stealing Babygros from Mothercare and concludes, 'Let's hope she gets a good grade in Home Economics' (68). Travis's priority is the school's being seen to thrive, and even pupils' suffering and misdeeds can be turned to this purpose.

The source of the social malaise on which *Fun City's* satire relies is exposed rather than identified or analysed. The pupils' activities take place offstage in an unseen school environment that is itself crumbling. In this case, the comedy has an intradiegetic audience in Kyle, who is amused at the idea of a door falling on one pupil and another getting an electric shock when turning on a changing-room shower which only ever produces cold water. Travis recommends reversed logic as a way of getting round the school's defects: 'Perhaps you should try switching on the lights, see if you get any hot water out of the sockets.' Despite his losing at arm-wrestling to Mr Shearer, Travis's view holds sway. His reporting Kyle to the police has, like his exercises, an origin in economics as well as pathology, as he claims to Shearer: 'we don't have the staff or the resources to deal with the likes of Kyle. He's an expensive commodity in educational terms and I'm afraid we can't afford him' (81).

The play's concluding image of Travis's stasis is a confirmation that the only change which has taken place is his attire: he is 'running on the spot, fully kitted up plus false nose and glasses' (83). At this moment Travis's character seems even more suited to an absurdist play. In Hines's drafts, the appearance in the headmaster's desk drawer of the 'novelty spectacles attached to a clown's red nose' is explained by means of an incident recounted by Travis in which a music teacher is driven to 'flip her lid', in his words, by her class mooing instead of singing: 'She put this on (*picking up the false nose and glasses*), sat down at the piano and started singing "Old Macdonald Had a Farm".' This extended example of reported action has been excised from the published stage-play, where Travis simply observes that 'If there were GCSEs in funny business, we'd have the best academic record in the country ... Some of [the pupils] even bring their own props with them to rehearse in class!' (81). This throwaway remark to account for the presence of the novelty spectacles satirises the system of school qualifications and awards, just as in *Speech Day*, Ronnie and his fellow-pupils imagine being awarded 'the detention prize' or one for 'the lads with the biggest appetite' (94).

The hints at the reality of Kyle's interiority in his laughing at the effects of the school's disrepair mark a shift away from the audience's having to gauge events from Travis's viewpoint, particularly after the boy's confession solves the mystery of the theft and establishes his guilt. Kyle's explanation of wanting the money to spend at Fun City is the culmination of this process. The difference from *Speech Day* in relation to historical context is apparent in this way. *Speech Day*'s setting in the early 1970s is made clear through the effects of the era's Conservative government under Edward Heath, with its unemployment, three-day weeks and strikes, while the threat of redundancy at work hangs over both Mr Warboys and Danny. The political figures of the era for whom Ronnie's grandfather has no time appear on his television in the form of two opposed figures: Harold Wilson, who would narrowly win two general elections for Labour in 1974, and Enoch Powell, whose anti-immigration and anti-Common Market pronouncements were notorious in the early 1970s, yet who endorsed Labour against the Conservatives in 1974. Like George, who says 'I soon decided that [Labour] wasn't the way, and I threw out' (105), it seems that Grandpa has given up on the Labour Party. In a late draft of *Speech*

Day, but cut from the broadcast version, another figure, foreshadowing an even greater bleakness to come, is mentioned in the scene in which Ronnie and his friends buy fish and chips. The chip shop is full of schoolchildren, whose presence is the subject of dialogue between the proprietor and a customer:

> PROPRIETOR: You know why, don't you? It's since they put school dinners up. A family with two or three kids at school can't afford it now, so they give 'em enough to buy a bag of chips or summat like that instead ...
> CUSTOMER: She'll go down in history as the patron saint of fish-and-chip shops, will that Missus Thatcher.

For *Fun City*, completed a decade later at the beginning of Thatcher's second term of office in 1983, the nature of schooling and the political context have altered. All of Hines's draft versions of the play include the detail that Wordsworth School is an 'inner-city comprehensive', although this specification has been omitted from the published script. Travis is shown to regret the old dispensation of the 11+ examination, with all of its inequalities, when he looks at a cricket team photograph: 'There was none of this nonsense then ... Grand bunch of boys ... Must have been the last year of the Grammar School intake' (70). The play relies on the early 1980s vogue for video games, while the advent of computers in education formed part of a market-driven discourse, as these notes resulting from Hines's research reveal: 'stand on your own two feet/ competitive world/technology rules ok'. The shift from manufacturing to service industries under the Conservative government is the play's backdrop, one which takes on an even greater role in Hines's post-industrial works of the 1990s such as *The Heart of It* and *Elvis Over England*. In *Fun City*, Travis is the mouthpiece of a parodically presented discourse of this kind as he and Kyle put forward different meanings for a particular word:

> TRAVIS: That's where the future lies, technology. The sunrise industries. [*Pause*] The dawning of a golden age of leisure.
> KYLE: My dad's always saying he's a man of leisure since he lost his job. (75)

The battle for meaning conducted over the term 'leisure'[75] is also implicitly present in relation to the adjective 'fun' of the title, particularly as Kyle is drawn to Fun City in order to play *Attack*, a 'video-game about nuclear war' (78) – the very subject of Hines's cautionary atomic-blast drama *Threads* of a year later, on which he was already at work when *Fun City* was completed. Kyle's being drawn to Fun City is not only for the sake of the game of destruction, however, as Mr Shearer argues of the arcade: 'They're home from home for some kids' (79). In *Fun City*, the title's derivation from the name of an amusement arcade is not made clear until over halfway through the play, presenting an irony directed against the (for once wholly) unidentifiable city in which the failing school is located, and against the nature of the game to which Kyle is drawn. Kyle's 'subjugated knowledges' and abilities,[76] uncredited at school, are deployed in this game in which 'you score points every time you destroy one of the enemy's missiles'. In a disturbing parallel with political history, since in November 1983 Britain became the first country to host US cruise missiles, Kyle's ambition is to be listed among the '*All Time Greats*' with the highest scores against the enemy's warheads (78). However, it is not the boy's preference which is the object of satire, but rather the power of militaristic discourse to represent itself even as a leisure-time option.

The play's restricted staging in a headmaster's office offers a stark contrast to the notionally worldwide effects of nuclear war, to which the play alludes. The logic that governs Kyle's being induced to confess to theft is structured like that of nuclear bargaining, since he does so in order to ensure his own survival. Travis himself invokes a Cold War scenario in his argument to Mr Shearer that most members of staff 'wouldn't care if [Kyle] was sent to Siberia' (81), at which Shearer is horrified: 'I gave him my word … He'll never trust me again' (79–80), and he concludes 'There are cheats at all games as far as I can see' (83). Travis's betrayal hints at consequences that will follow in the manner of an equally Cold War-era logic of escalatory tit-for-tat, after the play's end and outside the confines of the headmaster's study. Indeed, Willy Russell wrote to Hines suggesting that, since the putative television drama would offer the benefits of being filmed rather than shot in a studio, the action could be 'opened up' from the headmaster's office to take place 'in the whole school' with its 'myriad locations'.[77] In a carefully drafted response, Hines defended his vision for this one-act, one-location television play on the dramatic grounds that the restrictions of time and space serve to represent its 'claustrophobia'. This increases the audience's sense of the headmaster's 'isolation in "his" school' – it is clear for instance that he is never able to identify any of the pupils with whose cases he has to deal – as well as the sense of 'mounting hysteria' in his behaviour.[78]

In its final form, *Fun City* thus shows a kinship with Samuel Beckett's dramatic preference for similarly confined settings. This is particularly so of Beckett's play *Endgame* (1957), which is located in an 'empty room with two small windows' from which Clov, one of the two central characters, surveys a devastated terrain through a telescope.[79] While the setting of *Endgame* has been interpreted as that of a post-nuclear landscape, and *Fun City* is named for a place where playing at nuclear war constitutes 'amusement', both plays also include solipsistic elements.[80] The critic Hugh Kenner has argued that *Endgame* takes place within the space of an individual's consciousness, perhaps that of the other central character, Hamm.[81] In response to Willy Russell's suggestions, Hines composed a new draft of *Fun City* in which his compromise between restriction and a wider view of the school consists of 'opening up' the first scenes of the play to take place in the corridors, and, as if following Kenner's commentary on *Endgame*, within Kyle's imagination as he sits in Travis's study. The small change to the opening, by means of which the revised play begins with Kyle and Shearer advancing on Travis's room instead of our seeing him letting them in, alters considerably the audience's sense of whose story has priority. Hines's revised draft includes scenes that take place 'in Kyle's thoughts' and therefore adds to our engagement with the boy's viewpoint. Hines's plan was for the audience to gain a 'general picture' of the school's 'corridors, playground, playing fields, gym and hall' in this subjective manner, although the 'external action' would remain in the headmaster's study.[82] For instance, Travis declares of the sound of a dog howling in the corridor, 'It's a circus, that's what it is … I'm nothing but a ringmaster', prompting the dramatisation of Kyle's mental image of the headmaster 'in red tail coat and top hat cracking a whip at a circle of students prancing around him'.

The conceit of the ringmaster was added by Hines to his original version in order to accomplish its 'opening up', following Russell's suggestion. However, the making literal of metaphorical phrases from Travis's dialogue adds more to our sense of what Hines calls the headmaster's 'fascination' with Kyle, when these are ones that were already present. For instance, Travis's insistence to the boy that he does not 'understand what makes you tick' (69) is followed in the experimental draft version by Kyle's auditory image of 'the sound of a clock being wound up. Then silence'. Such a mechanical addition to the soundtrack would have contributed more to the play than the image of the ringmaster, which draws on what is already a personified image. As we have seen in relation to *Speech Day*, the presence of markers of school and industrial time, including clocks and bells, reveals their common purpose, and here the auditory image has multiple referents, to Travis's tightly wound temper as well as his wish to control, or even to wind up, his pupil. However, the representation of Kyle's inner world in such a way constitutes a challenge to what it is feasible to represent on stage and on television, and the published script includes none of these innovations. These draft experiments also exaggerate the play's genre as an absurdist rendering of real concerns, which are expressed in more considered and lengthy form in Hines's other works, including *Speech Day* itself.

Tony Garnett's comment that schools are 'potentially liberators of the soul', but in practice are 'prisons' where young people are 'disciplined for a work routine',[83] encapsulates the basis for Hines's ambivalence about education, as it is dramatised in *Fun City* and the earlier *Speech Day*. Thus in *Speech Day*, the schoolgirl Julie serves tea in the staffroom, prompting Mr Sanderson to foresee a future in which her gendered work continues on seamlessly after she leaves school: 'She'll make a lovely barmaid in a few years time, will Julie. I only hope she finishes up at my local' (95). In the case of Kyle in *Fun City*, Mr Travis tells the boy that his behaviour and hair have jeopardised his prospects: 'It's a buyer's market, I'm afraid, and there's no way I can sell you to an employer with a hairstyle like that' (70). It is a mark of the play's genre and its historical context that Kyle does not bother to retort that in the Thatcherite era to which Travis alludes, there are few jobs to choose from anyway.

Threads (1984)

A year after the release of *Looks and Smiles*, Mick Jackson, a science producer at the BBC, made a short documentary in the 'QED' strand entitled *A Guide to Armageddon*. The 30-minute programme focuses on the projected effects of a nuclear attack on a city, in this case London. In cold, analytical detail, the likely effects of the blast are outlined, using familiar markers of urban experience (parks, housing estates, public buildings) to bring the abstract geopolitical context of the Cold War into the realm of the plausible. Yet Jackson was left frustrated that the potential 'psychological effects' of the attack had not been developed with sufficient impact, believing that a feature-length drama was required in order to combine the human resonance, what he termed 'the here and now of everyday life', with the 'unimaginable' experience of nuclear apocalypse.[84] The BBC supported Jackson in the development of what was to become *Threads*, a horrifying documentary drama about the effects of nuclear war on Sheffield through the focus on two families, before, during and after the attack. The film was broadcast on 23 September 1984.

A Guide to Armageddon provided the documentary template for *Threads*, but Jackson's desire to broaden the scope of his earlier film led him towards the belief that he needed a writer who could help to conceive a 'realistic, socially conscious film', which might help people 'visualise the unthinkable'.[85] With these characteristics in mind, Jackson approached Hines, having admired his collaborations with Ken Loach. The director, who had travelled throughout America consulting a range of nuclear scientists, sociologists, social psychologists and political strategy experts, began the process of 'feeding' Hines 'research'[86] as the pair developed the project's scope to consider the long-term effects of nuclear war. The director and writer's research on civil defence strategy had led them to the conclusion that, in Jackson's words, 'the people who write these plans for coping with a nuclear war have no imagination'.[87]

Hines's experience of the collaboration was undoubtedly difficult. At the time of the film's broadcast, he recalled how: 'I withdrew into myself while writing *Threads* … and that is not my normal working behaviour. *Threads* took a year to write and I have never been involved in anything so mentally and emotionally demanding.'[88] Clearly the project marked a significant departure, at least superficially, from Hines's previous works. While *Threads* broke new thematic ground for Hines, the collaboration itself, since Hines was commissioned to write, marked a significantly different artistic practice to his previous working relationships, such as the free-flowing creative communion of his work with Loach and Garnett. Indeed, Hines's wife, Eleanor Mulvey, has recalled the on-set tensions between director and producer:

Barry spent quite a lot of time on set and, overall, it made Mick furious ... He was used to working with Ken Loach, and he deplored everything Mick did and looked down on it. He even disliked Mick for being middle-class and for wearing white shoes, but of course Mick knew exactly what he was doing, and was ahead of his time. Barry did admit that he was wrong, later, but he used to come off that set swearing![89]

Despite the strained nature of the creative partnership between writer and director, Mulvey does, in the same interview, identify what was perhaps the most successful element of the collaboration: 'Barry was a very politically aware person in every respect, and followed nuclear developments, but he was mainly concerned with class politics, inequality and injustices on a more domestic level. This is why Mick was so brilliant to insist on him writing it.'[90] Indeed, as Jackson intended, the film combines his own approach as a documentary filmmaker and his extensive awareness of the horrifying scientific and social-scientific dimensions of the nuclear threat, with Hines's artistic and political instincts: his ability to combine a structural analysis of human experience in its social context, with an affecting feeling for everyday lives.

In an interview ahead of the broadcast of *Threads*, however, Jackson was quick to assert that the 'concept of *Threads* is totally non-political', making the qualifying point that 'Our aim is to suggest what it might FEEL like for ordinary people to live through a nuclear attack'.[91] It is fair to suggest that Jackson was eager to protect his film against the charge of propaganda, given the contemporary nature of the nuclear debate, yet the use of 'ordinary people', the source of the film's pathos, is significant because rather than acting as a neutral, universalising framework, for Hines, as we have seen, ordinariness is deeply political. In showing the effects of a strategic power-play by a few remote politicians acting at odds with the interests of the majority, and destroying with a single act the deeply imbricated 'threads' of civil society, the film's premise unlocked for Hines a geopolitically existential dimension to his work. As Peter Bradshaw argues, *Threads* is the 'dark masterpiece for both' Jackson and Hines,[92] and the film represented a critical high point for both men. Jackson would go on to direct genre films in the United States, most notably *The Bodyguard* (1992), and *Threads* marked the end of Hines's most productive and artistically successful period, ushering in a fallow five years before the low-key broadcast of *Shooting Stars* (1990). As with so many of Hines's collaborations for the screen, the connection between *Threads* and the writer's screenplays as well as his unfilmed novels has been little explored. Perhaps understandably, critical attention has focused on the film's status as a document of Cold War culture and as an exemplary drama-documentary; our aim here is to augment these points of analysis with a wider consideration of Hines's contribution to *Threads*.

Threads centres on two Sheffield families, the working-class Kemps and the middle-class Becketts, connected by the relationship between Jimmy Kemp (Reece Dinsdale) and Ruth Beckett (Karen Meagher). Much of the early sections of the film concern the two families' response to the news that Karen is pregnant. This domestic drama unfolds alongside a global one, both diegetically (primarily through news reports) and extra-diegetically, through onscreen type and documentary voiceover provided by Paul Vaughan, of the *Horizon* science series. By this means we learn of the escalating conflict in the Middle East. These 'tensions' eventually result in the nuclear attack that constitutes the harrowing second half of the film, as, over a 13-year period, we follow Ruth and then her daughter Jane, through the struggles of the post-apocalyptic world.

The film opens with a voiceover explanation of the title alongside the image of a spider's web:

> In an urban society, everything connects. Each person's needs are fed by the skills of many others. Our lives are woven together in a fabric. But the connections that make society strong, also make it vulnerable.

Paul Vaughan, for Jackson a 'familiar voice of authority',[93] outlines the threads of contemporary society, the networks that underpin and give shape to the audience's experience of everyday life, before the narrative begins with Jimmy and Ruth sitting in a car on the edge of the city, positioned as fictional subjects of the documentary address. The film is therefore concerned with what happens when these threads are irrevocably destroyed, as David Seed argues:

> The opening sequence invites a special reading of every detail in the film as a synecdoche, as part of a system which locks into other systems. For instance, Sheffield is the main centre of steel production in Britain. Among the countless metal products depending on this industry are military hardware (the plane), domestic transportation (the car) and even the electronics of the media. ... A further system

is introduced in the casual conversation between Ruth ... and Jimmy ...: the seasonal cycle of nature. ... The destruction of this balance is imminent.[94]

The structural metaphor at the heart of *Threads* is one that evokes notions of shared reliance and interdependence within a specific and recognisable geographical framework: Sheffield. Sheffield, a city synonymous with the industrial working-class, is not a neutral, anonymous place but a city that in 1984 was beginning to feel the effects of Thatcherite recession. Indeed, the film alludes to this at numerous points both in terms of the plot, since Mr Kemp is a redundant steelworker, and more explicitly when a CND activist's warning that the bomb will destroy industry is met by a heckler: 'Industry? What industry? We ain't got no industry in Sheffield.' (See Figure 7.) The process of disaster in *Threads* might therefore be understood as an acceleration of this social and economic decline under Thatcherism.

Accordingly, much of the drama of *Threads* emerges from the destruction of the social and structural networks outlined in the

7 CND demonstration in Sheffield in *Threads*

opening. We are shown how the bomb tears out both the familiar, tangible 'systems' that govern daily existence and the recognisable structures of humanity that enable ontological and emotional clarity. Indeed, much of the horror of the final moment of *Threads*, a freeze-frame of Jane's face as she gives birth to a child, emerges from the realisation that the implicit acceptance of reproduction as initiating some sense of cyclical hope and progress, alluded to in the opening, is now reversed. This feeling is reinforced by the denial of Jane's point of view, as the viewer sees only the new mother's expression of primal fear and is invited to imagine rather than realise the object of her horror. In this scene, the birth signals the deepening of human misery as another child is faced with the horror of a post-apocalyptic society in which one's ability to work (one of the only words Jane knows) and survive is the overriding feature of human existence. As Sean O'Sullivan suggests, it is not difficult to extract from this bleak, hopeless conclusion an allegorical reading that suggests the film's critique of capitalism:

> We lack the ability to care about the general person and her general child, because all the indices of the human on which narrative drama depends would have been bombed out of existence. … when Margaret Thatcher would say, three years later, that there is no such thing as society, she was unwittingly speaking of this denied reverse-shot, of the society made of no things and only the ghosts of things, of the society of *Threads*.[95]

We will return later to the suggestion that the bomb initiates a destruction of narrative certitude and order, but it is important here to reflect on O'Sullivan's suggestion that the freeze-frame – foregrounding and making conspicuous Jane's horrified reaction but denying the audience's view of her child – crystallizes the tragedy of a ruthless, primitive society which has incontrovertibly destroyed the foundations of empathy and shared understanding while emphasising the impersonal physical effects of the attack on future generations. O'Sullivan's argument positions *Threads* as both an anti-Thatcher and an anti-nuclear war film. As we have intimated, this argument might be better made with a wider sense of Hines's oeuvre, a point suggested by David Rolinson's short piece on the film:

> Anxiety over a future of unemployment, which echoes Hines' earlier Sheffield-set film, *Looks and Smiles* (d. Ken Loach, 1981), is starkly

depicted in post-apocalyptic wastelands which could be read as a metaphor for social collapse in Thatcher's Britain.[96]

In our discussion of *Looks and Smiles* we pointed to the increasingly graphic depiction of 'wasteland' spaces, culminating in the collage of capitalist detritus and apocalyptic imagery that accompanies Mick and Karen's motorway trip from Sheffield to Bristol, and in this sense it is clear that Hines was developing an aesthetic critique of the human costs of free-market economics through the depiction of a displaced working class. A closer examination of the development of *Threads* reveals that these concerns were visible in his early work on the film and might be traced to the broadcast version. Moreover, as suggested earlier, such an analysis reveals the presence of long-standing markers of Hines's authorship that further illuminate the text's political complexities and nuances.

The first draft screenplay of *Threads* is, in plot terms, little removed from the final version. The fundamental difference is one of form, however, with all the strands of the narrative contained diegetically, since there is no voiceover nor typed intertitles. We will return to this point later, but it is important to register that in its first incarnation *Threads* was not a drama-documentary but a conventional television play which contained its Cold War themes within fictional parameters. This naturally places greater emphasis on character development as the dramatic elements are fleshed out to provide a structured narrative framework. As such, in the absence of the disruptive documentary register, so chillingly foregrounded in the later versions, the first draft bears a greater resemblance to Hines's more formally coherent previous works.

For example, Jimmy's aviary and his general interest in birds is a significant aspect of the film: it acts as a cultural signifier of his working-class identity, and his book *The Handbook of Foreign Birds* is retained by Ruth throughout her post-bomb life, serving as a reminder of Jimmy and all that he represented. When Ruth dies, Jane indifferently takes the items from her mother that are of practical use (a brush, a spoon and a scarf) and discards the book. As Sean O'Sullivan argues: 'We know that this book carries a huge and specific mnemonic and psychological value; to Ruth's daughter, it is generally without meaning.'[97] Here, the rejection of the book and the pre-war culture and value-system it represents is vital in communicating ontological rupture as the traces of the pre-apocalypse world fade away. However, in Hines's original script the aviary and the birds are not merely deployed as part of a symbolic system but are integrated elements of the representation of the Kemps' daily lives. For example, after Jimmy tells his parents that Ruth is pregnant he tends to his birds, and is joined by his younger brother Michael, who expresses a desire to inherit the aviary once Jimmy moves out. Jimmy rebuffs his younger brother on the basis that the birds would 'probably be all dead in a week if I left them with you', with an 'outraged' Michael promising that 'dad could help me'. A little later, Jimmy talks to Michael in more detail about the birds:

> JIMMY: See that? That's the first pair of Diamond Sparrows I've bred.
> MICHAEL: (*Pointing to a Gouldian Finch*) I like them best. Them with the purple breasts. (*Pause*) Will you take them with you if you go?
> JIMMY: (*Smiling at him*) I don't know. We'll have to wait and see. (12)

This scene not only offers a fuller insight into the dynamics and daily practices of the Beckett family, but also enables clearer connections to be drawn between *Threads* and Hines's other works. Here Jimmy is foregrounded as a nurturing 'expert' in the same mould as Mick in *Looks and Smiles* with his motorbike or Billy and the kestrel in *A Kestrel for a Knave*. More broadly, this appreciation for the natural realm and its foregrounded placement within an industrial working-class milieu evokes again *Kestrel for a Knave* but also *The Price of Coal*, *The Gamekeeper*, and *First Signs*, all texts which position such practices as sites of contemplation away from organised labour.

Similarly, there is a greater focus on the Beckett family in the first version, which in turn is played out in the terms of Hines's broader analysis of class relations. Mr Kemp's unemployed status as a former steelworker is more conspicuously contrasted with Mr Beckett's role as the manager of the steelworks, and the Becketts' response to Jimmy and Ruth's news also acts as a marker of their class status, as Mrs Beckett comments on their plans to rent a house: 'It's money down the drain paying rent. You're just lining someone else's pockets and nothing to show for it at the end' (16). This emphasis on private property as a marker of class status is tragically echoed after the bomb, when, just before the Becketts are killed by looters (an incident which is rendered in graphic detail in Hines's draft), Mrs Beckett tells her husband, 'the house is wrecked. Our Ruth's gone. A lifetime's work for nothing ...' (68). The Becketts' post-attack anxiety is therefore expressed in terms of the loss of their class status. This conflation of their middle-class lifestyle with a conservative, individualistic ideology is evident in the home too, when in another moment from Hines's first draft, Mrs Beckett and her daughter are discussing Ruth's unborn child's christening, and they see footage of anti-nuclear protests at Greenham Common:

> RUTH: (*Also watching the television*) Just look at that. It's disgraceful.
> MRS BECKETT: I agree. They should be at home doing something useful instead of carrying on like that.
> RUTH: (*Realising that they are at cross-purposes*) I mean the police, not the women. (21)

Later on Ruth describes how 'A few weeks ago I wouldn't have cared either, but now that I'm pregnant I feel different. … It makes you care about the sort of world that your children are going to be brought up in. It makes you angry, and protective, and frightened for their future …' (23). On one hand, the Greenham Common reference is significant because it shows the ways in which Hines initially sought to integrate the context of escalating tensions within the diegesis rather than through explicit documentary devices. On the other, it strengthens the notion that Ruth is positioned as a war survivor and in some way embodies the gendered resistance to the folly of nuclear war. This is symbolised both by the protestors at Greenham Common but also within the diegesis itself through the presence of the CND leader – it is significant that Jackson cuts between the speaker delivering her eloquent, left-wing case for peace, and Ruth's attentive reaction. As Daniel Cordle writes:

> The definitive shift of focus to Ruth is significant. It undermines the expectations we have of the narrative, but it is also representative of the way in which *Threads*, as David Seed points out, 'engages with the issue of gender to construct important functions for its female characters'.[98]

We should note how important this is to the 1980s Cold War context: anti-nuclear protest movements had, perhaps most dramatically at Greenham Common, been invigorated by their links with feminist activists. Anti-nuclear campaigners often presented the arms race as representative of the consequences of patriarchal thinking and institutions. The drama's shift toward female perspectives invokes this context.

Hines's initial plan to integrate the Greenham Common protestors explicitly would have made this theme even more conspicuous.
As Cordle suggests, the 'shift' to Ruth in the second half of the film,
after the bomb has been dropped, is of course significant in this
regard – as a pregnant mother, she is an embodiment of the tragedy
of the post-apocalyptic future. Yet in the early version Ruth's role
is even more advanced, as she provides a narrative focus for the
revelation of the effects of the attack.

Hines originally anticipated a much fuller exploration of the
dramatic shifts in everyday life after the bomb. For example, Ruth
encounters a family of farmers who give her food and drink and,
like that of Ruth's mother, their reaction to the bomb is primarily
framed in terms of economic loss, in a way which subsequently
appears to make the effects of the bomb more minimal: 'God knows
how we'll make a living. It was hard enough before. (*Pause*) Still, at
least we're here, that's something to be grateful for, I suppose' (86).
Ruth goes on to tell them that Sheffield is destroyed, which sets up
a dynamic between the displaced urban refugees and the compara-
tively unaffected rural, middle classes that is much more developed
in the first draft. In the final film this is hinted at though the character of Langley, a pensioner who is forced to take in Ruth and some
of her fellow refugees. Again, however, the theme is far less subtle
in its original form. For example, a landowner catches a group of
Sheffield refugees fishing in his lake:

> Come out, you buggers! Don't you know that this stretch of water
> is private? Can't you read? (*He points to a NO TRESPASSING
> board nailed to a tree.*) The fall-out's killed most of the stock already
> without you taking the bloody rest. ... Didn't you hear what I said?
> This is private water. (91)

Later on, the same man has a conversation with his wife as he spots
more intruders:

> MRS EVINSON: Who are these people, Ralph?
>
> Mr Evinson walks across to the window and looks out.
>
> MR EVINSON: Good lord! We shall have to do something about this. I
>   thought we'd come to some arrangement. (95)

The sense of sweeping annihilation, of a world changed forever that
is so central to the chilling broadcast version, is here far less defined:
there is still a residual sense of civilization or pre-bomb social

structures, as those with money and property attempt to maintain the status quo of class relations.

This class division is also played out in spatial terms. As Michael Mangan argues, one of the most effective elements of *Threads* is its evocation and then destruction of the specific cultural geographies of Sheffield, and more broadly the industrial North: 'The last stages of the film are set in desolate moorlands above and beyond the site that used to be Sheffield. The rubble of urban society is irrelevant in such times.'[99] Yet the city maintains its presence in Hines's original version, or at least its absence operates to define it. When some of Ruth's fellow refugees set up camp in a rural village, the dialogue of two local passers-by is couched in a highly conservative rhetoric, as Hines again uses the attack to magnify the class concerns of his other works:

> 1ST WOMAN: It's getting out of hand, isn't it? I mean, when's it going to stop? They're overrunning the place.
> 2ND WOMAN: I know. I feel ever so sorry for them. It's dreadful. But you've got to look after yourself and your own family first, haven't you? There's going to be no food left for anybody if they keep on pouring in at this rate. (93)

The lack of solidarity in this draft version foreshadows the increasingly individualistic and indeed anti-Thatcherite tenor of the rest of the film. Yet in this scene we can also see connections to the depictions of class struggle in *First Signs*, of ruthless, Darwinian free-market capitalism in *Billy's Last Stand,* and the media stigmatising of dole claimants that frames Mick's eroding self-worth in *Looks and Smiles*. Indeed, it is also worth noting *Looks and Smiles* as a referent for Hines's vision of post-war society because of the earlier text's focus on the military and the police set against the working-class. For example, in the draft version of *Threads*, the role of Clive Sutton (the local authority chief executive) is taken by a different character, Major General Gifford, who is described as the 'Regional Military Commander designate' (37). Gifford is an altogether more sinister figure than the bureaucratic Sutton, and in a pre-bomb scene he comments to his driver when passing the TUC rally: 'Some bloody agitators no doubt. It's a pity we can't run the buggers down' (41). This approach to civil disobedience foreshadows his later role in the post-attack world where he is literally 'Judge, Jury and Executioner', telling the looters who killed the Becketts:

You will be taken from this court and executed by firing squad. And let us hope that your deaths will act as a deterrent to others and show the community at large that law and order will be preserved at all costs in our efforts to rebuild a civilised society. The law of the jungle will not be allowed to prevail. Take them away. (82)

Again, the absence of the non-diegetic devices of voiceover and text, which in the final version summarise the increasingly harsh conditions of post-war South Yorkshire, forces Hines to create more dramatic episodes within the diegesis. For example, a scene reminiscent of the execution described in detail here is, in the film version, conveyed with a simple black and white image and accompanying text. While on one hand the diegetic marks of fictionalisation that underscore the first draft undermine the Cold War themes, on the other, they enable us to discern a much clearer sense of Hines's reading of the social, psychological and emotional effects of the bomb – precisely because these elements are dramatised and thus 'written' by the author rather than mediated through the documentary address.

This is particularly apparent in the much more developed stage directions of the first version, in moments in which Hines seeks to explore the broader societal effects of the attack. In examining these aspects of the screenplay, it is possible to identify a series of consistencies that offer insights into Hines's highly politicised reading of the bomb. In the moments following the blast, we follow separately both Ruth and Mr Kemp as they move through the bombed-out shells of their streets. As Ruth walks past a group of people listening to a radio broadcast, Hines notes that 'the listeners just stand there, lifeless, making no response to the broadcast. Ruth walks on' (68). Later on, Mr Kemp joins a 'gang' attempting to find food, and Hines suggests that '(t)here is an odd, demented quality about the group. No one speaks to anyone else. A man staggers and falls down. He lies still in the road face down. No one stops to attend to him' (70). Soon after this, a hysterical woman is taken away and passers-by are 'neither sympathetic nor unsympathetic, merely neutral in their attitude towards her' (81). As tensions rise between locals and refugees in the scenes mentioned earlier, we are told how the authorities break up an attack on the displaced people, Ruth among them:

The intruders move in amongst the refugees threatening them and telling them to get out. But no one moves. They have experienced too

much to be frightened by these men. Their stubborn, passive resistance disconcerts the intruders. They become less hostile and gradually
withdraw from the hall looking uneasy and sheepish.
  When they have gone, there is no sense of victory amongst the refugees. Nobody comments on the intrusion or looks triumphant. They
just carry on what they were doing before as if nothing has happened.
(96)

These moments are significant because they reveal a sense of the
hopeless, defeated apathy of the post-war condition. The struggle
to exist has eroded any solidarity or community that might have
existed before the attack, as the medical officer in the broadcast
version resignedly tells his colleagues in the bunker: 'it's back to survival of the fittest.' The common characteristic of Hines's description of daily life in these scenes is the absence of emotion and the
pervasive sense of catatonic singularity amongst peripheral characters, as citizens' lives consist of working to live. The volume of these
motifs strengthens the sense that Hines uses the war allegorically to
explore the themes of labour, society and capital that underpin his
other works of the period.

  Moreover, these moments establish the conditions of the final act
of *Threads*, as Ruth dies and the narrative focus transfers to Jane.
We have already mentioned the absence of emotion in Ruth's death
scene: necessity overrides grief for Jane, whose linguistic capabilities
have been severely diminished through lack of education, if not the
physical effects of the bomb, and she is only able to utter the words:
'Ruth, work, work, work, up'. The relationship between daughter
and mother here is one of labour rather than conventional love.
Hines advances the notion that emotion, like language, is environ-
mentally constructed and without adequate structures to support it,
it is replaced by an alien sense of unfeeling. Indeed, in the next scene
we see what appears to have once been a lecture theatre occupied
by a group of children like Jane, who stare blankly at an episode of
'Words and Pictures'. (See Figure 8.) This shell of a classroom, and
the overwhelming atmosphere of passivity, echo in extreme terms
the school scenes in *A Kestrel for a Knave*, as Hines's critical examination of education and its relationship to labour comes into focus.
Indeed, in the next scene we see Jane and others like her working in
this apparently educational space. The symbolism of their occupation is all too apparent, since 'the children are unpicking the seams
of old clothes and unravelling woollens, in preparation for making

8 The post-apocalyptic classroom in *Threads*

them into new garments' (182). As if to make the point explicitly, Hines directs the camera to 'Hold on a big close-up of the unpicking of threads' (182). The pervasive 'threads' imagery from the opening spider's web, and accompanying voiceover, to more subtle examples such as shots of telephone wires and a close-up of Mrs Beckett knitting for her unborn grandchild, have asserted the importance and meaning of the film's title, yet as we now see, the unravelling of threads has not merely resulted in the destruction of the infrastructural mechanisms that enable the proper functioning of society but the diminishing structures of feeling and emotion. The extremes of pain and joy are replaced by robotic functionality. Indeed, in a scene in Hines's first draft, in which Jane is abused in her care home, the stage directions indicate that:

> *Jane is not crying. She just stares ahead, wincing or twitching slightly at a particularly painful stroke. The main impression is not of pain or fear, but of a terrifying lack of feeling in one so young. We close on her face and listen to the sound of the cane.* (113)

This scene is a further example of the way Hines's stage directions offer an insight into his writerly authorship of *Threads*. More specifically, these moments of extended prose (particularly prominent in the first draft) can be read as a partial novelisation of the play, as though his early attempts at the narrative resulted unwittingly in a fragmented literary adaptation of Jackson's scenario. This is perhaps most effectively illustrated in the final moments as he describes Jane's journey to give birth:

> *That night. Jane is walking through town on her way to hospital. She is in pain. She is in a hurry. The baby is due. As she passes houses with lighted windows we glimpse televisions on inside. The streets are almost deserted. One or two people hurry by. They keep their eyes down and do not look at anyone. We see soldiers on a street corner. ... The officer knocks on the door of what appears to be a shop with its windows blacked out. The door opens slightly and someone peeps out, recognises the couple and lets them in. As the door opens wider, we hear music from inside. It is the same song which Jimmy and Ruth were listening to on the car radio in the first scene of the film. ... We hear the sound of a police siren in another part of town. We hear a gunshot, shouts, then silence. Jane passes some prostitutes standing in the street. They look old but they are only girls.* (118)

The short, percussive sentences describing the desolate landscape evoke immediately the similar passages of bleak desperation that accompany the climaxes of both *Kestrel for a Knave* and *Looks and Smiles* – the chilling fragments of post-apocalyptic life here mark the actualisation of the fatalism that underscores those novels as their young protagonists face a future of little hope. The images seem to evoke a sense of pre-explosion life that is wholly absent in the final version, suggesting that Hines came to imagine by stages what an absence of these details of everyday life would look like.

In drawing on the screenplay, and particularly its early development, we are able to understand better the ways in which Hines sought to interpret Jackson's vision of plausible nuclear attack drama in line with his own aesthetic and thematic preoccupations. However, by no means are we seeking to marginalise Jackson's role within the collaboration. Indeed, there can be no question that, as we stated at the outset, the effectiveness of *Threads* comes from its combination of Hines's feeling for everyday life and Jackson's craft as a documentary filmmaker. We have drawn a number of observations from Hines's early screenplay, which, apart from anything else,

imagines a post-war society that maintains a residue of normality
– indeed, there is a sense in which some 'threads' remain in Hines's
original vision for the script. Jackson's extensive scientific research
and consultation undoubtedly resulted in the removal of a number
of these plot lines. Carl Sagan, one of the many script advisers on
the project, praised *Threads*' treatment of the post-war world as
a 'realistic description, still erring on the side of minimizing the
consequences, but it's in the right ball park'.[100] Sagan was critical
of ABC's *The Day After*, an American TV film on the same subject
which had aired the previous year and was significantly more optimistic in its conclusion than *Threads*:

> It's everything that 'The Day After' promised but didn't deliver. I
> recently showed it to a conference of scientists and world religious
> leaders in Bellagio, and believe that it could play a significant role in
> actually doing something about the problem.[101]

The shadow of *The Day After* loomed large for *Threads* in the USA.
Furthermore, the media tycoon Ted Turner, a fierce campaigner for
nuclear disarmament, was forced to fund personally its broadcast
on his cable channel WTBS after advertisers and larger networks
rejected the play, partly as a result of the underperforming earlier
film. In line with Sagan's comments, Turner and his colleagues
sought to market *Threads* as a more authentic and chilling account
of a nuclear holocaust than its American forebears. The futuristic
realism of *Threads*, therefore, has clearly been crucial in defining
it critically as the most effective nuclear war film of its generation.
Hines's bleak vision of the post-attack work and its quotidian
framing clearly contribute to this, but there can be little doubt that
the film's sense of scientific authority is also a defining element.
Indeed, as suggested, while the first draft contains some scientific
allusions to the detail of nuclear war, there is a degree of implau-
sibility to a number of the dramatic scenarios within the narrative.
In the final version, the integration of the non-diegetic devices of
voiceover and text on the screen, punctuates the flow of the dramatic elements with markers of scientific context to assert the documentary 'authority' of the text and simultaneously to authenticate
the fictional world. In essence the development of the documentary
dimension involved the substantial re-contextualisation of Hines's
original screenplay so that it was at the service of the 'factual'
elements – drama is here re-imagined as a tool of documentary.

With this in mind, it is useful to draw again on Daniel Cordle's and Sean O'Sullivan's work on the film, both of whom suggest that Hines's script can be seen as bearing the traces of 'the kitchen sink form', which, for O'Sullivan, results in 'the familiarity of genre'.[102] Thus the recognised framework of working-class realism – Jackson had initially planned to use the cast of *Coronation Street* in *Threads* – is evoked to project a sense of comfort and reliability that is then shattered by the bomb. As Cordle goes on to argue:

> Before this moment of rupture, the world is coherent, and human experience is prone to sense-making by familiar narrative forms. Afterwards, experience can no longer be processed so easily. Part of *Threads*' innovation is to acknowledge how the sort of nuclear conflict threatened during the Cold War cannot be contained in narrative terms and is not susceptible to retrospective processing into a story. For such a conflict would destroy the very societies and cultures which make such narratives meaningful. *Threads* thus deals with the extinction of its own cultural form.[103]

To develop Cordle's point, then, we might suggest that one of the many 'threads' that the film seeks to untangle is that of narrative coherence itself, and that this process of disruption is enacted by the documentary address, which disturbs and fragments the coherence of the diegetic world that Hines constructs. To underline the radicalism of *Threads*, then, it is useful to draw on Colin MacCabe's structural analysis of the narrow parameters of realism in *Screen*, particularly the ways in which he persuasively argues for the inability of conventional cinematic language to effect a critical self-awareness of its own presence. To borrow MacCabe's phrase, rather than denying its 'status as articulation'[104] by constructing a plausible but enclosed diegetic space (such as that which is found in Hines's early screenplay), *Threads* repeatedly foregrounds its own construction and in the process denies viewers' attempts to form a coherent (and closed) site of dramatic engagement within the text. This in turn renders the horrifying concluding segments more significant because they operate dramatically without the usual points of engagement and coherence (we might think again of the denied reverse-shot) – yet simultaneously, the presentation of the dystopia is entirely plausible. It is also important to note here that in both the United States and Britain the film was broadcast as part of a suite of programmes about the prospects of nuclear war: *On the 8th Day*, a documentary which explored the ecological effects of nuclear winter, followed in Britain and America special discussion on the themes arising from both films. This extra-textual substantiating context therefore further reinforces the primacy of the text's documentary address over its fictional status.

In *A Guide to Armageddon* we can trace the origins of this effective clash of registers. Jackson uses still images which act as both markers of everyday life (and thus plausibility) and as documentary material, alongside actors playing 'normal people', in this case testing out a range of nuclear bunkers. These almost mundane episodes are intercut with actors blankly staring at the screen against a white background as the voiceover coldly describes the effects of a nuclear attack on their skin. The rhythmic deployment of differing documentary sources in a fictional setting that we see in *Threads* is glimpsed here in embryonic form. The documentary voiceover at the conclusion raises questions of the post-apocalyptic world for its viewer:

> What would you find? A world you recognised? Or a wasteland for which little in your experience would prepare you? Would the social fabric still be there? When after two weeks you crawl out of your trench or concrete bunker, it could be that your real problems will just be beginning.

In a sense, then, the film poses the questions that *Threads* would go on to answer. More specifically, Hines's dramatic scenario enables the humanisation of these abstract propositions, with Jackson's use of the documentary device ensuring that their chilling resonance is maintained. More broadly, however, and to return to the argument that *Threads* can indeed be read productively within Hines's wider oeuvre, we might suggest that it is not only the graphic depiction of the horrors of nuclear war that ensures the film is still watched by new generations of viewers. At its heart *Threads* is a film about power: its distribution, its abuse and its denial. The film's shocking conclusions generate the realisation of our frailty in the face of the inexorable forces of conflict, climate and, ultimately, capital. Reading *Threads* within Hines's work as a whole suggests that for the writer the film's focus on and critique of capitalist economic and social structures was its overarching concern, and the threat of nuclear war was subsidiary, a topical mechanism for the exploration of underlying and perpetual thematic concerns. Like so many of Hines's works, *Threads* is a film about now as much as it is a film about then.

Notes

1 Ken Loach quoted in Graham Fuller, *Loach on Loach*, London: Faber and Faber 1998, p. 58.
2 Barry Hines quoted in Rosalie Horner, review, *Daily Express* 19 May 1982, BHP/LOO 14
3 BHP/LOO 17.
4 Keith Harper, the *Guardian*, date unknown, 1977, BHP/LOO 18.
5 BHP/LOO 20.
6 Barry Hines, *Looks and Smiles*, London: Michael Joseph 1981. All page references in the text.
7 BHP/LOO 16.
8 John Hill, *Ken Loach: The Politics of Film and Television*, London: BFI 2011, p. 159.
9 Ibid., p. 160.
10 Fuller, *Loach on Loach*, p. 60.
11 Jacob Leigh, *The Cinema of Ken Loach: Art in the Service of the People*, London: Wallflower 2002, p. 130.
12 Ibid., p. 131.
13 Ibid.
14 Bordwell, *Narration in the Fiction Film*, p. 206.
15 Hilary Kingsley, review, *The Daily Mirror* 20 May 1982, BHP/LOO 14.
16 Sean Day-Lewis, review, *The Daily Telegraph* 20 May 1982, BHP/LOO 14.
17 Alan Brien, review, *The Sunday Telegraph* 19 December 1982, BHP/LOO 14.
18 Ibid.
19 Nancy Banks-Smith, review, the *Guardian* 20 May 1982, BHP/LOO 14.
20 Barry Hines, *Looks and Smiles* typescript, final draft, all page references in text, BHP/LOO 7.
21 Leigh, *The Cinema of Ken Loach*, p. 121.
22 Barry Hines, Programme notes for *Kes: The Musical* (Octagon Theatre, Bolton), September 1995, BHP/KES 19.
23 Barry Hines, *Looks and Smiles*: Annotated Production Script, Ken Loach Archive (BFI), KCL/15/1/4i.
24 Fuller, *Loach on Loach*, p. 60.
25 Leigh, *The Cinema of Ken Loach*, p. 131.
26 The location is in fact the now defunct Castle Square, a network of underpasses known locally as 'The Hole in the Road'.
27 Ibid.
28 Barry Hines, *Looks and Smiles* rejected scenes, BHP/LOO 14, p. 126.

29 Hines, BHP/LOO 14, p. 146.
30 Ibid., p. 151.
31 Ibid., p. 129.
32 Derek Malcolm, review, the *Guardian* 16 December 1982, BHP/LOO 14.
33 John Kirk, 'Figuring the Landscape: Writing the Topographies of Community and Place', *Literature and History* 15 (1) pp. 1–17: 7.
34 Kirk, 'Figuring the Landscape', p. 8.
35 Luke Spencer, 'British Working-Class Fiction: The Sense of Loss and the Potential for Transformation', *Socialist Register* 24 1988, pp. 366–86: 381.
36 Kirk, 'Figuring the Landscape', p. 8.
37 Schweitzer's renown as a campaigner against the atom bomb might underlie Hines's choice of name for the university tower, in this novel published the year before the broadcast of *Threads*: see James Brabazon, *Albert Schweitzer: A Biography*, Syracuse, NY: Syracuse University Press 2000 [1975], pp. 443–63.
38 BHP/UNF 5.
39 BHP/PRC 6.
40 Barry Hines, *Unfinished Business*, Harmondsworth: Penguin 1985 [1983], p. 71. All further page references in the text.
41 Hines made notes for a sub-plot on this topic, in which a series of x-rays reveals 'faulty work' at Phil's factory. The welder responsible 'blames bad material, poor wire, not enough time in which to do work', BHP/UNF 5.
42 See for instance Michèle Barrett on the possibility of tracing what she sees as capitalism's enlistment of a pre-existing patriarchal gender division, in her *Women's Oppression Today: Problems in Marxist-Feminist Analysis*, London: Verso 1980.
43 Patricia Craig, review, *Times Literary Supplement*, anonymous review, *Yorkshire Post*, both BHP/UNF 6; Hanna Behrend, 'Second Thoughts on an Unfinished Business', *Literarische Diskurse und historischer Prozess* 88, 1988, pp. 151–8: 151.
44 Fay Weldon, review, *Image* magazine; Netta Martin, review, *Annabel*, BHP/UNF 6.
45 See the hardback version of novel, published by Michael Joseph in 1983.
46 John Melmoth, 'Educating Lucy', *Times Literary Supplement*, BHP/UNF 6.
47 Gloria Steinem, the *Guardian* 17 October 2015.
48 As a *Guardian* quiz revealed in 2015, current 'mixed gender sports' are eventing, korfball and ice dancing (31 October 2015, *Weekend* p. 109).
49 See for instance Patricia Connolley's review article of several classic

books published in the early 1980s, 'On Marxism and Feminism', *Studies in Political Economy* 12, 1983, pp. 153–61.

50 Melmoth, 'Educating Lucy'.

51 Judith Butler, 'Imitation and Gender Insubordination', in Linda Nicholson, ed., *The Second Wave: A Reader in Feminist Theory*, London and New York: Routledge 1997, pp. 300–16: 308.

52 Craig, review.

53 Robert Nye, review, *Guardian*, BHP/UNF 6.

54 Behrend, 'Second Thoughts', p. 153.

55 Ibid., p. 158.

56 After the visit to Dave's family home, despite the fact that a flood of revelations takes place – Lucy discerns his mother's snobbery, intuits that his father has a threatening influence over Phil's engineering company, learns that her lover spent time with his estranged wife at Christmas and suspects that her role in his life as a 'married woman … *and* from a lower social class' is just 'another provocation' to his parents – we learn that she 'hardly spoke on the way home' and none of these matters is mentioned again (187–90).

57 Melmoth, 'Educating Lucy'.

58 'Women and the Capitalist Family: The Ties that Bind', *Proletarian Revolution* 34, 1989.

59 Carol Barron, review, *New Socialist*, BHP/UNF 6; Behrend, 'Second Thoughts', p. 153. Hines's research materials show that Barron was recommended to him as a former Sheffield Hallam mature student close in age to his fictional character, from whom he could learn the details of such an experience.

60 Among Hines's research materials are his notes on a University of Sheffield Politics Department seminar on this topic in 1980, in which students were encouraged not only to 'discuss distinctions between negative and positive freedoms' but also, as if issuing an instruction also to the novelist, to 'relate these themes to today's problems', BHP/UNF 5.

61 See Hayward's account of this incident as one of the 'hilarities' of the bosses' efforts at cleaning up, which is watched with 'humorous scepticism' by the workers, *Which Side Are You On?*, p. 141. It is missing from Hines's novel, where its equivalent is the description of Harry's cold and solitary working conditions at the pit conveyor belt, where he keeps a 'Girl of the Month' calendar 'turned permanently to August, because [he] liked the photograph of the girl walking out of the sea the best' (*The Price of Coal*, p. 75). Here, as in Harry's earlier longing thoughts of Raquel Welch, women 'symbolize a better kind of life' (21), as the vehicles in their objectified form of a hopeless male aspiration with which the reader is meant to sympathise.

62 Luce Irigaray, 'The Blind Spot of an Old Dream of Symmetry', in *Speculum of the Other Woman*, trans. Gillian C. Gill, Ithaca, NY: Cornell University Press 1985 [1974].

63 Barry Hines, *Two Men from Derby*, 'Centre Play', broadcast 21 February 1976; broadcast on BBC Radio Four, 23 October 1976.

64 See for instance John Hill, 'Barry Hines', BFI Screenonline, http://www.screenonline.org.uk/people/id/467744/index.html; *Act Two*, p. 6.

65 Peter Shepherd, Introduction, to Barry Hines, *Two Men from Derby* and *Shooting Stars*, Oxford: Heinemann 1993, p. vii; see also Towson, *Prompt Two*, p. 6.

66 Barron, review.

67 See Christine Delphy, *Close to Home: A Materialist Analysis of Women's Oppression*, Amherst, MA: University of Massachusetts Press 1984.

68 We will continue to refer only to 'Freda' for the sake of clarity.

69 Ian Sainsbury, review, *Morning Telegraph*, BHPUNF 6.

70 Radio play script, BHP/TWO 5. The radio play concludes slightly differently from the version in *Unfinished Business*, avoiding an expletive in favour of dialect: '"Well, this is not going to buy the baby a bonnet, standing here doing nowt". *She takes some clothes out of a tub and starts to mangle them. We hear the squeezed water running back into the tub. Fade down on the sound of the mangle turning.* (quietly) "What a life".'

71 Willy Russell, personal communication, 9 December 2015. The five directors of Quintet were Willy Russell, Jack Rosenthal, Jack Gold, Mike Ockrent and Kiffer Weislberg, while the other commissions for this putative series included plays by Jim Cartwright and Al Hunter-Ashton, as well as the poet Kit Wright, suggesting that Hines's work was viewed as part of a wider Northern tradition. Peter Terson, ed., *New Plays 2: Contemporary One-Act Plays*, Oxford: Oxford University Press 1988. All quotations are from this edition, page references in the text.

72 The apparently extreme decision to change the detail of the draft, in which Travis reports Kyle to his probation officer rather than the police, increases a sense of the play's hyperrealist mode. See BHP/FUN 3.

73 Hines's notes for reply to Russell, BHP/FUN 2.

74 Ibid.

75 See also Carol Ann Duffy's poem 'Education for Leisure', published in *Standing Female Nude* (London: Anvil 1985), a much darker exploration of Thatcher-era unemployment by means of this contested term.

76 Michel Foucault, *Power/Knowledge: Selected Interviews*, trans. Colin

Gordon et al., New York: Pantheon 1980, p. 82. Foucault claims that the bearers of such knowledges include 'the psychiatric patient, the ill person, the nurse and the delinquent', the latter designation encapsulating Travis's view of Kyle.

77 Letter from Willy Russell, 29 Feb 1984, BHP/FUN 2.

78 Hines's notes for reply to Russell.

79 Beckett's statement appears in the programme for JoAnne Akalaitis's 1984 production at the American Repertory Theater in Cambridge, Massachusetts, to which he objected for not following his stage directions (quoted in Jonathan Kalb, *Beckett in Performance*, Cambridge: Cambridge University Press 1989, p. 79).

80 Akalaitis's version of *Endgame* was staged at the height of Cold War fears of nuclear disaster in 1984, and took place in a subway station serving as a nuclear shelter in the aftermath of a war.

81 Hugh Kenner, *Samuel Beckett: A Critical Study*, Berkeley and Los Angeles: University of California Press 1968, pp. 159–60.

82 Hines's notes for reply to Russell.

83 Tony Garnett, interview with the authors, 9 October 2015.

84 Mick Jackson quoted in 'Threads at 30', BBC Radio Sheffield, broadcast on 23 September 2014, https://soundcloud.com/marky burrows/threads-at-30-a-bbc-radio-sheffield-special date accessed 30 September 2016.

85 Anonymous, 'End of the World Revisited: BBC's Threads is 25 years old', the *Scotsman*, http://www.scotsman.com/lifestyle/end-of-the-world-revisited-bbc-s-threads-is-25-years-old-1-773083   date accessed 12 November 2016.

86 Jackson, 'Threads at 30'.

87 Mick Jackson quoted in 'Visual History with Mick Jackson, Interviewed by: Robert Markowitz', Directors Guild of America, http://www.dga.org/Craft/VisualHistory/Interviews/Mick-Jackson. aspx?Filter=Full+Interview date accessed 12 November 2016.

88 Anonymous, 'A flash and Sheffield was no more', *The Star* 22 September 1984, BHP/THR 6.

89 Anonymous, the *Scotsman*.

90 Ibid.

91 Anonymous, BHP/THR 6.

92 Peter Bradshaw, '*Threads*: The film that frightened me the most', the *Guardian* (online) 20 October 2014, http://www.theguardian.com/film/filmblog/2014/oct/20/threads-the-film-that-frightened-me-most-halloween date accessed 20 October 2016.

93 Jackson, 'Threads at 30'.

94 David Seed, 'TV docudrama and the nuclear subject: *The War Game*, *The Day After* and *Threads*', in John R. Cook and Peter Wright, eds,

British Science Fiction Television: A Hitchhiker's Guide, London: IB Tauris 2006, pp. 163–4.

95 Sean O'Sullivan, 'No Such Thing as Society: Television and the Apocalypse', in Lester D. Friedman, ed., *Fires Were Started: British Cinema and Thatcherism*, London: Wallflower Press 2006, p. 240.

96 David Rolinson, 'Threads', http://www.screenonline.org.uk/tv/id/730560/ date accessed 23 October 2015.

97 O'Sullivan, 'No Such Thing as Society', p. 239.

98 Daniel Cordle, '"That's Going to Happen to Us. It Is": *Threads* and the Imagination of Nuclear Disaster on 1980s Television', *Journal of British Cinema and Television*, 10:1 2013, pp. 71–92: 88.

99 Michael Mangan ed., *Threads and Other Sheffield Plays*, Sheffield: Sheffield Academic Press 1990, p. 15.

100 Carl Sagan quoted in Steve Schneider, 'Cable TV Notes', *New York Times* 13 January 1985, BHP/THR 4.

101 Carl Sagan letter to Philip Daly, 4 December 1984, BHP/THR 4.

102 Cordle, 'That's Going to Happen to Us. It Is', p. 83; O'Sullivan, 'No Such Thing as Society', p. 235.

103 Corldle, 'That's Going to Happen to Us. It Is', p. 85.

104 Colin MacCabe, 'Realism and the Cinema: Notes on some Brechtian Theses', *Screen* 15:2 1974, pp. 7–27: 9.

4

Imagining post-industrial Britain

The Heart of It, the miners' strike plays, *Looking at the Sun*,
Shooting Stars, *Born Kicking*, *Elvis Over England*

As becomes clear over the course of this chapter, the exceptionally
divisive events of the miners' strike of 1984–85 had an acute effect
on Hines's writing, just as they did on the terrain and communities
of the South Yorkshire that he invariably depicts. The events proved
so resistant to Hines's efforts to represent them that none of the
three plays he wrote in the wake of the strike was ever produced.
His radio drama *Looking at the Sun* (1992), and novel *The Heart
of It* (1994), as the two instances of Hines's writing on the strike
which did appear in the public realm, portray the events from a pro-
foundly retrospective standpoint. Those elements of Hines's earlier
work, including his exploration of the role of a young man whose
abilities are never officially acknowledged, appear in the context
of post-industrial British life in Hines's television drama *Shooting
Stars* (1990), while his last novel, *Elvis Over England* (1998), marks
the efforts of its protagonist Eddie to escape the realities of redundancy by undertaking a musically inspired pilgrimage. Just as they
did in the early 1980s in *Unfinished Business*, the possibilities of
gender equality seem to offer Hines something of a way out of the
political impasse of the decade's later years: in his television play
Born Kicking of 1992, it is a young woman who has to contend
with the conflicting demands of intellectual and footballing success.

Writing the strike

Given Hines's political sensibilities, his family and geographical
background and the emphasis on coal-mining throughout his work,
it is surprising that it was not until 1994 that his published work
addressed the pivotal 1984–85 miners' strike. As we will show, his
novel *The Heart of It*[1] constitutes the culmination of a decade-long

struggle to represent the strike and the seismic political, economic and social changes that it brought upon Hines's class and his community. *Threads*, arguably the critical highpoint of Hines's career, was broadcast some six months into the strike and just three months on from the infamous 'Battle of Orgreave', which saw violent clashes between police and striking miners at the Orgreave coking plant, just a few miles from Hines's home. As we have already argued, the political flavour of Hines's post-apocalyptic vision of an irrevocably divided society can undoubtedly be read as reflecting an increasing anxiety with Thatcherite deindustrialization, and the effects on working-class communities. Yet, further attempts in the decade to build on the political and social critique of Thatcherism in the contemporary context of the strike and its immediate legacy would come to nothing. *The Heart of It* is Hines's only published miners' strike work, and therefore offers a valuable insight into the struggles of representing the experience of working-class communities in the late twentieth century.

Published in 1994, *The Heart of It* centres on Cal Rickards, a forty-something Hollywood screenwriter who returns to the Yorkshire mining village of his childhood to visit his mother, Maisie, and his father, Harry, a former miner, staunch communist and veteran of the 1984–85 strike who has since experienced a debilitating stroke. Initially, Cal shows little in the way of affection for the town or his family. He is preoccupied by the demands of his latest screenplay – a film about a mad scientist who turns a boy into a dog – and longs for the pleasures of his life in the South of France. His father, rendered largely mute as a result of his illness, manages only a few words to his son on his arrival: 'W-w-when-are-you-going-to-write-something-that matters?' (6), making explicit early on that Cal has sacrificed the politics of his background and upbringing in favour of what John Kirk – borrowing from Adorno and Horkheimer – terms 'the culture industry',[2] with its inherent vacuity and conservatism. Yet, as the novel unfolds, Cal learns more about the strike and Harry's and Maisie's involvement in the struggle, as he rekindles friendships with his former school friends, reads his father's diaries, and establishes a new-found openness with his mother. The novel also incorporates a lengthy flashback sequence in which Maisie recalls her doomed wartime affair with an Italian prisoner of war. The *Heart of It* then moves from Cal's distanced, outsider's gaze to an almost documentary reportage of strike stories alongside a deeper examination of his family's heritage and that of his community, until by the conclusion a newly politicised Cal resolves to write a novel about the strike.

Cal's reconnection with the community of his childhood sees *The Heart of It* as another of Hines's 'returning native' narratives, to use again Ian Haywood's useful phrase,[3] although Hines has updated the trope for the post-industrial age. Unlike *First Signs* and wider examples of post-war working-class writing, Cal's return is not that of the enlightened grammar school and university graduate to a traditional working-class community, as he instead finds a deeply fragmented and divided town haunted by the legacies of the strike. As Wally Hammond notes, the novel bears comparisons with one of the more thoughtful 'returning native' narratives of the 1960s, Albert Finney's *Charlie Bubbles* (1967), for its 'pained, rueful and melancholic' journey through 'deliberately engineered wastelands'.[4] In this sense what Cal finds is an actualised version of the decay gloomily anticipated in *Looks and Smiles* and the hyper-capitalist dystopia of *Threads*, with Cal's dislocated, outsider's perspective drawing into focus the sense of a community in ruins:

> They turned off the main road and drove around the council estate: street after street of shabby houses, some bricked up, some burnt out. An abandoned car. A police car. A gang of youths running away. A toddler in a vest paddling in a pothole. A pack of dogs snarling round the car when Cal slowed down to avoid a plundered cigarette machine lying in the road. (262)

Both the apocalyptic imagery and fragmented, list-like tone of the passage, complete with grammatical inconsistencies, bear striking similarities with the description of Mick's and Karen's impressionistically rendered journey through England as *Looks and Smiles* reaches its conclusion, while the similarities with Ruth's immediate experience of post-attack Sheffield in *Threads* are likewise conspicuous. To some extent, then, the novel represents the realisation of Hines's increasingly pessimistic analysis of class relations and the barbarism of the free market in Thatcher's Britain. In this sense, *The Heart of It* continues to reflect on the absence of meaningful, fulfilling labour in working-class communities – a concern throughout Hines's oeuvre but amplified in works such as *Looks and Smiles*.

For example, Cal's increasing interest in the strike and realisation of its legacy comes about partly through his reconnection with childhood friends, all of whom are ex-miners. Just as Mick's aspirations towards a steady career are sunk by the realisation of a likely future of low-paid, unskilled work in the service sector, in the wake of the closure of their pit, Cal's friends, we learn, have experienced a similar recognition of the precarious conditions of the post-industrial labour market. Firstly, Tommy recalls his varied casual employment after redundancy: 'I did all sorts after that. Pea-picking down in Lincolnshire. God, what a job that was. A van picked you up about four in the morning. Then when you got there, there was no guarantee that there'd be any work. Then if they set you on you'd be working in the pissing rain all day. And the wages!' (67) Interestingly, this is an almost verbatim anticipation of the experience of the redundant steelworker Eddie in *Elvis over England* who similarly singles out agricultural labour as the worst job he has undertaken. Another friend of Cal's, Charlie, juggles work as both a waiter and as a bouncer, and finally Jack, a local supermarket worker, relays his memories of the strike in a way that sees his 'face flushed' and 'fists clenched' (111). These vignettes of post-strike life reveal both the deep fragmentation of working-class labour and community and the turbulent psychological effects of the conflict.

The novel is therefore populated by characters who act as emblems of the traumatic and indelible marks of the strike. This can be seen most clearly in Harry, Cal's father. Harry, who named Cal after Marx (Cal reverts to Karl at the novel's conclusion), is revealed through his diaries and Cal's and others' memories of his father as a passionate and articulate union firebrand who was jailed during the strike. Harry is therefore linked directly to Hines's other mining fathers, Sam Renshaw (*First Signs*) and Sid Storey (*The Price of Coal*). Sam is positioned as the political and moral guide to his 'returning native' son Tom, whose intellectual equal he is, and he is heroised throughout the narrative for his leadership in the industrial action at his pit.

Meanwhile, Sid Storey, like Harry and Sam, is a deeply political anti-establishment figure: he is a vocal and articulate critic of the colliery management's surrender to protocol and class deference in the face of a royal visit in the first instalment of *The Price of Coal*, and, in the second, which records the fatal disaster at the same colliery just a few weeks later, Sid's political analysis is shown to be tragically prophetic. While both *First Signs* and *The Price of Coal* acknowledge uncertain prospects for the miners and their communities, Sam's and Sid's resilience, defiance and moral certitude in both texts identifies a clear source of hope for the future of organised labour and the working class more broadly. Almost twenty years later, however, the miner-father in *The Heart of It* is barely able to speak and is incontinent, functioning as an embodiment of the contemporary socioeconomic reality with which the novel presents us. Where Sid and Sam had offered self-confidence and optimism, Harry symbolises defeat and lost hope. In one of the novel's most moving scenes Cal is forced to wash his infantilised father, realising as he does so a new-found emotional and political consciousness:

> He returned from the kitchen with a bowl of warm water, then knelt down beside his father and washed him all over. He had forgotten about the mosaic of blue mining scars and seared shrapnel wounds covering his body. What a brave life he had led: five years fighting in the war followed by a lifetime of danger down the pit: the Enemy Within. Cal was proud to wash his feet. (94)

Here the elderly, failing body is presented as tangibly bearing the marks of the pit, which in turn are positioned as the scars of defeat for his community and his class – the allusion to the war underlining the totemic and injurious nature of the political struggle. Harry's naked vulnerability also points to a recurring theme in Hines's later works and of similar late twentieth-century representations of working-class communities: that of masculinity in crisis. Certainly, Cal's friends can be seen as equally bereft of a hitherto distinctly gendered labour identity, and Harry's own fragile body seems to consolidate the apparent erosion of an at least 'traditional' working-class masculinity. Yet, in keeping with Hines's characteristic ambivalence, the sense of an overarching post-industrial fragmentation is partially challenged by the ways in which *The Heart of It* privileges narratives of female empowerment as emerging from the strike. Hines foregrounds Maisie's prominent role during the strike in addressing meetings at home and abroad and raising funds, as a component of Cal's enhanced understanding of his parents' activism. As Cal leafs through her lecture notes he reflects on, 'His own mother turned teacher. He would have been so proud to have listened to her' (92). Christine, Cal's brother's ex-wife with whom Cal has a brief affair, develops the argument about the strike's effects:

It wasn't a total disaster, though, and a lot of people came out of it a lot stronger than when they went in. Especially the women. I mean, look at your mother. She was always a lovely woman, but totally dominated by your dad. She wasn't after the strike ended, though. They came out on equal terms. (80)

Inspired by Maisie, Christine goes on to describe how, through her own involvement in the strike, she 'became independent. I started to think for myself' (82). As John Kirk argues:

> ... a female working-class voice emerges strongly in this novel, finally eclipsing any sense of male dominance that some regard as the characteristic social arrangement in such communities.[5]

Kirk is right to suggest that the prominence afforded to female narratives as well as those of the emasculated, working-class men in *The Heart of It* is one of its distinctive and progressive features. It is not surprising then that Hines was invited to adapt the novel for Ken Loach, more specifically the aspect involving Maisie's doomed wartime affair and her experience of campaigning during the strike. Hines's archive reveals that as late as spring 2003 he had been offered a contract by Loach's *Sixteen Films* to develop this element of *The Heart of It*, renamed *Follow the Sun*, for the screen. The film would have reunited Loach and Hines well over twenty years after their last collaboration for *Looks and Smiles*. Yet it was not to be: correspondence in the archive reveals that, only a few months after undertaking the project, Hines pulled out saying that 'the idea had gone stale', 'there were too many drafts' and he'd 'spent too long on it'[6] – indeed, it was now almost twenty years since the strike and ten years since the publication of the novel.

Hines's difficulty in bringing the novel to the screen is reflected within the narrative itself, as Cal struggles to focus on his work as a screenwriter while uncovering the stories and legacies of the strike. In order to render this process, much of the novel is interspersed with fragments of Cal's latest screenplay, contrasting the Hollywood escapism of his professional life with the gradual re-awakening of his class-consciousness, as Cal oscillates between his fiction writing and listening to tapes, conducting interviews and reading diaries about the strike. In early sections of the novel, Cal's evident distance from the strike is illustrated by his tendency to render cinematically (in his imagination) the strike narratives of his family and former acquaintances. For example, when Christine, his brother's ex-wife, relays a story from Orgreave, Cal fails to engage with it directly and instead imagines 'a brilliant opening to a film', as he goes on to conceive:

> ... a close up of Joe lying on his back in a field with a skylark singing somewhere overhead. It looks idyllic, as if he raises his arms to block out the sun so that he can see the bird. Then the camera pulls back to reveal a field full of miners sitting and standing around in groups, talking, laughing, some eating sandwiches. The atmosphere is relaxed. In the background the police lines are forming up to keep the road clear for the coke lorries leaving the plant. There are thousands of them, reinforced by mounted police and dog handlers ... What a scene! It was like the build-up to the Battle of Agincourt in *Henry V*. (49)

A few pages later, Cal begins re-narrating an anecdote of his father's from the strike, relaying his memories of a 'scab'. Rather than focusing on the significance of Harry's actions, he is drawn to the superficial cinematic details of dialogue and accent:

> And to think that the union fought to get a sod – (no, cunt. His father would have said cunt). And to think that the union fought to get a cunt like that his job back.

> Cal switched it off, then played it back. His accent sounded stagey, like a southern actor playing a northerner. He believed the dialogue, though. (53)

Cal's playful and diversionary reanimation of the strike within his own memory is eventually superseded by a genuine desire to follow his father's advice and 'write something that matters', as he moves from Hollywood screenwriter to aspiring working-class writer. As John Kirk puts it:

> ... a powerful subtext emerges in the narrative highlighting the contradiction between representation and reality, whether in relation to the strike (its media construction, as opposed to people's actual experiences) or the film projects Cal is involved with.[7]

Kirk's suggestion that the novel itself acknowledges the struggles to represent the strike is worth developing. Indeed, Hines's decision to portray Cal as a screenwriter was perhaps more than a plot device to emphasise his initial distance from the class and community from which he is exiled, and might also point to Hines's own, decade-long struggle to dramatize the events of the strike, as he told Alfred Hickling ahead of the novel's publication:

I desperately wanted to write about the 1984–5 miners' strike. It was like a last stand the way communities pulled together in defeat. I attempted a couple of television scripts – both of which failed. It was because I was coming at the subject like a bull at a gate. My sympathies were too obvious, I need to adopt a more sceptical approach.[8]

As we suggest, Cal's sense of distance and initial cynicism enables Hines's desired 'sceptical' approach – yet what is perhaps most significant is that Hines refers to two failed previous miners' strike projects.

After the Strike and The Diggers

The scripts in question, *After the Strike*[9] and *The Diggers*[10] (both held in Hines's archive), might indeed be regarded as more politically explicit than *The Heart of It*, particularly when it is considered that both were conceived for television, with *After the Strike* written in the immediate wake of the strike. Moreover, both unproduced plays contain a number of elements which are integrated into *The Heart of It*, providing further evidence of the novel as a text which draws together Hines's previous attempts to narrate the strike, and of the fact that the novel is itself a reflection on the process of representing authentically and ethically its tumultuous effects.

For example, one of the most arresting scenes in *After the Strike* is a brutal re-enactment of the 'Battle of Orgreave' in which Hines dramatises the disproportionate police force and unprovoked violence against the miners. In the build-up to the scene Hines's stage directions describe the protagonists in their environment:

> Although it is still early, it is warm and the sun is rising in a clear sky. The pickets are dressed mainly in T-shirts, jeans and trainers. Eddie and Bonk are sitting down. Pete is lying on his back enjoying the sun on his face. He listens to a skylark singing over the fields and shields his eyes as he tries to see it. (24)

The scene echoes clearly the one mentioned earlier which Cal imagines as Christine describes Orgreave in *The Heart of It*. The connection is furthered when it is considered that Pete from *After the Strike* is remarkably similar to Joe, Christine's ex-husband (and Cal's brother) in *The Heart of It* – following their arrest at Orgreave the conditions of both characters' bail mean that they are forced to leave their homes, and Hines has them moving to Scarborough where they begin affairs and eventually leave their wives. To confirm the parallel, Pete's wife, like Joe's, is called Christine. Thus in Hines's published miners' strike novel, *The Heart of It*, he depicts as problematic an imagined televisual or cinematic adaptation of the 'Battle of Orgreave', yet the adaptation is presented in almost exactly the same terms in his own unproduced miners' strike play conceived almost ten years before. The distance from the strike and the struggle to tell its stories in *The Heart of It* is therefore not only Cal's, it is Hines's too.

After the Strike is, however, a valuable example not only of Hines's wider, unproduced and unpublished work – that tells us much about his concerns and development as a writer – but it stands as a rare contemporary representation of the strike from an insider's perspective. The play is focused primarily on the experiences of Eddie and Joyce Wragg and those of their family and friends during and in the year following the miners' strike – it therefore deals with the central events of the strike in South Yorkshire, such as the Battle of Orgreave (as told in flashback) and with its immediate legacy, describing the weakening of the trade union movement and an increasingly divided community.

In *After the Strike*'s flashback scenes, Eddie is a striking miner and his wife, much like Maisie in *The Heart of It*, becomes a prominent activist, travelling to Germany to campaign on behalf of the movement. As the play begins, in the present (late 1985), Eddie is campaigning against his sacking for militancy during the strike, 'standing outside the pit gates with a collecting bucket and a placard which reads: SUPPORT SACKED MINERS' (1), before Hines moves to a scene involving Eddie's wife, Joyce:

> Joyce Wragg, Eddie's wife is attending an 'A' level Sociology class. On the board we see a main heading STRATIFICATION, with sub-headings, a) Social Mobility, b) Class Inequalities. The lecturer is sitting at his/her desk dictating notes to a group of students of widely differing ages. (1)

We then return to Eddie, who is 'folding up the ironing board' before opening a 'thick scrapbook' entitled 'THE MINERS' STRIKE 1984–85'; the book is shown to contain 'photographs', 'cuttings' and 'regular diary entries on the progress of the strike' (1). Eddie begins to read one of the entries and in the process triggers a flashback to the strike. These opening scenes therefore establish a number of thematic concerns which are later developed in *The Heart of It*. Most obviously, *After the Strike* presents us immediately with contrasting images of post-industrial gender roles. Jobless Eddie outside the pit and then undertaking a domestic task is bereft of agency, while his wife is positioned in an academic context, building on her experience of the strike to develop her interest in the politics of social justice. The period 'after the strike' is one of progress for Joyce and regression for Eddie, with the flashback device embedding within the narrative structure a retrospective, nostalgic gaze. For the male characters the strike is therefore elegiacally historicised, while for female characters like Joyce – and by extension Maisie in *The Heart of It* – it functions as a platform towards political activity and the imagination of a possible future. The gendered power shift is identified explicitly as having its origins in the strike, when Joyce and Eddie argue towards the end of the play:

> EDDIE: … it's gone to your head since you went to Germany. Dashing about. Organising this and organising that. God knows what you'll do when it's all over.
>
> JOYCE: Well, I'll tell you what I'm not going to do. I'm not going to be at your beck and call for a start. I'm not going back to the kitchen sink and running the hoover up and down all day.
>
> EDDIE: What are you going to do then, join Women's Lib? Go and live at Greenham?
>
> JOYCE: I might do. And I'll not ask you either if I do. I've had my eyes opened during this strike and neither you or anybody else is going to shut them again. (84)

Hines again aligns an erosion of male working-class agency with empowerment for the female characters whose existence had been previously firmly rooted in the home. The reference to Greenham Common is also noteworthy, particularly given our previous discussion of *Threads*, and furthers the sense in which Hines's portraits of Thatcherite decay position women as offering a resistance and resilience that is absent in their male counterparts.

After the Strike might also be seen to connect to *Threads* and, indeed, *Looks and Smiles* for its pointed representation of an authoritarian, unaccountable state, shown here through graphic images of police violence. For example, when Eddie is photographed and then beaten after being arrested, his protests to the police that their actions are 'illegal' are met with a sinister response:

'Nothing's illegal in here' (54). Similarly, the depiction of the Battle of Orgreave is unflinching, deploying a militaristic discourse to describe the tactics of the police, the like of which has since been deployed in representations of the strike such as *Our Friends in the North* (1995) and David Peace's 2004 novel *GB84*, but would undoubtedly have shocked audiences had the play been broadcast in 1986, as intended. Before the clash the police sergeant ominously tells his men: 'Get ready, pick your targets ... Pick your targets ...' (25), and Hines then goes on to describe how the 'front line of pickets are battered by shields and truncheons and kicked as they push against the police' (25).

While such an account of Orgreave would now, thirty years since the strike, appear accurate, there can be no question that at the time such cultural representations of contentious recent history would be deemed 'unfilmable'.[11] Indeed, ahead of the publication of *The Heart of It*, Hines reflected further on his unfilmed plays:

> I desperately wanted to write about the strike. Before I wrote television scripts for the BBC but they did not work. They were just documentaries, where everyone knows the end. ... If it had been a script it would have been someone more involved in the strike, an NUM militant. This way, it gives people the chance to tell their own stories rather than it becoming a polemic.[12]

Hines was therefore mindful of the potential for his realist, televisual attempts to narrate the strike to veer towards didacticism. The novel form, with its dispersal of voices and the detachment of its protagonist, resists the possibility of appearing as 'documentary' reportage, although *After the Strike,* even in its unproduced state, is a remarkable portrayal of the effects of the strike on working-class communities and undoubtedly gives voice to a sense of collective anger. Indeed, despite the representation of Eddie as disempowered, Hines finishes with a tone of hope: Eddie's friend, Bonk, informs him that he and his fellow miners have voted to go on strike until Eddie is reinstated at the pit, and the final scenes show Eddie's defiance. Eddie delivers a speech at a benefit event where he attacks Norman Willis, the General Secretary of the TUC, and Neil Kinnock, leader of the Labour Party during the strike (from whom Hines had in the previous year received a letter of praise for *Threads*), aligning their perceived treachery with that of the scabs who had returned to work:

But miners have got long memories. We know about the betrayals of
1926 even though we weren't there. We know who scabbed then and
who betrayed us, like our children and grandchildren will know who
scabbed and betrayed us during this strike. They won't be forgotten
and they won't be forgiven. Are you listening Willis? Are you listening Kinnock? I hope you are, because you've got a lot to answer for.
(*applause.*) And finally, don't get despondent. Keep your heads up.
Management will try all kinds of tricks to break your spirit now
that they think they've got the whip hand. But don't let them get you
down. The fight goes on. You'll remember this dispute for the rest of
your lives and you'll be proud to have taken part in it. But learn the
lessons from it, and don't think this is the end of the story because
it's not. It's only the end of a chapter. There's a lot more to be written
yet. (86–7)

After the Strike is therefore a deeply oppositional text which leaves
the reader in no doubt of its political sympathies. *The Diggers*,
another unproduced play, written some nine years later, is no less
clear in its position on the strike. However, it does reflect Hines's
desire to move away from a direct, documentary-style restaging
of events, with the focus on a rock band made up of two striking miners, Scott and Joe, and two middle-class teenagers from
Sheffield, Matthew, a university student, and Alice who is studying
A-levels at a suburban grammar school. Again, Hines uses a flashback structure to return to the events of 1984–85 from the lens
of the present day. In this case, Matthew has become a rock star
and is playing a concert in Sheffield, thus triggering memories of
the band and the strike. In Hines's synopsis he seems conscious of
the need to underplay the script's political dimension: 'The story is
treated obliquely and didacticism and dour political rhetoric will
be avoided at all costs.'[13] Instead, crucially, Hines emphasised that
the music 'is the narrative, set against the backdrop of the miners'
strike'.[14] This illustrates the extent to which Hines was keen to
guard against charges of substituting polemic for literariness.

However, despite the play's overt emphasis on the eponymous
band, *The Diggers* draws heavily on *After the Strike* for its themes
and narrative content, and bears similarities with many of Hines's
other politically focused works. For example, on a surface level,
it borrows many details from the earlier play: it is set at the same
fictional 'Foxmoor Colliery'; the representation of an Orgreave-
like clash with the police is portrayed in vivid terms as in *After the*

Strike; Scott's father is revealed as a 'scab', which generates tensions in the family and community, just as similar betrayals are emphasised in *After the Strike*; Scott is killed while 'coal picking' in an incident which mirrors the one in which Eddie and Joyce's son is injured; and Hines uses the same name, 'Tolson', for a police character in both plays. As in *The Heart of It*, Hines also uses the perspective of outsiders to inject, as he called it, a 'sceptical' point of view of events, which might work to counterbalance or at least to work through objections to his own sympathies. This is most obviously found in Matthew's, and, to a lesser extent, Alice's, interactions with their band mates about the strike:

> JOE: … People are going skint, going without food, going into debt to fight for their jobs. If they break the strike and the pit closes down, what do you think we're going to do?
> ALICE: Can't you find a job somewhere else?
> JOE: (*driven beyond endurance*) Where, you stupid cow!!?
> ALICE: Don't you call me a cow!
> JOE: You're supposed to be educated and you know fuck all.
> MATTHEW: You're exaggerating. All this stuff about the police. Where do you think it is, Russia?
> SCOTT: You know fuck all about it. (21)

This exchange also connects *The Diggers* back to Hines's wider thematic interest in the tensions between formal education and localised wisdom and experience found throughout his work. In this case, Joe's political philosophy, shaped by experience of his working-class community and the strike in which he is involved, comes into conflict with the naïve perspectives of his middle-class, educated band mates, albeit with a lack of feminist awareness. The exchange is also significant in further marking Matthew's remoteness from the strike – while he is a student in Sheffield, the city that housed the NUM's headquarters, he views the strike as though it is an abstract conflict taking place in a foreign country, a trope developed when Matthew meets the record executive, Ronnie Gee:

> MATTHEW: Have you heard about Scott?
> GEE: Yeah. I read about it in the paper. Tragic … I can't believe what's going on up there. It's like a fucking war zone.
> *He pauses. He can see Matthew is upset.*
> GEE: You're not a miner are you?
> MATTHEW: No …

GEE: I didn't think you were. You sound like you're from down here
somewhere ... Foreign country up there. More like fucking Russia.
(49)

Thus, Matthew's status as outsider is here foregrounded geographically, as well as socially and politically, as Hines redeploys the codes
of North and South which underpinned Tom's experience of class
difference in *First Signs*. Matthew subsequently adopts the role of
a cold and detached observer of the post-industrial North in the
present-time narrative as his chauffeur-driven car returns to familiar
sites from his time with The Diggers. Matthew points out Orgreave,
'where they had the big battle with the police' (38), but the stage
directions tell us that his companion, Ronnie Gee, 'couldn't care
less about Orgreave' (38). It is therefore from Matthew's perspective that the post-industrial conditions of South Yorkshire 'after
the strike' are witnessed by the viewer, just as Cal observes the
'wastelands' in *The Heart of It*. Hines's stage directions describe
how 'Matthew is being driven through the industrial area of the city.
Many of the factories have been demolished. Others stand empty
with FOR SALE signs outside' (52), while later his journey takes
him towards the coal fields:

> *Matthew's limo drives slowly down the lane towards the colliery.*
> *It stops at the gates and* MATTHEW *gets out and surveys the scene.*
> *The colliery is closed, the pit yard silent, the buildings derelict, the*
> *winding gear still.*
> *The remains of the pickets' cabin is still standing at the side of the*
> *lane, with faded slogans visible on the walls. An eerie scene.* (53)

These sections take place after we have witnessed numerous strike
scenes in flashback: scenes that convey the violence and poverty of
the conflict, but also its moments of humour and camaraderie. To
revisit the now ghostly ruins of the same places in the film's present
tense, with the dislocated individual Matthew – complete with his
limousine and all that it represents – as our guide, doubly emphasises
the collective tragedy of the events of the previous decade. Thus *The
Diggers* is significant for its attempts to critique the sense of an outsider's perspective on the strike, and can be seen as further evidence
of Hines's self-conscious attempts to work through the problematic
questions of representation and realism in his strike narratives.

Matthew's extraction of capital from the tragedy of the strike is
given coherence when he persuades Alice to play a gig in the wake

of Scott's death. In the audience is Ronnie Gee, who subsequently signs Matthew as a solo artist:

ALICE: Go on! With Scott dead and Joe in hospital? You're out of your mind.

ALICE *makes for the door.* MATTHEW *grabs her and pulls her round.*

MATTHEW: It's a chance to tell people what's really happening. That people are dying in this strike.

ALICE *still does not look convinced. She shakes her head.*

ALICE: It's an insult ...

MATTHEW: It's not an insult. It's a tribute. I think we should do it. (45)

ALICE *is convinced to take part and* MATTHEW *addresses the audience:*

MATTHEW ... People are being killed out there! Families starved into submission. Communities destroyed by a Government determined to defeat the miners even if they have to kill them to do it!
    ... And remember. The miners united will never be defeated! (*wild cheers and applause from the audience*) O.K. This one's for you Scott ... (45–6)

Matthew's appropriation of the strike's motto, his sensationalised reporting of the events around Scott's death and his cynical conversion to a hard-line anti-government position are all directed towards an attempt to seize the emotion of the collective struggle for his own ends. Alice and Matthew's bittersweet performance is a triumph as Matthew signs his record deal as a result, and in this sense Hines anticipates the way in which performance, as a discourse of individualism, operates in contrast to images of collective working-class defeat in post-industrial fiction. While films like *Billy Elliot* (Stephen Daldry, 2000) and, to a lesser extent, *The Full Monty* (Peter Cattaneo, 1997) and *Brassed Off* (Mark Herman, 1996) evoke industrial struggle as an emotive backdrop for individual success, Hines's use of flashback and his privileging of Scott and Joe's positions as young, striking miners in contrast to their economically comfortable and socially remote friends, furthers his project of emphasising the lingering, corrosive effect of the strike on working-class communities and works to resist superficial narratives of recovery.

Slate

In *The Diggers* Hines experiments with genre as a means of enabling a more multi-dimensional perspective on the themes of the strike. Another unproduced television play, *Slate*,[15] written around 1987, is similarly inventive in its attempts to bring into focus the fundamental political and social significance of the conflict. *Slate* is a period piece which attempts to tell the true story of the so-called 'Great Strike of Penrhyn', which took place at the Penrhyn Slate Quarry between 1900 and 1903. The screenplay represents a span of several years, charting the formation of the first trade union for the quarrymen, general elections, riots at the quarry as well as a broadening out of the narrative to incorporate scenes in parliament in which the strike is debated. Such is Hines's commitment to detail that the exchanges between the prime minister Herbert Asquith and Gerald Balfour, at the time president of the Board of Trade, are drawn from Hansard.

However, despite the commitment to a historically accurate representation, the retelling of this significant struggle of British working-class history, just two years after the miners' strike, underlines its allegorical potential. Indeed, Hines treats a violent uprising at the quarry in a similar fashion to representations of Orgreave in his other miners' strike works, to the extent where one character, Samson, is forced to leave Bethesda, and his partner Sioned, after he is banished from the quarry following the events of the strike. Samson's forced geographical displacement (to Liverpool, in this case) mirrors that of the Joe/Pete character in *The Heart of It* and *After the Strike*.

Further parallels are found in the representation of picket-line treachery and 'scabbing', as one of the central characters, Edward, returns to work, much to the horror of his brother, Robert, and father, Morgan, who claims: 'You'll be a traitor for the rest of your life' (80). The film ends as Robert murders his brother – an uncharacteristically sensationalist conclusion and illustrative of the enhanced dramatic possibilities of allegory. These harrowing portraits of familial disunity are similarly explored in *The Diggers* when Scott's father makes the decision to return to work.

While *Slate* shares the plot details of Hines's other miners' strike narratives, it also returns to the fundamental, underlying questions of class, power and labour present in *After the Strike*, *The Diggers* and *The Heart of It.* For example, in the final moments of the play, a philosophical Morgan attempts to console his angry son, Robert:

> ROBERT: Once the traitors went back and accepted their twenty pieces of silver, it was like a sword in our side and we couldn't staunch the wound.
>
> MORGAN: At least you went back together, with pride and dignity. That's the main thing. And don't forget that your original demands for a decent living wage, the right of combination and the other grievances remain just as valid now as when you went out on strike. (*pause*) Penrhyn didn't beat you by argument or reason, he won by sheer economic power, that's all. He could afford to hold out longer. It's as simple as that. (*Pause. Morgan looks out over the hills.*) My father would never have believed it. The very idea of a union would have been unthinkable in his day. We've made tremendous strides Robert, let's not forget that. You've set an example to the working people of Britain, and I'm proud of you. (132)

Hines here uses the historical perspective on the quarry strike of 1900 to unlock and illuminate the structural forces that underpin the miners' strike of 1984–85. He draws on a sense of hope found in collective struggle from the previous strike, as Morgan rousingly speaks to the present from the past, while moving beyond the surface detail of contemporary representation of class struggle to reveal its underlying perpetuity. It is sobering, however, that Hines has to go back so far in time to derive any positive message from the very formation of unions.

Looking at the Sun (1992)

During the period between the strike and the publication of *The Heart of It*, one of Hines's mining-related projects did appear in the public realm. *Looking at the Sun*[16] was a radio play, broadcast on BBC Radio 4 in 1992, one which follows the fortunes of an ex-miner, Stewart, and his wife Lisa, as they move away from Yorkshire so that Stewart can take up a job in a nuclear power station. However, Lisa becomes friendly with an elderly neighbour, Mr Ellis, who was forced to retire as a result of what he believed to be a radiation-related illness. As Lisa learns more from Mr Ellis about the apparent dangers of nuclear power, she becomes convinced that the radiation from the power station will harm Stewart, their daughter Alison, and their unborn child, who at one point in the play Lisa attempts to abort. The play ends with Lisa leaving Stewart.

Like *Slate*, *Looking at the Sun* is not directly about the miners' strike, but its presence is felt throughout. For example, the opening scene suggests that Stewart and Lisa's move is one of economic necessity and not choice, shown here in Stewart's conversation with a colleague:

> DAVIE: I could never leave Yorkshire. My home. My family. My friends. Everything I've got is here. I could never give all that up.
> STEWART: I can't see as you'll have much choice. You've got to follow the work these days. Industrial gypsies. That's what we are.
> DAVIE: I know, but going over to the nuclear industry though. It's like a Rangers player going over to Celtic.
> STEWART: I'm glad to get a job in any industry, I can tell you. Ours won't be the last pit to close. The coal industry's dead as far as I can see. Hey! Come on! Drink up. This is supposed to be a celebration, not a wake. (1)

This exchange develops the theme of geographical displacement, of individuals being uprooted from their homes and communities in response to the demands of the market, as represented in the texts already discussed, as well as in *Looks and Smiles* and, in allegorical terms, in *Threads*. The nuclear power industry is therefore depicted as an unsatisfactory replacement for the coal industry in both sociological and later scientific terms, as Lisa, much to her husband's annoyance, listens to a speech by an anti-nuclear campaigner, Melanie Lee:

> It seems to me that the nuclear industry is holding us to a kind of industrial blackmail. No nuclear power. No jobs. As if there were no alternatives. Of course there are. Nuclear power stations only produce twenty percent of our electricity. We don't need it. We've got coal reserves to last hundreds of years. We've got oil and gas, and we've got the longest coastline in Europe to develop wind, tidal and wave power. If we had an energy policy based on coal, conservation and renewables, it would be safer. It would create new jobs. And it would ensure jobs for the affected by the phasing out of nuclear power.[17]

This is the most didactic point of the play and implicitly makes the point that the programme of pit closures is a political rather than scientific or economic strategy. Lee articulates Hines's ideological sympathies in precisely the same way as the CND campaigner in *Threads* does, connecting abstract ecological and political concepts to tangible questions of class and social justice. Moreover, the gendered aspect of anti-capitalist resistance is again present here, building further continuity from *Threads* as well as connecting to the representations of enhanced political agency for women in *After the Strike* and *The Heart of It*.

Taken together, these texts constitute an interdependent ecology of miners' strike narratives. That only two appeared in the public realm emphasizes both the controversy of the subject and the feeling, evidenced through the multiple parallels that exist between these works, that Hines's view of the strike was both holistic and ever evolving and, as we have argued, that the struggle became a representational one. *After the Strike* is a play of anger and immediacy; *Slate*, an attempt to use the veracity of historical record to illuminate the contentiousness of the contemporary moment; *The Diggers* tries to sweeten the pill of the struggle; *Looking at the Sun* recalls the recent industrial past, shows us the unsatisfactory nature of the present and points to an uncertain future; with *The Heart of It* marking a summative point to this cycle of responses to the events of 1984–85, and is a text which, tellingly, points to the impossibility of writing the strike.

Shooting Stars (1990)

In this section, we discuss two of Hines's plays, *Shooting Stars* (1990) and *Born Kicking* (1992), which centre on football and its representation in relation to class, economics and gender. Although the form of a football match might appear to offer a ready-made dramatic structure,[18] neither of the plays takes a conventional form in this respect, and matches are only made visible in the form of fragmentary moments. The structural principle of ambivalence that we have traced in other examples of Hines's work also appears here. Both of the plays are torn between registering football's self-expressive qualities on the part of the players and its significance for working-class spectators, alongside an awareness of the fact that the game not only fails to offers a solution to the hardships of ordinary people's lives but distracts them from trying to find one. Thus both plays continue the dramatised debate that runs throughout Hines's writing life about the social role of football and footballers.

Shooting Stars centres on Vic (John Brobbey) and Gary (Chris Hargreaves), friends who have been driven to theft by their impoverished status, accompanied by Gary's younger brother Sean (Frank Lauder), a youthful natural at confidence trickery. When a prank goes wrong, the three end up holding to ransom the local football celebrity, Calvin Clark (Gary McDonald), whose initial antagonism towards his kidnappers turns into a grudging sympathy and respect so that, when he is eventually freed, Calvin does not reveal the names of his captors to the police. Hines completed the screenplay based on Dixie Williams's original idea, after that writer's death in 1989. The filmed version failed to find a theatrical release, 'bewilderingly' so, in the phrase of an enthusiastic reviewer,[19] and was first broadcast on Channel Four on 17 May 1990. It was directed by Chris Bernard, whose earlier films include *Letter to Brezhnev* (1985), and, following the pattern established with *Speech Day* and *Fun City*, Hines's script has been published in a volume with *Two Men from Derby* as a pair of plays 'adapted for schools'.[20] In the case of *Shooting Stars*, this adaptation entailed age-appropriate cuts such as removing obscenities from the characters' dialogue, thus reducing the menace apparent in the film, and cutting out many of its sexual references, an omission which lessens the sense of rivalry, crucial to the plot, between Gary and Calvin. In apparent continuation of such a reduction, the blurb describes the kidnappers as 'children', which itself elides the play's carefully constructed contrast between its one genuinely youthful character, the pre-teen Sean, and his late-teenage brother Gary.

Hines planned *Shooting Stars* to be set in Sheffield, as shown by its reference to Radio Hallam, altered in the television play to Radio City.[21] In the televised version, filmed in Manchester, the northern urban setting is bleak yet generalised and is never named. The opening sequence consists of a montage of shots of mounted police at a football match, fans congregating while a notice offering 'DHSS estimates' is visible in the background, and the as-yet unidentified hands of the protagonists are shown in close-up as they try to break into parked cars. The characters' accents support this impression of a non-specific, underprivileged Northernness. While the footballer Calvin Clark has clearly come from London to play for City, Gary and Sean are Mancunian, their friend Vic Liverpudlian. The least sympathetic characters, the football club director Bob Southgate (Keith Allen) and the stolen-goods fence Mr Groves (Stratford

Johns), speak in the tones of received pronunciation. *Shooting Stars* retains signs of its layered authorship, and some elements refer back to the earlier work of the original writer and to the play's director. Dixie Williams wrote one other television drama, *Vampires*, a 1979 *Play for Today* about two young brothers, Stu (Peter Moran) and Davey (Paul Moran), who imagine they see in their everyday life in Liverpool vampires like those in the Hammer Horror film *Dracula: Prince of Darkness* (1966), starring Christopher Lee, which they have watched on late-night television. The real horrors in the brothers' lives are more mundane, including their mother's efforts to bring them up on her own after their father's death, and her encounter with a violent boyfriend.

In *Shooting Stars*, the relation of the everyday to imagination is reversed, and reality itself assumes a fantastic aspect. As in the director Chris Bernard's *Letter to Brezhnev*, in which an unexpected love affair between a local woman and a Soviet sailor takes place against the backdrop of Thatcher-era Liverpool, in the televised version of *Shooting Stars* realist cinematic techniques are used in the service of a plot that relies upon exaggeration. The same familial situation as in Dixie Williams's *Vampires* is evident here: Paula Gibson (Sharon Duce) is a single mother to Gary and Sean, and is forced into uncongenial work to support her family. In *Vampires* Stu wears joke-shop fangs to scare his younger brother Davey, while in *Shooting Stars* the stakes are higher, since it is the real criminality in which Gary engages that the younger Sean participates in without fully understanding. Albeit by accident rather than design, Gary leads his brother and friend Vic into the kidnapping of Calvin Clark.

Like Hines's novels *The Heart of It* of 1994 and *Elvis Over England* of 1998, the setting of *Shooting Stars* is that of a post-industrial Britain. This time the context is that of the early 1990s, during the recession whose long-term effects are also evident in the later novels. The settings of *Shooting Stars* are notable for the contrasts they offer between poverty and privilege, an opposition that also structures the plot.[22] For instance, while much of the action takes place in a block of derelict council flats, filmed in Manchester's Brunswick estate, the visiting manager of Hamburg football club stays in a luxury hotel; the local nightclub is called Millionaires, but outside it young men try to rob the parked cars.[23] Gary leads Vic and Sean in a series of scams and thefts to supplement what he describes as his paltry wage of £27.50 per week (67), while by contrast the football star Calvin, who is from a similarly deprived background, drives a Porsche, wears designer clothes and is the subject of a £3 million transfer deal. Although Gary is represented as a threateningly self-contained young man who directs the group's operations, the plot turns on the consequences of his soft spot for a local girl, Alison Connor (Jane Hazlegrove). The lengths to which this unreciprocated fondness lead him are necessary for the plot's extremity, but also support the impression of his pathology. Indeed, as a review argues, Gary's role as both 'psychologically stunted *and* socio-economically deprived' is crucial to the plot's structure.[24]

Alison wins a radio quiz for which the prize is an evening with the local football team's 'top scorer', Calvin Clark, before he is transferred to play for Hamburg. Gary's jealousy leads him to follow Alison and Calvin on their night out, resulting in a spur-of-the-moment decision to kidnap the footballer and demand a large ransom from his club. The action that was motivated by Gary's sexual jealousy turns into one about a more general rivalry between the two men. Indeed, the notion of the ransom is a 'McGuffin', a device without narrative purpose or outcome, although its logic of trying to cash in a footballer for his monetary value is not dissimilar to that of the financial manoeuvres undertaken by the City director Bob Southgate. The kidnap itself is the pretext for men from different walks in life being forced to interact with each other over the course of eight days in a confined space. This play ostensibly about the football star system is, rather, one about the 'enterprise culture' of the era, a term used by the fence Mr Groves,[25] and a class structure based not only on heredity but on wealth.

Elements familiar from Hines's other works appear in *Shooting Stars*, including questions about the value of football in the context of its commercialisation, and a concern for unrecognised and 'subjugated' kinds of knowledge. In the world of the play, no one seems to notice that Sean is not at school, and education itself is shown to be subject to market forces as summed up in a material way. Gary takes his stolen goods to the fence Mr Groves, played by Stratford Johns in a pointedly different role from that of *Z Cars*' Detective Inspector Charlie Barlow, for which he became famous. Groves turns down the offer of blank video cassettes and asks instead for school uniforms, to Gary's mystification:

GARY: What?

GROVES: Riverdale and Bloomfield particularly.

GARY: Never heard of them.

Groves smirks.

GROVES: No, I don't suppose you have, Gary. They're private schools.

(38)

While education is for sale here in a socially sanctioned sense, the uniforms are to be sold as stolen goods. This apparent distinction collapses in the play's reconsideration of the notion of 'theft': Gary steals goods in order to sell them, but something has been stolen from him too, as Mr Groves's 'smirk' suggests. In each case, what would now be called the forces of neoliberalism hold sway, as Mr Groves satirically puts it: 'in today's enterprise culture one must respond to the fluctuating demands of the market place' (39).

Shooting Stars represents a different world from that of the self-contained white working-class communities of Hines's plays from the 1970s, including *Speech Day* and *The Price of Coal*. By contrast, *Shooting Stars* acknowledges the multicultural nature of late twentieth-century Britain, set within its political context of IRA campaigns, to which the kidnap is initially ascribed, and the end of the Cold War. The cast list describes both Calvin and Vic as, in the discourse of the era, 'West Indian', and in the film they are played by, respectively, Gary McDonald, known for his *EastEnders* character Darren Roberts, as well as the role of 'Ethnic' in the television play *London's Burning* (1986), and John Brobbey, who followed his work in *Shooting Stars* with roles in crime dramas of the 1990s.[26]

The plot of *Shooting Stars* works towards revealing that apparently widely divergent social positions are based on arbitrary distinctions, and that their moral values are the opposite of what they might seem. This pattern follows the logic of Mikhail Bakhtin's notion of carnival with its temporary reversals, which he describes as being enacted in annual festivals or, in the modern period, in literary works.[27] Even in the plot of Hines's play, such reversals are both temporary and largely invisible to the world at large. The play's title itself conveys this mixed meaning, with its connotations of both football prowess and flashes of brilliance that exist only fleetingly. The crossing of paths on the part of those in high and low social positions that such reversal relies upon takes place at the play's opening. An initial change of scene takes us from Gary, Vic and Sean robbing a car in the 'wasteland' around the City Football Stadium, in which they find a gun in the glove compartment, to a group of women on their way to a match. Not only does this imply a link between these different actions and groups of people but it also represents a gender reversal. The acknowledgement in *Shooting Stars* of football's interest for women, who are 'keen supporters and never miss a home game' (31), is a new one in Hines's oeuvre which reaches its logical conclusion in *Born Kicking* two years later, where the football star herself is female.

In the present play, the encounter that follows between Sean and the City director Bob Southgate implies an unexpectedly shared interest in money-making. Sean offers to 'look after' Southgate's car, which we take to mean that he won't try to rob it, and he is rewarded with 'a pound coin' for his 'cheek' (32). This exchange is followed by a scene that confirms the unexpected similarity between Southgate and Sean in relation to their respective quests for money. We hear only the former's side of a telephone conversation, in which it is clear that the football club owners are concerned about its financial situation, not to mention its inability to win any games:

> SOUTHGATE: Tell them it's a routine enquiry and there's nothing to worry about ... Okay, Clive? Just keep calm. The last thing we want to do is panic our shareholders ... We're losing three-one. (34)

This linking of financial with football prowess, by means of which the 'score' goes down in symmetry with the club's bank balance, is one with a long history in Hines's work. The function of such a link is both symbolic and analytical. It reveals hubristic bad faith on the part of directors like Southgate, Vickers in *Tom Kite* and Victor Grace in *Born Kicking*, for engaging in the transformation of football from 'being a weekly antidote to the ills of capitalism' into 'the very embodiment of this competitive system', and these characters' narrative downfall registers this.[28] Hines's unease about football becoming big business prompted comic critique as early as 1967 in his radio play *Continental Size Six*, where a United fan claims of Mr Clegg, the manager of the rival City team, that 'You've only got to wave a cheque at that Cleggy and he'll sell anybody. He'd sell his grandmother if she had one leg and could head a ball.'[29] Thirty years on in *Shooting Stars*, the extent of a manager's viewing players as tokens of exchange is revealed by Bob Southgate, not just by his agreeing to Calvin's transfer to Hamburg to solve a 'serious cash-flow problem' (42), a decision made without consulting the player, but because he sees Calvin's life itself in monetary terms. When the arrangements to make the ransom payment go awry and Karl Gutke (Helmut Griem), the Hamburg manager, is worried that Calvin's life might be at risk, Southgate responds, 'Well, if it comes to the worst, at least we're insured' (92). Gutke's reaction, a look of 'disgust', repeats the gesture of viscerally registered morality on the part of Mr Shearer at his boss Mr Travis's similarly treating his pupil as an object in *Fun City*.

The play's introduction of racial difference into a plot about working-class masculinity at first assumes the form of a staged conflict, although later a real quarrel occurs on these grounds. Initially it is an element of a confidence trick on the part of Gary and his friends, which takes in the reader or viewer as well as the audience within the play, since it is not clear at first whether the argument is genuine. Vic encounters Sean as if by chance in an electrical goods shop, where they watch the football results on a television and argue about Calvin Clark, who has scored for City although his team lost the match:

> VIC: Brilliant, that Clark.
> SEAN: You what? He's rubbish … I've seen better players on a Subbuteo pitch.
> VIC: Why don't you shut your mouth?
> SEAN: Make me. (36)

The scene's ambiguity is emphasised in a draft stage direction: 'During this scene there is no indication that Vic and Sean are in collusion. Their argument and fight should appear genuine.'[30] Under cover of the scuffle that follows, Gary, who has entered the shop 'in the background', steals a video camera and leaves unnoticed. The mock altercation seems to depend for its convincing nature on the boys' respective ethnicities, since Vic praises Calvin while Sean, otherwise unaccountably, insults him.[31] Their differences in other respects, in terms of their age and size, make the argument, as the stage direction has it, 'absurd'. The performance seems to be orchestrated by the eerily unostentatious Gary, whose role and even his name resemble that of the playwright himself.[32] The reader's inability to detect Gary's intentions is emphasized on another occasion when he pretends to hold up Alison with a concealed weapon in the

'Asian video shop' where she works, as the stage direction emphasises: 'We cannot tell if he is holding the gun or not' (44). In the
televised version, this ambiguity is absent, and the fact that the stick-
up is clearly recognized as a joke by Alison and the viewer lessens
the risk of Gary appearing unsympathetic. Yet it is the plot device,
if not the psychology, of Gary's feelings for Alison which often has a
different effect, that of turning jokes into real affronts. Vic identifies
himself with Calvin when he and Gary speculate on whether Calvin
and Alison will be attracted to each other on their blind date:

> VIC: She'll fancy him. All the birds do. He can have any bird he wants.
> GARY: Yeah, 'cos he's famous, that's all. They wouldn't want to know
> if he wasn't famous.
> VIC: Do you think she'd fancy me if I was famous?
> GARY: You! You haven't got a chance! (53)

The role of racial difference as a marker of status is unspoken but
implicit here, adding to Gary's conviction that fame is all that dis-
tinguishes Calvin, otherwise women 'wouldn't want to know'. It
equally underlies his extreme disdain for Vic's putting himself, as
another black man, in Calvin's place: without the latter's fame, as
Gary puts it, 'You haven't got a chance!' This riposte is a late substitution made by Hines for the screenplay's original, 'She wouldn't
fancy you if you were fucking Prince!', one that would have made
the racialised nature of Gary's envy more overt.

The implicit elements of the dialogue as it appears in both published script and film are made overt later in *Shooting Stars* when
Calvin is held hostage. After his collection of the ransom payment
goes wrong, Gary turns 'viciously' on Calvin, accusing him of thinking his three captors are 'no-hopers' (to use the published script's
decorous substitute for the screenplay's 'shites'):

> CALVIN: You said it.
> GARY: Well, we're not, see! And you can have all the suits, and all the
> cars and all the money in the world, but you're still a black bastard!
> VIC: Hey! Watch it, man!
> *Gary rounds on Vic.*
> GARY: What's the matter with you? You on his side or something?
> (89)

Gary's racist outburst expresses sexual jealousy, made to sound
here like a revulsion at miscegenation. Calvin has already pointed

out the irreducibility of racism, against Vic's insistence that 'It's rich and poor that counts, not black and white', anticipating Gary's phrasing but from the opposite perspective: 'When a guy on the other team calls you a black bastard … all the money in the world don't protect you!' (77). Gary's challenge to Vic in the quotation above, 'You on his side or something?', uses the vocabulary of football 'sides' in order to refer to other kinds of division. He disavows the racial difference he has just invoked in claiming to have suggested, rather, that Vic, as a kidnapper, has unaccountably developed a loyalty to the hostage. Gary's effort to appease Vic in these terms takes the form of the 'token minority best friend defence': 'I'm not talking to you! You're different. You're one of us'.[33] This moment makes it hard to feel positively about Gary's football skills as revealed in the informal game that follows, or Calvin's exonerating, if 'sarcastic', remark, 'Not bad for a white kid' (90).

The denouement of *Shooting Stars* seems to support Gary's insistence that only fame sets Calvin apart from the young men who kidnap him, since the definition of a celebrity as 'a person who is known for his well-knownness' might aptly apply to this footballer whose prowess is never fully represented.[34] Gary gives an 'equally impressive' display of football skills to that shown by Calvin during their 'kick-about', unlikely as this may seem, when the comparison is with a first-division professional described by the Hamburg manager as 'the man that I want' (34). Hines's drafts reveal that the writer was determined to present Gary's subjugated skills in one form or another, and details about his propensity for kick-boxing and breakdancing were replaced with the final version's showing him to resemble Calvin in football prowess. Despite his present status, Calvin has a background similar to that of his captors. Vic's 'job in a restaurant' turns out to be one of a series of unskilled roles, since all he does is 'wip[e] tables in a paper hat', to which Calvin responds defensively, 'Hey, I wasn't brought up in Buckingham Palace, you know. I lived in a flat like this. I worked in a sausage factory when I left school' (76).[35] Yet it is Gary who is sufficiently cosmopolitan and adaptable to be able to count in German and use chopsticks, rather than Calvin, who can do neither. Calvin himself acknowledges their equality, by overlooking the criminality of Gary's behaviour in letting him escape from the police and then failing to point him out in an identity parade.

As a reviewer argues, the focus on the similarity between Calvin and his kidnappers risks the play seeming to 'shoot at the wrong target', since those who benefit from inequality, Southgate and even Gutke as 'the people who manipulate footballers', assume secondary roles in the plot.[36] The only narrative superiority granted to Calvin takes place in the play's final lines as he leaves City football ground for the last time. Gary and the others are nowhere to be seen, but Alison asks for Calvin's autograph 'for a friend'. He adds his address in Hamburg to the signature, 'just in case she wants to write to me' (105). The screenplay's stage direction, absent from the published script, makes this meaning plain: 'There is a suggestion that the relationship could continue.' Thus *Shooting Stars* concludes in a way similar to *Letter to Brezhnev*, in which Elaine's letter to the Soviet president enables her to imagine a life in a different country, on the basis of an unlikely romance distant from Thatcher-era Britain. In *Shooting Stars*, the object of Alison's affection is not a Soviet sailor, as in *Letter to Brezhnev*, but a Hamburg-bound black Briton.

The extra element that Calvin's blackness adds to the scenario of a working-class man who has become a wealthy and famous footballer is one that sometimes exceeds the generic capacities of *Shooting Stars*. It complicates the mixture of admiration and jealousy that Gary feels for Calvin, and the nature of his antipathy makes Gary unsympathetic in a way that endangers the play's balance. Calvin's concluding act of generosity in not identifying Gary to the police might thus seem unaccountable. The play's female characters, after the promising start in which women are shown to be enjoying a match while the men are outside the stadium, are represented for the most part in the opposite way, as inessential to the narrative. As we have argued, the play's action is shown to be orchestrated by Gary, even when its structure emerges through contingency. During the chaos that follows his unplanned ramming of the car in which Calvin is taking Alison home after their night out, Gary panics because 'Things are getting out of control' and 'he just wants to get away' (60). Only a performative utterance reveals Gary's 'brainwave' about what to do with the injured Calvin: 'We're holding him to ransom', he says (62). The statement is one of description as much as intent, constructing a purpose to Gary's having brought Calvin to a derelict council flat 'by circumstance rather than design'. Gary's insistence that Calvin can't be set free because 'he'll turn us in' makes the kidnapping into an educational rather than a plot-related event, since this is precisely what Calvin does not do by reason of undergoing the ordeal. Later, having regained his composure, Gary justifies his actions to Alison by using satirically the discourse of free market economics: 'We're helping ourselves, like the Government says' (65).

As is fitting for his role as a figure for the playwright, Gary's plan is followed by all the other characters. This is particularly true of Alison. Her ineffectual protests about the kidnapping, and Calvin's exonerating her of any blame, make her seem overly accepting of Gary's plan and his threats. Neither she nor Paula, Gary and Sean's mother, has any agency in the narrative. Paula inhabits a subplot about women's 'underpaid, menial jobs', as Hines puts it in the introduction to the published script (viii), since hers is that of dressing up to deliver kissagrams. She is seen in costume variously as a traffic warden, a French maid and a nurse, suggesting that any of these women's jobs could become occasions for sexualised commerce. When Alison's night out with Calvin is interrupted by Paula surprising a twenty-first-birthday party in one of her kissagram costumes, she defends her friend against Calvin's charge that such women must be 'right slags … showing themselves off in public' (56), by implying that there is a similarity between what Paula and Calvin do 'in public': 'She's just trying to earn a living. We can't all earn thousands of pounds a week kicking a football around, you know' (56). The persuasiveness of her assertion is revealed when Calvin punches Gary for calling Alison in turn a 'slag' at the end of their evening out. The fact that this fight leads to Calvin being kidnapped suggests that his 'arrogant and insensitive' (56) demeanour towards Alison warrants the narrative punishment and education that follows. When Gary and Vic discuss the ransom money they might stand to gain, Sean plaintively muses that 'I'm going to give my share to my mum so that she can give up work and stop at home' (75). Although this represents an apparently selfless wish on Sean's part, it also implies that, as a mother, Paula would be better off not working at all. This makes the tawdry inequalities of recession-hit Britain in 1990 seem very distant from the radical gender politics of 1983's *Unfinished Business*.

Born Kicking (1992)

Hines's football-based narratives focus on different aspects of the game: *The Blinder* (1966) centres on incompatible life choices, *Continental Size Six* (1967) on the excesses of fandom, *Two Men from Derby* (1976) the significance of being talent-spotted, and *Shooting Stars* relies upon the star status of its footballer protagonist. *Born Kicking* has what seems to be a more conventional plot: that of a novice's entry into the professional football system and a confrontation with its temptations and pitfalls. Yet that very structure is thrown into question by the fact that the protagonist is a woman, whose footballing triumphs are always also gender-related ones. In a continuation of the radical separation between women's lives and men's established in relation to football in *Continental Size Six*, where it jeopardises the protagonist's marriage, and *Two Men from Derby*, in which it offers a wife her only possibility of escape, in *Born Kicking* the Football Association's rules are altered more easily than the social rules of gender division. The film of *Born Kicking*, directed by Mandie Fletcher, was broadcast on BBC's 'Screen One' series on 20 September 1992, and, despite its seeming suitable at least to be a text for schools as in the other instances we have encountered, the script has not been published.

The plot of *Born Kicking* centres on the 18-year-old A-level student Roxanne Reddy (Eve Barker), whose football skills astonish Archie (John Albineri), the Swifts' team talent scout, when he sees her playing in an informal women's match at a local park. Roxanne's abilities quickly win over the Swifts' director, the pointedly named Victor Grace (Denis Lawson), as well as the less easily-persuaded team manager Eddie Lang (George Irving), of whom Victor observes, 'His gruff exterior hides a heart of stone'. Grace uses his business contacts to influence the Football Association to change its rules excluding women from men's professional teams, and Roxy – thus nicknamed, as she tells her friend Kate (Julie Hewlett), because Grace says it makes 'good commercial sense' – is signed up to play for the Swifts. It is the tension between Roxy's femininity and her footballing vocation, rather than the vagaries of her sporting fortunes alone, that constitutes the narrative dynamic. Thus Roxy's matches with the Swifts, realised through details that Hines spent much effort in perfecting through a series of drafts, are not only a test of her football flair but of her ability to withstand the laddish behaviour of her male teammates. Throughout the play, such chauvinism is set in parallel to the commercial pressures that follow upon Roxy becoming the first female professional. A man in the crowd at a Swifts match observes of her that 'she's more interested in fashion these days', and it is the temptations of a glamorous life that constitute the internal obstacles to a sporting career in Roxy's case. Thus femininity is the cause of both vulnerability and liability for Roxy, in an expansion of the uneasy combination in *Shooting Stars* of Calvin Clark's undergoing discrimination as a black man, yet also enjoying the unwonted luxury of football success. In neither case is a change of class identity through wealth the only hazard.

In an instance of a patriarchal double-bind, as a footballer Roxy is seen both to typify and to lack conventional feminine attributes. Thus we learn about the nickname 'Georgie Breast' given by men to female footballers, but Roxy is also confronted by newspaper reporters who want to know if she is a lesbian. While sexist behaviour of this kind is satirised, the play nonetheless exhibits its own anxieties about the spectacle of a footballing woman. Roxy is constructed in reassuringly heterosexual terms, as her affair with Victor Grace emphasises, and is conventionally feminised, as revealed in the very first dialogue between her and her school friend Kate:

KATE: What are you wearing [tonight]?
ROXANNE: I don't know yet … I was going to wear my leather skirt.
KATE: That! It's more like a wide belt than a skirt.
ROXANNE: I can't now though. I got a kick on my leg.

In an earlier draft, the mark on Roxy's leg was not a bruise but a love bite,[37] the extent of the play's investment in compulsory heterosexuality threatening to turn its protagonist into someone too experienced for the 'innocent high spirits' that the stage direction describes in relation to her and Kate.

In a redoubling of the subsumption of football by finance that we have encountered in *The Blinder*, *Tom Kite* and *Shooting Stars*, Victor Grace embodies a tension between romantic and business interests where Roxy is concerned. Their affair functions in part to remind the audience that Roxy is not the 'six-foot dyke' who Eddie Lang initially expects, while equally exemplifying the temptations to which she is subject. It also reveals the inextricability of personal and public life in Grace's case. His first move towards Roxy is prompted by her enthusiasm for modelling the 'leisurewear' his company promotes, represented in the film by a lingering close-up on their clasped hands after the deal is agreed. In a direct hint at the ambiguity of his role in a draft, Grace makes the decision to take on the role of her business manager at the moment he sees Roxy in a new dress,[38] although in the final screenplay he is prompted to do so by her father's concerns. Grace's claiming to his wife Joanne that his relationship with Roxy is 'business, that's all', becomes true only when the younger woman no longer furthers his financial interests. Albeit more reluctantly than Bob Southgate in *Shooting Stars*, Grace accepts the offer of a £5 million transfer fee for Roxy, when she has become the Swifts' star striker, as a way out of both the negative publicity following their affair, and his company's cash shortfall. Roxy's protest against being 'treated like merchandise' in this way is realised by her refusal to go along with the transfer.

The difficulty of Grace's position after Roxy rejects the transfer is conveyed most economically in the filmic terms of Hines's screenplay. Grace's wish that Roxy should be edged out of the first eleven conflicts with his wanting the Swifts to do well, as shown by means of a series of reaction shots to Roxy's final, triumphal game, making visible the fact that 'Victor Grace is in an agony of indecision'. The reaction shots are not limited to Grace but include those of all the significant figures in Roxy's life, as if drawing the play's narrative threads cinematically together. While her father and two younger sisters respond with unselfconscious delight to Roxy's success, this is the first time that Roxy's mother has acknowledged her daughter's chosen career. Mrs Reddy is a version of Hines's staple figure of a mother whose ambitions for her children centre on education at the expense of all else. In this case, the profundity of Mrs Reddy's (Carole Hayman) conviction that football is a 'waste' of Roxy's abilities means that for most of the film's duration she refuses to speak to her daughter, thus adding to her sense of isolation. The same phrase is used by the Swifts' scout Archie, who warns Roxy not to 'waste' her talents – but in reference, rather, to her footballing skills. Thus the contradictory tests that face Roxy as a female footballer come from both sides of her life, the familial and the professional.

The play itself is torn between critiquing the transformation of football from a 'beautiful' to a financial game, and ensuring that the audience always wants Roxy to win at a sport even as it is shown to be tarnished. The same is true of the story of female emancipation that constitutes *Born Kicking*'s plot, since Roxy's success as a footballer has its fullest expression in the detail of sponsorship and merchandise. After Roxy's signing, the advertisements for Brut and *The Times* at the Swifts' home ground are replaced with ones for Chanel and *Cosmopolitan*, 'Roxy' dolls go on sale, and young girls buy her photograph from the Swifts supporters' shop. As the 'grumpy old Director' Mr Radley (Norman Bird) demands about the spectre of a female footballer, 'But where's it going to end? They'll be in the boardroom if we're not careful!'

However, as Radley's remark, expressive of male panic, suggests, the play uses the elements of its Thatcher-era backdrop to support a disruptive plot. This is despite the fact that *Born Kicking* is Hines's least specifically located play, in terms of either time or place. It is set in a scarcely identified London, as the heart of the speculative property developments of the early 1990s, of which Grace's wryly named 'Leisuredome' complex is an example. Although the era's poll tax and council tenants' 'right to buy' their houses are mentioned in the dialogue and stage directions respectively, the play offers a 'fantasy', as one reviewer puts it,[39] about the rescinding of the Football Association's rules which, even in the new millennium, continue to prevent women from playing in men's teams. Despite the nightclub openings, rap songs and shampoo advertisements with which Roxy is expected to engage, she is also shown to inspire other women, who range from schoolgirls to the club's cleaners, to rebel against the status quo, and her friend Kate counsels Roxy against giving up football in just such terms: 'You've opened up things that weren't possible before.' In this sense, Roxy's role bears a structural resemblance to that of Hines's female characters in his miners' strike plays, who similarly find empowerment in unlikely circumstances. As Roxy recounts in the voiceover to footage of a little girl juggling a football, even Mrs Reddy has been positively influenced by her daughter's example and has signed up for night school. Roxy's most sympathetic teammate, Joseph Foster (Anthony Warren), is a black defender who takes her part against his 'embarrassing' colleagues, and her plight is implicitly likened to his. At a Swifts' away match, another team member observes to Roxy, of 'the hooligans on the Kop' who have been singing sexist versions of football chants, 'At least they're not throwing bananas at you'. Thus the backlash on the part of white men against women and ethnic minorities which we saw in *Shooting Stars* has come closer to being offset by an alliance between different disadvantaged groups in this play.

As he did in *Unfinished Business*, Hines has attempted in *Born Kicking* to represent the life of a young woman by showing her experience from within, including its instances of sexism and discrimination, unsuitable romance, maternal conflict and, in Roxy's case, close female friendship. He also constructs what are some of the most detailed and stylised sets of shot descriptions of any of his screenplays in relation to the play's central football matches: Roxy's first for the Swifts where she scores a goal which is barely acknowledged; an away game where she is subject to a series of sexist fouls; one in which she plays for the reserves after a suspension, is served a red card and is at her 'most miserable'; and the final, 'magical' match 'of her life', as the stage direction has it, in which she is a substitute but, having been brought on to the field in the game's final moments, scores a winning penalty goal. Mandie Fletcher's film follows these directions exactly, from Hines's instruction that the first match should be shot in a 'mixture of slow-motion and actual speed' footage, a technique used in the filming of all the subsequent games, to the structuring of the final match by means of a series of 'action shots intercut with reactions' to Roxy's game. Hines notes in pencil on one of the draft screenplays that the film's conclusion is to be 'told in pictures', that is, in the form of still photographs, as is evident in the televised version, following the screenplay's directions:

> *END CREDITS CONTAINING:*
> 1. *A still of JOHN HUDSON: The Swifts captain holding up the FA Cup in front of the Royal Box. ROXY is standing behind him holding her cup winner's medal.*
> 2. *CLOSE-UP OF ROXY. PULL BACK to reveal her wearing England kit on an England team photograph.*
> *FADE OUT.*

It is by this visual means, and in a reprise of the ending planned for *Tom Kite*, the film about a jaded footballer which was never made, that Hines's screenplay combines its portrait of an individual's triumph with one that is more general and utopian. Thus it is implied that the 'brilliance and creativity' which football had once allowed manual workers to experience away from their jobs could equally become open to women, outside their experience of subordination.[40]

Elvis Over England (1998)

Elvis Over England was Hines's last published novel, appearing in 1998 to mixed reviews.[41] It was never filmed, despite the expectations of several reviewers as well as those of Hines himself.[42] This is even more surprising since the text includes not only material with eminently visual potential but also its own soundtrack in the form of the songs by Elvis and his contemporaries, which the main character Eddie Brooks plays during the course of the road-journey plot. While some critics found the novel to be a 'softly comical and gently affecting' portrait of one of Hines's 'working-class dreamers', others claimed that its protagonist Eddie becomes 'increasingly unlikeable' and that his 'love of Elvis', on which the plot turns, 'is virtually his only redeeming feature'.[43] The polarised nature of these responses is summed up by the fact that some reviewers likened Eddie to a version of Billy Casper in later life, while others saw in him instead a middle-aged Jud.[44] Eddie's description of himself as 'fat, fifty-five and fucked' (153) reveals the novel's representation of a particular image of post-industrial masculinity. After 35 years in the steel industry, followed by 'short spells as a driver, as a security guard and on building sites', and, 'worst of all, seasonal agricultural work' (127), Eddie is unemployed. The plot's road journey is undertaken by Eddie in a crimson 1953 Cadillac Eldorado convertible, the very make of car that Elvis drove, bought with the entirety of his redundancy pay-off. The goal of his journey turns out to be Prestwick in Scotland, the only place where Elvis, en route back to the USA after his military service in Germany, set foot in Britain.

As Eddie drives forward towards Prestwick in the novel, he casts his mind backward, and we learn by means of these memories the importance for him of such a destination. This secular pilgrimage, accompanied throughout by the lyrics of Elvis's and other songs from the 1950s, seems to have its starting point in South Yorkshire, as readers of Hines's fiction might expect. However, despite the inescapability of geography in the novel's world, the hints at location are limited to such small details as Eddie's work in an unnamed steel foundry, his mention of Chatsworth as the kind of home of which its owners would want a painting, the novel's Alhambra cinema,

called thus after Hines's local in Barnsley, and the presence of a
fictional US army base at Wharncliffe, a location named after the
village Wharncliffe Side on Sheffield's outskirts, and a nineteenth-
century steelworks in the city centre.[45] Eddie's journey to Prestwick
takes place on the 'old A1'. It seems that he joins the road quite
far north, but the villages he passes through, including one named
Mayfield, are themselves fictional.[46] It is in part by reason of its unidentifiable location that the characters' dialogue does not possess
what Christopher Hart refers to as Hines's customary 'vernacular
fizz'.[47] If *Elvis Over England* is viewed in the terms of Mikhail
Bakhtin's notion of the chronotope, in which the road journey is a
'metaphor made real', Hines's novel is one of its modern exemplars,
in which time is at least as important as space. Bakhtin argues that
'in the chronotope of the road, the unity of time and space markers
is exhibited with exceptional precision and clarity',[48] although in
the present case, Eddie's route is predetermined, since he knows by
heart the sequence of towns en route to Prestwick, and the sights
and individuals he encounters gain significance only for the sake
of their relationship to his past. Hines's notes for his composition
make this priority clear: 'Describe Eddie's feelings through what he
sees as he is travelling north.'[49]

Elvis Over England opens on a funeral, at the moment when
the burial of Eddie's mother Stella is interrupted: 'The bearers were
lowering the coffin when the telephone rang' (1). Ironically it is the
vicar's mobile phone which causes this disruption, and although
Eddie's nephew audibly whispers about the call that 'It's from God',
it does not convey a divine message. Rather, it communicates the
unwelcome intrusions of late twentieth-century modernity, a consistent theme in the novel, even into a ceremony such as this. The
novel's road journey is sparked off by the unsatisfactory funeral of
Eddie's mother, redoubling Eddie's sense that she 'deserved better'
during and at the end of her life (2).

Thus it is this sense of retrieving or revisiting what has been lost
that prompts Eddie's odyssey. His visit to Stella's house in the wake
of the disappointing send-off allows him also to start to reinhabit
his own past by trying on the Teddy Boy jacket he used to wear as
a young man in the 1950s. It is followed in the present by a series
of domestic contretemps, including an argument with his sister
Brenda, then falling out with his wife Pearl, both of which re-enact
youthful conflicts. These arguments, and the resulting absence of

sympathetic interlocutors, impel Eddie to leave home. This double movement, of a journey forward which is also one into the past, is summed up by the fact that the day he sets off, following a chronology whose detailed workings-out are apparent in Hines's archive, is the twentieth anniversary of Elvis Presley's death on 16 August 1977.[50] Although the reader does not know this at first, Eddie's journey is itself the retracing of a plan to drive to Prestwick he had made forty years earlier with his late best friend Jet, whose grave he visited after his mother's funeral. Thus Eddie's journey is undertaken in the shadow of death, as well constituting an unconscious attempt to evade it.

Elvis Over England's setting in 1997 is one that appears even more alien and degraded than that of *The Heart of It*, located some five years earlier, and its focus on post-industrial life more pronounced. The novel appeared just after the election of Tony Blair's Labour government in 1997, which ended nearly two decades of Conservative rule in Britain. In a 1998 interview published to coincide with his new book, Hines revealed he was already disenchanted with the new government, claiming that 'ministers are more concerned with image than substance' and that 'Labour should be more committed to socialism'.[51] Just as they were absent from the world of *The Heart of It*, the fruits of socialism are scarcely in evidence in the present novel. The former sites of industry in *Elvis Over England* are now those of leisure and consumption, and we learn that 'sports centres and shopping malls [have] replaced the steelworks' (47) where Eddie once earned his living, while houses are marketed as 'executive dwellings' (85). Even children's swings, that signifier of a transition out of youth in *Looks and Smiles*, are tainted here. Eddie recalls his children playing at the local recreation ground during 'the good years', when he 'was earning high wages at the rolling mill and working hard for the family', but the unsatisfactory present intrudes upon his memories: 'He smelled burning plastic, opened his eyes and sat up. Somebody had set one of the swings on fire' (69).

Although the children responsible for the fire are fascinated by Eddie's Cadillac and his invented claim that it belonged to Elvis, they are also the 'hooligan toddlers' of a reviewer's phrasing.[52] One boy has 'a ferret round his neck', while a little girl is 'wearing Dracula teeth' (70). Later, sleeping drunkenly in the Cadillac, Eddie mistakes a 'prowler in a hooded sweatshirt' for the Grim Reaper, that more ominous 'figure in the hood' (72–3). All his encounters with youth are menacing. Yet Eddie's own self-ascription is that of a child, one of a different, innocent kind, modern to their postmodern, and he spends much of his road journey looking back at his misunderstood younger self. Eddie considers his return to his mother Stella's house after her funeral to be the action of 'a hurt child running home' (10), where finding the Teddy Boy jacket provokes his 'jubilant cry', like that 'of a child receiving exactly what he wanted at Christmas' (13). Pearl's calling her husband a 'big kid' for wanting to wear the jacket at all is a recognition of the beginning of his return to the past.

It seems therefore that young people themselves embody the contradictions of the post-industrial 1990s. When Eddie returns to the council estate where his mother lived, he comes upon 'Two fly boys, one black, one white, doing deals into mobiles outside a burned-out house', to whom he offers the advice, 'You're wasting your talents here, you two. You should be down London, in the City. You'd make a fortune' (5–6). The boys are purveyors of the postmodern era's inauthenticity and its emphasis on the circulation of profit unmoored from labour. As one of them puts it, 'We've just branched out into counterfeit, if you're interested. Double your money, if you see what I mean' (6). Eddie is indeed interested in this literalised means of making money, and his roll of fake banknotes becomes the measure of whether a situation merits actual or fraudulent payment. Another pair of young men, whose conversation Eddie overhears in a roadside café as his journey begins, are identified only by means of their baseball cap logos:

> 49ers instructed Yankees how to make gas meters run backwards in order to obtain free gas. Then with the aid of a salt pot, Yankees demonstrated the correct way to climb through a cat flap. (76)

These two pairs of young men are partly embodiments of the difficulty of finding meaningful work, as is evident in Eddie's ruminating on another occasion about 'the things people had to do to make a living these days; begging and busking and such like and doing crap jobs for fuck-all an hour' (50). His violent encounter on the road with a lorry driver who has been pressured by his employers into unsafe routines is resolved by their agreement that the contemporary era offers 'either overwork or no work' (105). As well as this recourse to Hines's customary theme of safety sacrificed for profit, evident in the 'Back to Reality' episode of *The Price of Coal* and hinted at in *Unfinished Business*, the young men whom Eddie encounters in the present novel also embody once more those 'subjugated knowledges' which are neither acknowledged nor rewarded within capitalist social formations.[53] In these cases, in contrast for instance to that of Ronnie in *Speech Day* or Kyle in *Fun City*, the 'knowledges' are very reduced. Like the 'girl in a baseball cap' (70), one of the threatening children at the recreation ground, these young men's American-inspired 'baseball caps and baggy trousers' (76) are presented as another facet of postmodern decline. Since their headgear conveys 'random stylistic allusion'[54] when divorced from its baseball context, the irony of the slogans' basis in American history, including the Gold Rush of 1849, and the American Civil War, rings out more clearly. Such irony represents another contradiction, since American culture infuses both Eddie's journey and Hines's novel, from its title onwards. It seems that the young men's distance from the culture they appear to emulate emphasises the hopelessness of their situation, while for Eddie it has the opposite function: that of giving his pilgrimage a depth of personal and social meaning.

Eddie's estrangement from his wife takes place by reason of his violent argument with their nextdoor neighbour, followed by his spending the redundancy payment which Pearl had regarded as their 'nest egg. Something to fall back on' (63). It is a mixture of personal and socio-historical circumstances which drives Eddie away from home. In place of the community of miners and their families in *The Price of Coal*, Eddie's profound estrangement from his neighbours is symbolised by their playing the wrong kind of music. While the whole of Eddie's journey north takes place to a 1950s soundtrack, that issuing from next door is another unwelcome intrusion from the contemporary world: 'Bhum. Bhum. Bhum. The beat came pounding through the wall' (58). Eddie takes a sledgehammer to the two houses' dividing wall, in a way that emphasises the music's aesthetic affront: 'He picked up the beat and hammered in time' (62). The origin of Eddie's anger is made clear in his skill at knocking the wall down, since

> he had worked in the demolition business after being made redundant, but when they were contracted to destroy the buildings in which he had worked all his life, he couldn't face it and handed in his notice. (62)

Just as he was expected to assist in 'destroying' what had been his livelihood, so Eddie demolishes his own home life. Later, he surveys

Pearl's makeshift repairs and considers his a 'broken home' (73). We do not see Eddie living there again during the course of the novel; indeed, as Claus-Ulrich Viol argues, the Cadillac becomes his home instead.[55]

While Eddie has no job, Pearl has too many. It is Pearl who, as she says, 'has kept us going for the past five years' (64). She is an early-morning office cleaner, has a 'morning shift at a primary school' as a lollipop lady, and we learn that Eddie can avoid her questioning him about the Cadillac because every evening 'she set off for the White Hart about quarter to seven, so … there would be no time for an argument' (41). The reader is wrong-footed into believing that Pearl is a regular at the pub, yet soon learns that she does not go there as a customer but as an employee, 'wearing her barmaid's uniform of black skirt and white blouse' (42). Women's work is shown to be gruelling yet insubstantial, and Eddie views it with both envy and resentment. It is hard to credit his criticising the abandoned Pearl for being 'always so tired' by contrast to a different kind of barmaid, the Elvis fanatic Sue, with whom he enjoys a brief romantic encounter in Scotland (193). While in *Unfinished Business* it is Lucy's husband Phil who cannot understand what else she might want from life, here such a question comes from Eddie's wife: 'We've been married thirty-odd years. We've had two kids. We've got grandchildren. What more do you want, for God's sake?' (34). Hines's experiments with representing women's experience of education and work, as we have traced them in relation to *Unfinished Business* and *Born Kicking*, are not in evidence here.

Music is integral to *Elvis Over England* and to several other examples of Hines's writing, including *Speech Day*, with its satirical conclusion of radical folk songs and Blake's 'Jerusalem', as well as the unproduced play *The Diggers*, its title the name of the protagonists' rock band. The author's interest in developing a way of narrating musical experience is evident from his earliest writings. In Hines's first novel, his university dissertation 'Flight of the Hawk', the protagonist Jack experiences certain kinds of dancing as a kinetic art form. While he loves 'the free experience involved' in rock and roll 'twisting', and sees jive and even ballet as akin to the expressiveness of football, Jack disdains ballroom dancing for its resemblance to the routine of work, its 'mechanical precision' seeming to him like a 'well-oiled piston-rod'.[56] Hines's 1960 story

'I Went to a Jazz Concert', published when he was a student at
Loughborough Technical College, develops the theme from 'Flight
of the Hawk' of specialised aesthetic tastes.[57] In the latter, Jack
values the improvisational music of a 'modern jazz group', to which
a mystified friend responds, 'Hey up, Malcolm Sargent, what's
tha know about music anyway?' In 'I Went to a Jazz Concert', as
in *Elvis Over England*, the experience of listening to music takes
the narrator back to childhood. The 'pipes down the front' of the
vibraphone remind him 'of the organ at the Wesleyan Chapel and
being sent home for piling the hymn books on it instead of passing
them down'.[58] The presence of music in *Elvis Over England* is even
more extensive than in any of these earlier examples, and acts as
their culmination in uniting the novel's construction with its plot.
In the novel, the lyrics of Elvis's and others' tracks assume narrative
importance, while the reader is relied upon to 'perform' the 'tonal
shape' of these culturally paradigmatic songs as they read.[59] Such
a use of what Viol calls 'verbal music'[60] is a means of conveying
Eddie's interiority as well as his interactions with the outside world
on his pilgrimage to Prestwick. It acts to unite past and present,
since hearing a track in the present frequently takes Eddie back to a
moment where it was played in the past.

Music accompanies Eddie's journey from its outset, increasing
its 'mythic' appearance and giving the novel the appearance of a
film screenplay. While Jane Feuer argues that dream sequences in
film musicals draw attention to the oneiric nature of the medium
in which they feature,[61] the distinction between dreams and
dream-like reality is blurred even further in *Elvis Over England*.
Here, the fantastic is represented by means of realist techniques.
This is different from the introduction of metafictional or surreal
elements as they appear in *Speech Day* and *Fun City*, although
in each case the genre blurring arises from the crises of capitalism. The dream-like quality of *Elvis Over England* is initiated by
Eddie's acquiring the Cadillac. We do not gain access to the act of
purchase itself, which takes place in a gap between two episodes.
In the earlier of these episodes, Eddie accuses Pearl in bed late at
night of a romantic nostalgia for his late friend Jet, in an argument
which ends only because a neighbour demands through the wall
that they 'keep [their] voices down' (34). A line space in the text
is followed by a passage narrated in a variety of registers from
Eddie's viewpoint:

Is it a bird? No! Is it a plane? No! Is it the twister? No! It was Eddie
cruising the estate in a 1955 crimson convertible with the hood down.
A convoy had built up behind him as he drove slowly down the
middle of Attlee Drive. (34)

Since it follows immediately on from the bedroom argument
between Eddie and Pearl, the status of this startling change of scene
and mood is at first unclear, to the extent that it appears to be
Eddie's dream or a fantastic wish fulfilment. On a road so British it
is even named for a former prime minister appears a quintessentially
American car. Some of the sequences that follow as Eddie drives
north in the Cadillac appear equally unlikely if approached in terms
of conventional realism. Yet they create meaning in other ways. This
is true of the episode in which Eddie in the Cadillac encounters a
young man who is, following that informal service occupation of
the 1990s, a squeegee merchant, as well as being a self-confessed
'encyclopedia of Elvisology' (132). The boy agrees to sing in public
Elvis's 'American Trilogy' while Eddie holds up a queue of drivers
by failing to move off at a traffic light. The initially 'hostile, captive
audience' is won round by a mixture of Eddie's threatening physical violence and the boy's rendition of the song itself, so that, at
the song's end, 'there were tearful eyes in many vehicles' and the
singer is rewarded with 'emotional applause' as well as a bucketful
of coins. Such a scenario is unlikely in social-realist terms, and in
a review Harry Ritchie singles it out as one of the novel's incidents
that he 'didn't buy',[62] but it possesses psychic and generic coherence of another kind. The lyrics to 'American Trilogy' are quoted at
length, by interleaving them into the narrative in italics, with a view
to making the reader a part of the raptly listening audience. While
the words commemorate and 'give meaning' to the deaths of Elvis
and Jet,[63] they also migrate into the voice of the narrator:

> So *hush little baby, don't you cry.*
> And the traffic travelling in the opposite direction seemed to hush a
> little too as it passed by. (134)

What is significant here is not the implausible idea that the traffic
might really 'hush' in response to the song but Eddie's subjective
reaction, registered in the use of 'seemed'. Indeed, the comment
about the traffic seems to be his wishful thinking as much as narratorial observation. The lyrics, in an arrangement by Mickey Newbury
which Elvis included in his concerts from 1972 onwards, unite three

nineteenth-century songs from both sides of the American Civil War into 'a grand patriotic medley'.[64] Through the song's musical affirmation of reconciliation, Eddie regains a sense of a 'community of kindred souls' in the form of the listening drivers,[65] one that he has lost from the realms of both family life and work.

Other episodes, including the extreme incident of the sledgehammered home wall, which rely on improbability and coincidence can also be viewed as possessing their own significance of a non-realist kind. In Scotland, Eddie chances upon a pub hosting a 1950s theme night held in honour of the twentieth anniversary of Elvis's death, to which his response emphasises the unlikely nature of such an occurrence: 'He couldn't believe it … He had fallen asleep and woken up in 1956' (170). The Elvis karaoke offered at the pub as part of this anniversary celebration might appear to be another 'symptom of postmodernism', if it is seen only to be offering an opportunity to 'try out different masks'.[66] However, Eddie's karaoke rendition of 'Heartbreak Hotel' is shown instead to be one 'full of passion' and genuine feeling,[67] conveyed by the same method of interleaving lyrics with narration as in the 'American Trilogy' episode:

Well I'll be,
I'll just be so lonely, baby
Jet, Elvis, his father and mother, all gone. And now Pearl … (170).

The pub audience are described as recognising an expression of authentic feeling which goes beyond mimicry in Eddie's performance: 'Nobody sang along with him. It wasn't party time. They had never seen a lonelier man in their lives' (175). Eddie transcends not only the postmodern repetitions of karaoke but also this existential loneliness by another fantastical action, that of vanquishing a pair of skinheads who burst into the pub and try to disrupt the Elvis commemoration by 'insulting the music and the occasion' (178). It is the swastika tattoo on the back of one of the skinhead's hands that brings the past forcefully back into the present for Eddie, who declares of its Nazi associations, '"Millions of people died because of them bastards. My dad …". He paused, too choked to continue for a moment or two' (181).

However, the father whose fate Eddie is moved by is not his stepfather Jack, who brought Eddie up and whose wartime suffering in Burma the novel details, but Ray, the biological father he never knew: 'My dad was a pilot on bombing missions over Germany …

He was reported missing and my mother ... my mother never knew what happened to him up to the day she died' (181). Hines's notes made during the process of the novel's composition show that he envisaged this moment as Eddie's 'com[ing] to terms with the past' in his act of 'tell[ing] about his father'.[68] Yet when Hines wrote this aide-memoire, it seems that he imagined the father with whom reconciliation would take place to be Jack and not Ray, since the story Eddie was to relate was one about being 'a prisoner of war'.[69] Indeed, Eddie's earlier efforts to understand Jack's actions lead the reader to expect that the reconciliation will be with him. Although in the published novel Jack was a soldier in Burma rather than a prisoner of war, since such extreme suffering might have altered its balance of sympathies, the lack of affection he showed his stepson meant that this possible fate surfaces in Eddie's childhood wish that Jack 'had been captured and died like the soldiers building the Burma railway' (16). Just as his wartime experience has been commuted to one of military rather than prison-camp hardship in the novel's final version, so Jack has been superseded by Ray. Eddie's being able to 'let Elvis (his father) go', which Hines claimed would be 'explained by the 'scene on [the] airfield ... at end of book', has a quite different meaning in the published version's conclusion, since Eddie plans to set off to Ray's hometown of Chicago.[70] His step-father Jack has become irrelevant and appears irredeemable. Rather than the return to reality that Hines initially planned by means of Eddie accepting Jack's behaviour and relinquishing Ray, the novel concludes with a resumption of fantasy.

Two elements of *Elvis Over England* were judged by critics to be unassimilable: Eddie himself is portrayed in terms that are unsympathetic, as reviewers variously describe his unappealing traits of 'solipsism, his forlorn wish to be "a somebody"', 'bullying egoism' and 'jealous violence'; while Eddie's journey north is judged by another reviewer to be 'pointless'.[71] As we have argued, these troublesome aspects of the novel make more sense when it is viewed as non-realist, and in relation to Eddie's efforts to reconsider his past. While Eddie's anger and violence seem to repeat those aspects of his father Jack's behaviour that he most hated, the pilgrimage to Prestwick is one of penance for his role in his best friend Jet's death. These two aspects of his memorial journey are united by a third element which is only gradually revealed, that of Eddie's biological father being not Stella's husband Jack but Ray, the American GI stationed in Britain during the war with whom his mother had an affair while Jack was away in Burma. Thus Eddie's interest in Elvis Presley and the novel's extensive incorporation of music in verbal form does not arise simply from a nostalgic effort to recapture his youth at a time of mid-life crisis. Embracing Americana is also a means for Eddie to retain a link with the father he never knew. The image of Elvis is also a way for Eddie to enact his class identity in the post-industrial era. Hines notes, from his reading as well as his own experience, that the phenomenon of Teddy Boys constituted a 'reaction against the suffocating nature of early 1950s society', while Van Cagle argues that Elvis's personal style was a 'flamboyant indicator of class contradictions', since such features as the singer's outsized diamond rings and Cadillac 'satirized upper-class pretensions'.[72] In the present novel, Eddie's car alone represents an equivalent 'contradiction' in starkly visual terms within a British landscape. Indeed, as Cagle argues, the image of Elvis represented in Hines's novel is a specifically British construction.[73] Thus Eddie's suppressing an impulse to invoke 'Dixie' during his journey is not due to its controversial links to Confederate slave-owning, as might be the case in an American context, but to his self-consciousness about acting a role.

In contrast to the idealised paternal figure of Ray, from whom Stella heard no more after his taking part in the Battle of Britain, Jack returned traumatised from a gruelling war spent in Burma only to be confronted with his wife's illegitimate son. Jack's history seems to be told by an omniscient narrator, since we learn about the homecoming from his own point of view. However, such a perspective in fact relies upon Eddie, who finds Jack's love letters to Stella after her death, and which include Jack's own use of verbal music: '*the only thing that keeps me going in this rotten hole is thinking about you … and whistling that song "Stella by Starlight" over and over again*' (110).[74] In the event, it is the vision of Eddie, seen from outside as a 'little boy standing in the hall doorway, staring across the kitchen at him' (112), that spoils Jack's return. Yet the closeness of the third person narrative voice to Eddie's viewpoint, as it exists throughout the novel, is not, as it might at first seem, disrupted here. This is Eddie's reconstruction of Jack's return, as well as his effort to understand the stepfather who rebuffed him: 'Poor bugger, Eddie thought, putting himself in Jack's place. By the time you're grown up yourself and understand these things, it's often too late' (112).

The absence of quotation marks and the free direct discourse of the second sentence emphasise the narrator's closeness to Eddie. Jack's history, although Hines meticulously researched the experience of soldiers and prisoners-of-war in Burma, exists in the published version in a sparse form and only to illuminate Eddie's pathology.[75]

The last act of retrieving and laying the past to rest undertaken by Eddie is one that concerns his own actions and includes a late revelation for the reader. It occurs at the conclusion of Eddie's journey and that of the novel itself. In the form of a 'musicalized flashback',[76] we learn that the teenage Eddie, late for a date with Pearl, found her 'jiving with Jet' at the local Cats Eyes danceteria. Eddie ominously took the upbeat romantic lyrics of Elvis's 'All Shook Up' – 'I'm in love/I'm all shook up' – to describe instead his experience of jealous anger. Pearl and Jet are 'rocking together by the juke box to "All Shook Up". Eddie certainly was' (207). He delays going to Jet's assistance when a fight breaks out between him and another boy who asks a reluctant Pearl to dance, by watching from the stairs and even silently urging the assailants on: 'That's it. Let him have it'. But the fight turns suddenly more dangerous and Jet is stabbed, suffering what Viol calls 'the cliché Teddy Boy death'.[77] It is a quick and sudden end that Hines defended as such to his editor Jenny Dereham at Michael Joseph, when she urged him to make such a decisive event in the novel's trajectory more detailed.[78] Dereham found the scene of Jet's death 'quite a bit too soft', and suggested an addition in which the stakes are much higher to explain the fight's escalation: the unwelcome suitor might 'manhandle [Pearl] to the floor; Pearl might stumble and he might pull her up roughly … which would make her cry out'. Hines's dissenting reply illuminates the fact that 'We see the action coldly through Eddie's jealous eyes. We are not on the dance floor in the thick of it', and, as he adds, invoking an autobiographical element, 'believe me, as an ex-Teddy boy who has frequented such places, *more than enough* violence has happened to make Jet intervene'.[79] Indeed, the same sketchy representation of a fight over a girl appears in *Looks and Smiles*, where, as in this novel, it is significant for its role in the plot rather than its detail. In *Elvis Over England*'s present time, Eddie twice addresses the same phrase to the absent Jet: 'It's taken us a long time, kid, but we finally made it' (209, 211), referring both to his arrival at Prestwick, and to the admission of responsibility for his friend's death. Such an admission leaves Eddie free to contemplate not returning to Pearl but taking a flight from Prestwick to see if any trace of his American father can be found – via a return journey to Sue at the Scottish pub while awaiting his passport.

It seems that Hines and Eddie alike are somewhat adrift in the post-industrial world of the novel's setting in the Britain of 1997. The novel's image of Elvis offers not so much an escape from this setting – since, as the title has it, he is flying 'over' rather than away from England – but a means of accessing an individual's psyche and past, in place of the industrial labour and strife of Eddie's earlier life and Hines's earlier works. The mode of narration, with its third person voice focalised through Eddie, cannot help but imply a close-ness between protagonist and implied author. Eddie's fondness for performance, including taking on the role of a Texan at a motorway service station, and concern for how he is seen by others, makes third person narrative particularly appropriate.

Such closeness of narration equally means that Eddie's view-point, with its gendered sense of self-pity, is never really ironised. One reviewer calls the novel 'misogynist', an overstated recognition, perhaps, of Eddie's tendency either to blame or venerate women in stereotypical fashion.[80] It is notable that the novel's heroic figures from the past, particularly Jet and Ray, are all male, while the unsat-isfactory ones of the present are female, including Eddie's sister Brenda, various women who fail to respond to his advances during his journey, and Pearl herself. On his arrival at Prestwick, Eddie's automatic sympathy with what he takes to be a put-upon husband, 'in trouble already and they haven't even taken off yet' (210), makes him appear to be suffering from the post-industrial backlash against feminism as analysed in the early 1990s by Susan Faludi.[81]

A more metafictional effect of the close relation between pro-tagonist and narrator in *Elvis Over England* is Eddie's pilgrimage's resemblance to a drive-by of the concerns of Hines's entire body of work. It is as if Eddie's picaresque encounters encapsulate the journey that Hines's politically inspired writing took, concluding, as we have seen, with his being poised to leave Britain altogether. In Hines's earlier works, the notion of industrial injury is a cause for anger. Thus in *Speech Day* the handyman George claims that it is the memory of 'burns on their arms from metal splashes' suffered by his steelworker colleagues that 'makes [his] blood boil' when he contemplates his sell-out workmate, the Mayor Joe Brannigan.[82] The notion of steelworkers' injuries of this kind reappears in *The*

Gamekeeper, where George denies the right of his son's school-teacher to call his job 'cruel' since she has never 'come home in an ambulance with metal splashes on her'.[83] In both these texts, the 'splashing' of molten metal onto workers' bodies is symbolic of the human cost of manual labour. In *Elvis Over England*, by contrast, it is the absence of even this marker of work that Eddie laments. Thus he describes his soft hands, which used to be as 'tough as old boots' when he was working: 'That's what you get working with molten steel' (59). Purposelessness trumps industrial hardship for Eddie, who concludes, 'When they take your work away, they take away your life!' (60).

The mnemonic effect of Eddie's driving north behind an army truck, which reminds him of both Jack and Ray, prompts him also to ruminate on the theme of enlistment as a dangerous way of avoiding unemployment, as is familiar from *Looks and Smiles*: 'Eddie thought about the young soldiers in the back of the truck and wondered how many of them would have joined up if they'd been able to get a job' (108). The question of land ownership which underlies class and economic inequality, evident throughout *The Gamekeeper*, appears in relation to a farmer on whose land Eddie trespasses. At first Eddie acts out a role, claiming in cod John Wayne style to be a landowner from the USA: 'It's mighty different to the bitty little fields you got over here of course. My land stretches as far as the eye can see', but concludes by pretending to be 'Eddie McBrooks' of Scottish descent so that he can cite the victims of the Highland clearances, as a figure of the human cost of private land ownership: 'We were driven from our rightful land by the English way back in the eighteenth century' (114–15). Even *The Gamekeeper*'s complex representation of the shooting of game birds reappears in *Elvis Over England*, in a way that makes clear it is the fate of working men that these deaths encode. Eddie takes the distant sound of gunfire to be 'a twelve-gun salute to Elvis', but is told by the hitchhiker he has picked up that it is, rather, a shooting party since 'the grouse season's just started ... I tried to get a job beating, but they said they didn't need anybody else' (123). Shooting emphasises the prevalence of unemployment, as does the landscape that Eddie drives through. The working men's club and the recontoured muckstack from *The Price of Coal* have undergone a wholly denaturing refurbishment this time, the former into a 'heritage centre', the latter now a ski slope (198).

None of these elements is made into a plot device, and they exist simply at the level of signifiers or thoughts on Eddie's part. Hines's paring down of the road-journey narrative in favour of that concerning Eddie's past and his subjective world is evident in his notes for a possible but eventually discarded elaboration of the grouse-shooting episode: 'Redundant miners beating on grouse moor – Eddie knows one of them', while other sensationalist plot lines were also abandoned.[84] Several of these involved mishaps concerning the Cadillac, as the literal vehicle of the story, being stolen or hijacked, and Eddie's retrieving it or fighting the thief.[85] Just as the character of Arthur Scargill was excised from 'Back to Reality' in *The Price of Coal*, although his name remains in the verbal trace of graffiti, so Hines's notion of including implicit references to the miners' strike in this novel of over a decade later was not followed through. He experimented with the idea of having Eddie drive through North Yorkshire to Scargill, a village whose road sign was altered to include the additional legend 'is a bastard', or, in reference to a nearby hamlet, 'Scargill 0, Reeth 12'.[86] Such apparent antagonism seems to be meant as an expression of hopelessness, directed by locals against the miners' leader who could not bring them victory. Not including any detail of this kind shows the extent to which the novel's political backdrop is itself subordinate to Eddie's retrieval of a personal past.

Notes

1 Barry Hines, *The Heart of It*, London, Michael Joseph 1994. All page references in the text.

2 Max Horkheimer and Theodor W. Adorno, 'The Culture Industry: Enlightenment as Mass Perception', in *Dialectic of Enlightenment: Philosophical Fragments*, ed. Gunzelin Schmid Noerr, trans. Edmund Jephcott, Stanford: Stanford University Press 2002, p. 94.

3 Ian Haywood, *Working Class Fiction: From Chartism to Trainspotting*, London: Routledge 1996, p. 111.

4 Wally Hammond, review, *Time Out* May 11, BHP/HEA 21.

5 John Kirk, 'Figuring the Landscape: Writing the Topographies of Community and Place', *Literature and History* 15 (1) pp. 1–17: 9.

6 Notes on script, BHP/HEA 17.

7 Kirk, 'Figuring the Landscape', p. 9.

8 Alfred Hickling, 'Tales dug deep from the heart', *The Yorkshire Post* 7 May 1994, BHP/HEA 21.

9 Barry Hines, *After the Strike*, all page references in text, BHP/ATS 1/2.

10 Barry Hines, *The Diggers*, all page references in text, BHP/DIG 2.

11 In October 2016 the Home Secretary, Amber Rudd, rejected a campaign to initiate a statutory inquiry into the events at Orgreave.

12 Unknown author, 'Writer returns home after putting miners' strike in print', *Barnsley Chronicle* 7 May 1994, BHP/HEA 21.

13 Barry Hines, *The Diggers*: Synopsis, p. 6, BHP/DIG 1.

14 Ibid.

15 Barry Hines, *Slate*, all page references in the text, BHP/SLA 1.

16 Barry Hines, *Looking at the Sun*, broadcast on BBC Radio Four, 13 August 1992, all page references in text.

17 Page unlisted.

18 See Jack Rosenthal's definition of drama, indebted to that of his university tutor, the Shakespearean scholar John Danby, as consisting of 'a protagonist trying to score a goal and an antagonist trying to stop him', in the BBC 'Timeshift' documentary *Jack the Lad*, 2004.

19 Anonymous review, the *Listener* 24 May 1990.

20 Barry Hines, *Shooting Stars* and *Two Men From Derby*, London: Heinemann 1993, p. 29. All further page references in the text.

21 This reference remains in the published play, suggesting that the latter was based on a late version of the screenplay but not the shooting script. Other small references to the original setting remain in the film, including Alison telling the DJ during the radio quiz that she lives in 'Highfields', a suburb of Sheffield.

22 Jonathan Cribb, Richard Joyce and David Phillip describe the increase in income inequality that started in the 1980s as, by 1990, 'the largest increase' of this kind 'seen in recent British history', one that was 'larger than the rise that took place in other countries at the same time', *Living Standards, Poverty and Inequality in the UK: 2012*, London: Institute for Fiscal Studies 2012, p. 2.

23 The nightclub's original name, Toppers, was altered to Millionaires by Hines in a late draft to enhance the impression of social extremes.

24 Review, the *Listener*, BHP/SHO 7.

25 As Simon Frith argues, this 'ideological term' emerged in late 1980s Britain to refer to a cultural and financial willingness to emulate North American risk-taking on the part of individuals for the sake of financial profit (in Michael Payne, ed., *The Blackwell Dictionary of Cultural and Critical Theory*, Oxford: Blackwell 1997, p. 59).

26 The generalising historical term 'West Indian' (not to mention the nickname 'Ethnic') has been replaced by 'African/Caribbean', as the British Association for American Studies notes. See 'Language and the BSA', http://www.britsoc.co.uk/media/25564/EqualityandDiversity_ LanguageandtheBSA_RaceMar05.doc.

27 Mikhail Bakhtin, *Problems of Dostoevsky's Poetics*, ed. and trans. Caryl Emerson, Minneapolis: University of Minnesota Press 1984.

28 Guy Howie, 'Football under Capitalism: The Rich Exploit a Working-class Sport', *Socialist Appeal* 15 September 2014.

29 *Continental Size Six*, BBC Radio 4 'Afternoon Theatre', 12 April 1967.

30 BHP/SHO 5.

31 In the shooting script and published version, although this is not the first time we have encountered Vic, the stage direction describes him as 'a black youth', as if ensuring we are aware of the ostensible reason for the mock fight.

32 'Billy', the name of two of Hines's protagonists, as well as 'Gary' and even 'Eddie', from *Elvis Over England* and *After the Strike*, are near-homophones for 'Barry', emphasising these characters' roles as autho-rial alter egos of various kinds. In a reverse formation, Hines takes an uncredited cameo as the physiotherapist for the football team in the films of both *Shooting Stars* and *Born Kicking*, as if revealing his writerly role of easing the characters into action. In *Shooting Stars*, it is at the moment that the physio moves aside that we first see a close-up of Calvin Clark, the film's star, as if in enactment of Hines's role in his creation.

33 Bradford Plumer, 'Rick Santorum: A Brief History of the "Some of My Best Friends" Defense', *New Republic* 16 June 2011.

34 Daniel J. Boorstin, *The Image: A Guide to Pseudo-Events in America*, New York: Vintage 1961.

35 This detail was subject to small but symptomatic alteration in the screenplay drafts. 'Sausage factory' was changed to 'bakery', then 'West Indian bakery' in the television play, as if to emphasise the particular nature of Calvin's disadvantage, BHP/SHO 4/5.

36 Anonymous review, *The Times* 17 May 1990. Several reviewers comment on the difficulty of taking the kidnap plot light-heartedly in view of real-life threats in the early 1990s to kidnap such players as Liverpool's John Barnes, to whom they frequently compare the fictional Calvin.

37 BHP/BOK 2.

38 Ibid.

39 James Rampton, review, the *Independent* 21 September 1992.

40 Harry Pearson, quoted in Peter Stead, 'Brought to Book: Football and Literature', in Rob Steen et al., eds, *The Cambridge Companion to Football*, Cambridge: p. 249.

41 Barry Hines, *Elvis Over England*, London: Michael Joseph 1998. All page references in the text.

42 See for instance an anonymous review in the *Bradford Telegraph and Argus* ('Teddy boy Eddie and his Elvis fixation', 25 April 1998) praising the novel's 'visual promise', and one by Stephen Dyson in the

Birmingham Evening Mail (15 May 1998), urging the reader to 'watch out for a TV adaptation'; in an interview with the *Barnsley Chronicle* Hines observed that 'there might be a film in it', 'Much to be angry about'. All from BHP/EOE 10.

43 Respectively, Ross Fortune, *Time Out*; Tom Adair, *Scotland on Sunday*; Anonymous, the *Sun-Herald*; Lottie Moggach, *Yorkshire Evening Post* 7 May 1998, all BHP/EOE 10.

44 Simon Glover argues for Eddie's likeness to Billy, review in the *Yorkshire Post*, Justin Warshaw for one to 'Billy's nasty elder brother Jud', in 'The king at Prestwick', *Times Literary Supplement* 27 July 1998, BHP/EOE 10.

45 The nearest US Air Force bases to Sheffield during the war included Goxhill in Linconshire and Burtonwood in Lancashire, but most were located further south.

46 Hines wrote in response to a question from his editor Jenny Dereham at Michael Joseph that Mayfield was an 'archetypal market-town that everyone can identify with' (BHP/EOE 8), including its run-down high street in which the tattooist's Eddie visits is situated between 'a charity shop and a bookmaker's' (77).

47 Charles Hart, review, *Daily Telegraph* 6 June 1998.

48 Mikhail Bakhtin, 'Forms of Time and Chronotope in the Novel', *Discourse in the Novel*, trans. and ed. Michael Holquist, Austin: University of Texas Press 1981, p. 98. In an interview, Hines claimed to have read Hunter S. Thompson's rather different kind of road-journey novel *Fear and Loathing in Las Vegas* fifty times while working on *Elvis Over England* (*Metro*, BHP/EOE 10).

49 BHP/EOE 7.

50 Ibid.

51 'Much to be angry about'.

52 Simon Evans, 'Cadillac man on Elvis trail', BHP/EOE 10.

53 Michel Foucault, *Power/Knowledge: Selected Interviews and Other Writings, 1972–1977*, Brighton: Harvester 1980, p. 82. Following his usual methodology, Hines collected newspaper reports about long-distance lorry drivers' safety being jeopardised by employers' ruthlessness, including one from the *Observer*, 'Tired truckers cause hundreds of road deaths', BHP/EOE 10.

54 Fredric Jameson, *Postmodernism: Or, the Cultural Logic of Late Capitalism*, Durham, NC: Duke University Press 1991, p. 19.

55 Claus-Ulrich Viol, *Jukebooks: Contemporary British Fiction, Popular Music and Cultural Value*, Heidelberg: Winter 2006, p. 163.

56 BHP/BLX.

57 Mr B. Hines, 'I Went to a Jazz Concert', *Thesaurus: A Magazine of Creative Writing by Loughborough* Students 3, March 1960, pp. 8–10.

58 Ibid., p. 8.
59 Viol, *Jukebooks*, p. 163.
60 Ibid., p. 161
61 Jane Feuer, quoted in James R. Walters, *Alternative Worlds in Hollywood Cinema: Resonance Between Realms*, Chicago: University of Chicago Press 2008, p. 31.
62 Harry Ritchie, 'Unsteady Eddie', *Metro*, BHP/EOE 10.
63 Viol, *Jukebooks*, p. 163.
64 'Readers' Poll: The 10 Best Elvis Presley Songs', *Rolling Stone* 21 January 2015.
65 Viol, *Jukebooks*, p. 165.
66 Kevin Brown, *Karaoke Idols: Popular Music and the Performance of Identity*, Bristol and Chicago: Intellect 2015, p. 102; Johan Fornäs, quoted in ibid.
67 Fornäs, in Brown, *Karaoke Idols*, p. 102.
68 BHP/EOE 7.
69 Ibid.
70 Ibid.
71 BHP/EOE 10.
72 BHP/EOE 7; Van M. Cagle, 'Flaunting It: Style, Identity, and the Social Construction of Elvis Fandom', in Steve Jones and Joli Jensen, eds, *Afterlife as Afterimage: Understanding Posthumous Fame*, New York: Peter Lang 2005, pp. 48, 41.
73 Ibid., p. 34.
74 This jazz standard first appeared in Lewis Allen's 1944 film *The Uninvited*, its lyrics composed later in 1946. Although the film fittingly concerns uncertain parentage and a young woman haunted by her late mother's legacy, the timing of its release makes it easier to imagine in *Elvis Over England* that Ray, who calls the usherette Stella with her torch 'Stella by spotlight' (140), would be more familiar with the song than Jack.
75 Hines's notes on several historical accounts, such as Richard Rhodes James's *Chindit* (London: John Murray 1980), are included in his archive. At an early stage, Hines planned that Eddie himself would read such works, thus learning 'what his father went through', although this does not take place in the published version, since the plot's emphasis has moved away from Jack to Ray. Alongside these notes are interview questions that Hines posed to the widow of a Burma veteran, including some about the frequency of letters sent and received, a matter crucial to the plot, since information about Jack's experience appears only by that means. BHP/EOE 7.
76 Viol, *Jukebooks*, p. 208.
77 Ibid., p. 161.

78 BHP/EOE 8.
79 Ibid.
80 'NC', *The List*, 30 April–4 May 1998, BHP/EOE 10.
81 Susan Faludi, *Backlash: The Undeclared War Against American Women*, New York: Three Rivers Press 1991.
82 Barry Hines, *Speech Day*, in Michael Marland, ed., *The Pressures of Life: Four Television Plays*, Harlow: Longman 1977, p. 106
83 Barry Hines, *The Gamekeeper*, Harmondsworth: Penguin 1975, p. 66.
84 BHP/EOE 7.
85 Ibid.
86 Ibid. The detail of Hines's writing habits is starkly shown in the archival material for *Elvis Over England*. Each page of his notes about social and historical material, on youth cultures, the war in Burma and GIs in Britain concludes with a single line written in different ink summarising the fictional outcome of this investigation. Thus Hines's reading and other activities, including his driving from Sheffield to Prestwick and visiting the airport's Graceland bar, constitute sources of inspiration rather than simply background research.

Conclusion

The death of Barry Hines was announced on 20 March 2016, and the tributes in print and on social media were heartfelt and wide-ranging. Hines's work was lauded by well-known personalities such as the actor Kathy Burke, who likened him to 'JK' (Rowling), while the Barnsley-born novelist Joanne Harris noted how she 'hated and loved him at the same time for writing the world I saw every day, and for giving me hope to escape it', and the footballer-turned-actor Vinnie Jones referred to *A Kestrel for a Knave* as 'the book that changed his life'.[1] However, it was the words of condolence from ordinary people that were most affecting: those who had read Hines's work as children and had taught it as teachers, those who had discovered a lifelong love of literature through *A Kestrel for a Knave*, or those who had been scarred and moved by the power of *Threads*. A writer who we had thought had been forgotten, whose work we had been studying, scrutinising, discovering (and re-discovering) in preparation for this book, was suddenly and joyfully remembered. In testimony to this, in the days following Hines's death, *Kes* was cited by Paul Mason in a comment piece for the *Guardian* about the death of the white working class, and in the same publication the sports writer Richard Williams revisited *The Blinder*, finding it a 'powerful portrait of how football looked and felt 50 years ago'.[2]

Hines, it seems, has become relevant again. Nicola Wilson argues that a retrieval of working-class writing's heritage has characterised twenty-first-century culture, which had been lost to a 'generation growing up in Thatcher's Britain amid the "death" of class as an ideology and political tool'.[3] Part of Wilson's evidence for this loss is the disappearance of *A Kestrel for a Knave* as a set text from the school syllabus, although it remains an option frequently chosen by teachers for pupils of Billy's age. The retrospective currency of

Hines's work in the wake of his death likewise seems to emerge from a collective sense in which it has brought into focus the absence of a place-specific, working-class culture of writing in contemporary Britain. Unlike many of his contemporaries, Hines's focus on class issues was unerring and fundamental, and he rarely strayed from his native South Yorkshire for source material. As the Barnsley-born poet Ian McMillan reflects, Hines challenged the notion that the working classes were not 'fit for literature … [by] placing us centre stage', and for Tony Garnett, Hines 'only ever wrote about what he knew' and was 'the voice for his community'.[4] This might suggest that today such voices are silenced or that they no longer exist. For Hines, the local was a site replete with poetic and political energy and inspiration, in his own words:

> the view from my window is very inspiring. What? they say. Those horrible blocks of flats, all those mucky factories and all that smoke pouring out? Those ramshackle houses down there, that faceless council estate? Well, yes, I say. Most people live and work in places like that. And I can't think of anything more important to write about. Can you?[5]

This book has been concerned with exploring these interconnected issues of class, space and place in Hines's writing, and more broadly in anatomising the practice and purpose of working-class film, television and literature, through one of its most prolific and committed exponents. Our argument here is that Hines's works are reaching a new audience, and there is evidence that his unpublished and unperformed works are also attracting attention, from researchers, reading groups and dramatists. The Barry Hines Papers offer a glimpse into Hines's working methodology, as well as the manifest level of what might be called the genotext of his works, following Julia Kristeva's usage: that is, a record of the documents and drafts that were tried out, edited, included or discarded, only to appear in what is their often fruitfully ambiguous final form.

Notes

1 Kathy Burke, 'RIP #BarryHines our generation's JK,' 20 March 2016; Joanne Harris, 'RIP, Barry Hines: I hated and loved him at the same time – for writing the world I saw every day, and for giving me hope to escape it,' 20 March 2016; Vinnie Jones, 'The Q&A', the *Guardian* Saturday magazine, 11 June 2016.

2 Paul Mason, 'The problem for poor, white kids is that a part of their culture has been destroyed', the *Guardian* 12 April 2016; Richard Williams, 'A glimpse of a forgotten game: How Barry Hines painted a portrait of football's past', the *Guardian* 4 April 2016.

3 Nicola Wilson, *Home in British Working-Class Fiction*, London: Routledge 2015, p. ix.

4 Mark Hodkinson and Tony Garnett. 'Barry Hines obituary: Author of A Kestrel for a Knave', the *Guardian* 23 March 2016.

5 Barry Hines, *This Artistic Life*, Hebden Bridge: Pomona 2009, pp. 3–4.

Bibliography and Filmography

Works by Barry Hines

Novels (all first published London: Michael Joseph)
The Blinder, 1966
Elvis Over England, 1998
First Signs, 1972
The Gamekeeper, 1975
The Heart of It, 1994
A Kestrel for a Knave, 1968
Looks and Smiles, 1981
The Price of Coal, 1979
Unfinished Business, 1983

Published screenplays and plays
Fun City, Peter Terson, ed., *New Plays 2: Contemporary One-Act Plays*, Oxford: Oxford University Press 1988
Kes, ed. Lawrence Till, London: Nick Hern 2000
The Price of Coal, ed. Allan Stronach, London: Hutchinson 1979
Shooting Stars and *Two Men from Derby*, ed. Peter Shepherd, London: Heinemann 1993
Speech Day, Alan Durband, ed., *Prompt Two: Five Short Plays*, London: Hutchinson 1976, edited version
Speech Day, Michael Marland, ed., *The Pressures of Life: Four Television Plays*, Harlow: Longman 1977
Threads and Other Sheffield Plays, ed. Michael Mangan, Sheffield: Sheffield Academic Press 1990

Short stories and essays
'Different People', *Thesaurus: A Magazine of Creative Writing by Loughborough Students 5*, May 1963, pp. 23–5

'I Went to a Jazz Concert', *Thesaurus: A Magazine of Creative Writing by Loughborough Students* 3, March 1960, pp. 8–10
This Artistic Life, Pomona: Hebden Bridge 2009

Television plays

Billy's Last Stand, Play for Today, John Glenister, broadcast on 4 February 1971
Born Kicking, Screen One, Mandie Fletcher, broadcast on 20 September 1992
The Price of Coal, Play for Today, Ken Loach, broadcast on 26 March and 5 April 1977
Shooting Stars, Chris Barnard, broadcast on 17 May 1990
Speech Day, Play for Today, John Goldschmidt, broadcast on 26 March 1973
Threads, Mick Jackson, broadcast on 23 September 1984
Two Men from Derby, Centre Play, John Glenister, broadcast on 21 February 1976

Films

The Gamekeeper, Ken Loach 1980
Kes, Ken Loach 1969
Looks and Smiles, Ken Loach 1981
The Navigators, Ken Loach 2001 (as 'script editor')

Radio plays

Billy's Last Stand, BBC Network 3, 12 August 1965
Continental Size Six, BBC Radio 4 'Afternoon Theatre', 12 April 1967
Looking at the Sun, BBC Radio 4, 13 August 1992
Two Men from Derby, BBC Radio 4, 23 October 1976

Unpublished and unperformed works by Barry Hines

Scripts and screenplays

After the Strike, 1985
The Diggers (also known as *Walking Wounded*), 1989
Last Shift, 1974
Private Fears, 1990
The Promise, *c.*1975
Slate, 1987
Springwood Stars, 2000
Tom Kite (also known as *Injury Time/Man of the Match*), 1977

Dissertation
'Flight of the Hawk', novel, Loughborough College 1964

Primary works by other authors
Novels and plays
Beckett, Samuel, *Waiting for Godot*, New York: Grove Press 1953
Braine, John, *Room at the Top*, London: Eyre and Spottiswoode 1957
Sillitoe, Alan, *The Loneliness of the Long Distance Runner and Other Stories*, London: W.H. Allen 1959
Storey, David, *This Sporting Life*, Harmondsworth: Penguin 1963 [1960]

Television plays and films
Bar Mitzvah Boy, Michael Tuchman, Play for Today, broadcast on 1976
if..., Lindsay Anderson 1968
Letter to Brezhnev, Chris Bernard 1985
The Loneliness of the Long Distance Runner, Tony Richardson 1962
Room at the Top, Jack Clayton 1959
Saturday Night and Sunday Morning, Karel Reisz 1960

Secondary works

Alcalá, Roberto del Valle, 'Class, Embodiment and Becoming in British Working-Class Fiction: Re-reading Barry Hines and Ron Berry with Deleuze and Guattari', *College Literature* 43 (2) 2016, pp. 375–96

Babington, Bruce, *The Sports Film: Games People Play*, New York: Wallflower Press 2014,

Bakhtin, Mikhail, *The Dialogic Imagination*, trans. and ed. Michael Holquist, Austin: University of Texas Press, 1981

Barrett, Michèle, *Women's Oppression Today: Problems in Marxist-Feminist Analysis*, London: Verso 1980

Behrend, Hanna, 'Second Thoughts on an Unfinished Business', *Literarische Diskurse und historischer Prozess* 88, 1988, pp. 151–8

Berger, John, 'Why Look at Animals?', *About Looking*, London: Vintage 1992 [1977]

Bordwell, David, *Narration in the Fiction Film*, Wisconsin: University of Wisconsin Press 1985

Brass, Tom, *Labour Regime Change in the Twenty-first Century: Unfreedom, Capitalism and Primitive Accumulation*, Leiden: Brill 2011

Brown, Kevin, *Karaoke Idols: Popular Music and the Performance of Identity*, Bristol and Chicago: Intellect 2015

Burt, Jonathan, 'John Berger's "Why Look at Animals?": A Close Reading', *Worldviews* 9 (2) 2005 pp. 203–18

Burt, Jonathan, *Animals in Film*, London: Reaktion 2002

Butler, Judith, *Gender Trouble*, New York: Routledge 1990

Cagle, Van M., 'Flaunting It: Style, Identity, and the Social Construction of Elvis Fandom', in Steve Jones and Joli Jensen, eds, *Afterlife as Afterimage: Understanding Posthumous Fame*, New York: Peter Lang 2005, p. 51

Cardullo, Bert, *Loach and Leigh, Ltd: The Cinema of Social Conscience*, Newcastle: Cambridge Scholars Publishing 2010

Cixous, Hélène, *The Speculum of the Other Woman*, trans. Gillian C. Gill, Ithaca: Cornell University Press 1985 [1974]

Connolley, Patricia, 'On Marxism and Feminism', *Studies in Political Economy* 12, 1983, pp. 153–61

Cordle, Daniel, "That's Going to Happen to Us. It Is': *Threads* and the Imagination of Nuclear Disaster on 1980s Television', *Journal of British Cinema and Television*, 10:1 2013, pp. 71–92

Cribb, Jonathan, Joyce, Richard and Phillip, David, *Living Standards, Poverty and Inequality in the UK: 2012*, London: Institute for Fiscal Studies 2012

Delphy, Christine, *Close to Home: A Feminist Analysis of Women's Oppression*, Amherst: University of Massachusetts Press 1984

Evans, Eric, 'Landownership and the Exercise of Power in an Industrializing Society: Lancashire and Cheshire in the Nineteenth Century', in Ralph Gibson and Martin Blinkhorn, eds, *Landownership and Power in Modern Europe*, London: HarperCollins 1991

Faludi, Susan, *Backlash: The Undeclared War Against American Women*, New York: Three Rivers Press 1991

Forrest, David and Vice, Sue, 'Archival Traces of the North', in Julia Dobson and Jonathan Rayner, eds, *Mapping Cinematic Norths*, Oxford: Peter Lang 2016

Forrest, David and Vice, Sue, 'A Poetics of the North: Visual and Literary Geographies', in Ieuan Franklin et al., eds., *Regional Aesthetics: Mapping UK Media Cultures*, Palgrave 2015, pp. 55–67

Foucault, Michel, *Power/Knowledge: Selected Interviews and Other Writings, 1972–1977*, Brighton: Harvester 1980

Foucault, Michel, *Discipline and Punish: The Birth of the Prison*, trans. Alan Sheridan, New York: Vintage 1979

Fuller, Graham, *Loach on Loach*, London: Faber and Faber 1998

Garnett, Tony, *The Day the Music Died: A Life Lived Behind the Lens*, London: Constable 2016

Garnett, Tony, 'Working in the Field', in Sheila Rowbotham and Huw Beynon, eds, *Looking at Class: Film Television and the Working Class*, London: Rivers Oram Press 2001

Genette, Gérard, *Narrative Discourse: An Essay in Method*, trans. Jane E. Lewin, Ithaca: Cornell University Press 1983 [1980]

Hanna, Mark, 'Playwright for Today: Barry Hines', *Cherwell* 3 February 1978

Hayward, Anthony, *Which Side Are You On? Ken Loach and His Films*, London: Bloomsbury 2005

Haywood, Ian, *Working Class Fiction: From Chartism to Trainspotting*, London: Routledge 1996

Hill, Jeffrey, *Sport and the Literary Imagination: Essays in History Literature and Sport*, Oxford: Peter Lang, 2006

Hill, John, *Ken Loach: The Politics of Film and Television*, London: BFI 2011

Hines, Richard, *No Way But Gentlenesse: A Memoir of How Kes, My Kestrel, Changed My Life*, London: Bloomsbury 2016

Hoggart, Richard, *The Uses of Literacy*, Harmondsworth: Penguin 2007 [1957].

Horkheimer, Max and Adorno, Theodor W., 'The Culture Industry: Enlightenment as Mass Perception', in *Dialectic of Enlightenment: Philosophical Fragments*, ed. Gunzelin Schmid Noerr, trans. Edmund Jephcott, Stanford: Stanford University Press 2002

Howie, Guy, 'Football under Capitalism: The Rich Exploit a Working-class Sport', *Socialist Appeal*, 15 September 2014

Jameson, Fredric, *Postmodernism: Or, the Cultural Logic of Late Capitalism*, Durham, NC: Duke University Press 1991

Kalof, Linda and Fitzgerald, Amy, 'Reading the Trophy: Exploring the Display of Dead Animals in Hunting Magazines', *Visual Studies* 18 (2) 2003, pp. 112–22

Kirk, John, 'Figuring the Landscape: Writing the Topographies of Community and Place', *Literature and History* 15 (1) 2006, pp. 1–17

Knight, Deborah, 'Naturalism, Narration and Critical Perspective: Ken Loach and the Experimental Method', in George McKnight, ed., *Agent of Challenge and Defiance: The Films of Ken Loach*, Connecticut: Greenwood Press 1997

Lacey, Stephen, *Tony Garnett*, Manchester: Manchester University Press 2007

Leigh, Jacob, *The Cinema of Ken Loach: Art in the Service of the People*, London: Wallflower 2002

Lorenz-Meyer, Dagmar, 'The Politics of Ambivalence: Towards a Conceptualisation of Structural Ambivalence in Intergenerational Relations', *Gender Institute New Working Papers*, 2, February 2001

MacCabe, Colin, 'Realism and the Cinema: Notes on some Brechtian theses', *Screen* 15:2 1974, pp. 7–27

McGowan, Lee, 'Marking Out the Pitch: A Historiography and Taxonomy of Football Fiction', *Soccer and Society* 16:1 2015, pp. 76–97

O'Sullivan, Sean, 'No Such Thing as Society: Television and the Society', in Lester D. Friedman, ed., *Fires Were Started: British Cinema and Thatcherism*, London: Wallflower Press 2006

Peim, Nick, 'The History of the Present: Towards a Contemporary Phenomenology of the School', *History of Education* 30 (2) 2001, pp. 170–90

Russell, Dave, *Looking North: Northern England and the National Imagination*, Manchester: Manchester University Press 2004

Seed, David, 'TV Docudrama and the Nuclear Subject: *The War Game, The Day After* and *Threads*', in John R. Cook and Peter Wright, eds, *British Science Fiction Television: A Hitchhiker's Guide*, London: IB Tauris 2006

Sobchack, Vivian, *Carnal Thoughts: Embodiment and Moving Image Culture*, Oakland, CA: University of California Press 2004

Spencer, Luke, 'British Working-Class Fiction: The Sense of Loss and the Potential for Transformation', *Socialist Register* 24 1988, pp. 366–86

Spicer, Andrew, 'Restoring the Screenwriter to British Film History', in James Chapman, Marc Glancy and Sue Harper, eds, *The New Film History: Approaches, Methods and Sources*, Basingstoke: Palgrave Macmillan 2007

Stead, Peter, 'Brought to Book: Football and Literature', in Rob Steen et al., eds, *The Cambridge Companion to Football*, Cambridge: Cambridge University Press 2013

Stephenson, William '*Kes* and the Press', *Cinema Journal* 12: 2 1973, pp. 48–55

Thompson, E.P., 'Time, Work-Discipline and Industrial Capitalism', *Past and Present* 38 1967, pp. 56–97

Turnbull, Simone, 'The Portrayal of the Working Class and Working-class Culture in Barry Hines's Novels', unpublished PhD thesis, Sheffield Hallam University 2014

Vice, Sue, 'Barry Hines's Unproduced Miners' Strike Plays: An Archival Study', *Journal of British Cinema and Television* 8 (2) 2011, pp. 204–17

Viol, Claus-Ulrich, *Jukebooks: Contemporary British Fiction, Popular Music and Cultural Value*, Heidelberg: Winter 2006

Whannel, Gary, 'Winning and Losing Respect: Narratives of Identity in Sport Films', *Sport in Society: Cultures, Commerce, Media, Politics*, 11: 2–3 2008, pp. 195–208

Williams, Raymond, *The Country and the City*, Oxford: Oxford University Press 1975

Willis, Andy, 'Jim Allen: Radical Drama Beyond *Days of Hope*', *Journal of British Cinema and Television* 12:2 2008, pp. 300–17

Wilson, Nicola, *Home in British Working-Class Fiction*, London: Routledge 2015

Archives

Barry Hines Papers, Special Collections, University of Sheffield
Ken Loach Archive, Reuben Library, British Film Institute
Jack Rosenthal Papers, Special Collections, University of Sheffield
Willy Russell Archive, Liverpool John Moores University Library

Index

Lightning Source UK Ltd.
Milton Keynes UK
UKHW011541150819
347946UK00005B/277/P

9 781784 992620